Arguments For Socialism

Paul Cockshott and David Zachariah

2012

ISBN: 978-1-4716-5894-5

Contents

Preface

This book is made up of a collection of polemical articles written by us over the period since the fall of 'die Mauer' and the crisis of the European socialist movement brought on in its wake. They record an attempt to argue through the theoretical challenges that this period has posed:

* Why did both Leninist communism and social democracy come to crisis?

* What were the economic weaknesses of both and what economic policy should a future socialist movement adopt to overcome these?

* How can the struggle for popular democracy be integrated into the goals of a new movement?

The articles were written for a variety of publications or occasions. Rather than presenting them in chronological order we have organised them into topics. The first section, Foundations, deals with the fundamental theoretical resources that the socialist movement has available to it in facing its current problems.

The socialist project and the working class provides some foundational arguments for socialism and the capacities required to advance the socialist project. It argues why the working class necessarily remains a central component in the class composition of socialist political forces.

21st Century Marxism is an article published in Junge Welt that tries to draw up the theoretical problems and methods of investigation available now, trying to distinguish these from those in past periods. A theme of this, and subsequent articles in the Foundations section, is a re-emphasis on the importance of scientific socialism, a socialism that is not afraid to rest on the results of today's scientific knowledge.

How physics is validating the Labour Theory of Value also published in Junge Welt argues that the methods of physics are now being applied to the economy, the so called 'econophysics' and are in the main validating the results of the labour theory of value.

Historical Materialism or Subjectivism published in Open Polemic argues against certain readings of Marx that are associated with the 'Neue Marx-Lekture' or value-form school. It argues that these assumptions handicap the re-establishment of Marxian political economy as a science that we can use to change the world.

Competing theories wrong or not even wrong published in Vlaams Marxistisch Tijdshrift continues the argument that the labour theory of value

6

produces strong empirically verifiable results whereas the competing subjective theory of value is unfalsifiable and yields no useful macro economic predictions.

The second section of the book includes a series of shorter more popular polemics.

Against Nationalism attempts to explain why nationalism has to be the enemy of socialist ideology, and why socialist should be consistent internationalist. *Beyond anti-imperialism* argues that the profound changes of imperialism during the 20th century require reconsidering anti-imperialism as a distinct strategy. *Against Republicanism* argues against the romanticisation of the republican form of government by some on the British left. Whilst living as they do in a monarchy, the republic seems something radical, the article says that this is a false path to set out on, our goal should not be the Republic – something deliberately borrowed from Rome by the wealthy founding fathers of the USA but a radical democracy. *Democracy without Politicians* takes this theme further spelling out how a radical democracy or demarchy could operate.

A third section looks at the major strategic questions facing the left in Europe and what have been the past failings of the socialist movement. Famously the early 20th century socialist movement split after the 1917 revolution into Social-democratic and Leninist wings. We look at the failings of both of these.

Limits of social-democratic politics argues that the relationship between social democracy and the state, and in particular its reliance on the capitalist sector of the economy for tax raising, fatally undermined its long term progressive goals. The paper was presented at the annual conference organised by Arbetarrörelsens Forskarnätverk.

Six theses on the problems of the communist movement published in Open Polemic shortly after the fall of the USSR argued that the crisis of world socialism was due primarily to economic failure and that its collapse of was due to causes in its economic mechanism, but which are not inherent in all possible socialisms. It goes on to argue that the political failures of the Left today stem from the lack of a programmatic conception of how a socialist economy should be operated along with the lack of a viable constitutional program.

Reform and Revolution in Leninist Politics addresses what has been a perennial issue on the Left, but does so by introducing a number of new concepts about the nature of different periods: stable, restructuring and revolutionary and emphasises the need to have a practical intervention programme that is specific to the current conjuncture.

The review of Mike Macnair's *'Revolutionary Strategy'*, engages with a leading theoretician of the Communist Party of Great Britain, who is trying to revive classical German Social Democracy. Whilst this approach has some strengths when contrasted to much of the Left, it is criticized for having a conservative attitude to democracy, limiting its aims as historical Social Democracy did, to a parliamentary republic. Since 1945 this state form has proven to be the most perfect superstructure for capitalist economy. Along with this political conservatism goes an unwillingness to set out distinct socialist economic goals.

Ideas of Leadership and Democracy, an address given in Stockholm in 2010, continues the critique of both historical social-democracy and the far Left for their failure to put forward a genuinely democratic programme. It argues that the constitutional policies of the far left remain an uncritical idealisation of the Soviet form of government. The talk goes on to propose a concrete socialist economic programme for the Left in Europe today.

The final section of the book addresses socialist economics.

Venezuela and Socialist Economic Policy, published in Junge Welt, is the result of a visit to Venezuela in 2007. It looked at what measures would have to be taken by a socialist government in Venzuela to effectively transform the economic system there from a capitalist to a socialist economy. It looks at issues monetary policy, taxation policy and property rights asking how a socialist government could set about the abolition of exploitation.

Economic Factors in the failure of Soviet Socialism looks at the economically catastrophic policies pursued by the Gorbachev government in the USSR and how and why these led to economic and political collapse.

The review of Spufford's *'Red Plenty'*, looks at a novel set in the Khruschev era in the USSR. The novel's hero is the idea of cybernetic socialism advocated by Kantorovich and Lebedev in the 1950s and early 60s. Spufford's book recounts the transition from the hope and excitement of the 50s to the disillusion and demoralisation of the 70s.

Against Mises, is a reply to the arguments of the Austrian school economists according to which socialist economy is bound to collapse into inefficiency due to the alleged impossibility of socialist economic calculation.

A Critical Look at Market Socialism, does what it says on the label. It examines the claims of market socialism to be a viable alternative to capitalism, especially through a critique of the work of Yunker, a prominent US theorist of market socialism.

Towards a New Socialism, is an interview with the installation artist

Oliver Ressler about the book of the same title, written by Cottrell and Cockshott. It provides a concise synopsis of the ideas of socialism advocated in that book.

David Zachariah wrote *The socialist project and the working class*, *Democracy without Politicians* and *Limits of social-democratic politics*. The article *Beyond anti-imperialism* was written jointly. Paul Cockshott wrote the other articles.

Part I.

Foundations

1. The socialist project and the working class

Why socialism?

People on the Left are united in their goal of a society in which every individual finds approximately equal means for the full development of her diverse capacities. This egalitarian goal is blocked by vast and persistent social inequalities in living standards, employment, working conditions, health, education, housing, access to culture, means of development, and the fruits of social labour etc.

What distinguishes socialists from the rest is their recognition that the specific way in which society is organised to reproduce itself also reproduces these social inequalities. It does so by two broad types of mechanisms: (i) exclusion and (ii) exploitation. In the former mechanism a group of people is systematically barred from means of development, e.g. through institutional racial separation or mass unemployment. In the latter mechanism the produce or means of subsistence of one group of people is systematically extracted and appropriated by another.

Karl Marx considered the extraction and appropriation of the social surplus produced by the working population to be the "innermost secret" of each civilization:

> *The specific economic form, in which unpaid surplus-labour is pumped out of direct producers, determines the relationship of rulers and ruled*, as it grows directly out of production itself and, in turn, reacts upon it as a determining element. ... It is always the direct relationship of the owners of the conditions of production to the direct producers – a relation always naturally corresponding to a definite stage in the development of the methods of labour and thereby its social productivity – which reveals the innermost secret, *the hidden basis of the entire social structure* and with it the political form of the rela-

tion of sovereignty and dependence, in short, the corresponding specific form of the state.[1]

By controlling the productive assets of society, an economic class – slave owners, landlords, state managers, capitalists – can extract and appropriate the surplus of the producing classes, i.e. goods and services over and above consumption of the exploited. These exploitative relations are maintained and codified in different forms of property established and defended by the state.

In a society dominated by the capitalist mode of production, rights to own productive assets are universal and equal. But the ownership of the assets is highly concentrated and unequal, leaving wage-labourers with few options but to sell their ability to work to a class of capitalists. They appropriate what their employed workers produce, sell it for a profit and purchase the social surplus produced by the working class collectively.

In the process wealth, and hence the power to command labour, is accumulated in a capitalist society. The unequal and concentrated ownership of productive assets persists through the dynamic of market competition between firms, which destroys low-productivity firms and benefits capital-intensive ones, and the reinvestment of the surplus product, which further concentrates capital assets and raises competitiveness. Furthermore, unemployment persists for a substantial section of the working class as a result of the unplanned and anarchic nature of capitalist production and exchange. Through these mechanisms of exclusion and exploitation, social inequalities are reproduced in a society of juridically equal individuals.

Consequently, establishing a society that no longer reproduces social inequalities requires destroying the mechanisms of exclusion and exploitation and transforming the organisation of social production. For socialists, such as the great physicist Albert Einstein, this means the establishment of collective forms of ownership of productive assets and surplus appropriation:

> I am convinced there is only one way to eliminate these grave evils [of capitalism], namely through the establishment of a socialist economy, accompanied by an educational system which would be oriented toward social goals. In such an economy, the means of production are owned by society itself and are utilized in a planned fashion. A planned economy, which adjusts production to the needs of the community,

---

[1] Karl Marx, *Capital vol. III*, Part VI, Ch. 47, 1894. Emphasis added.

12

would distribute the work to be done among all those able to work and would guarantee a livelihood to every man, woman, and child. The education of the individual, in addition to promoting his own innate abilities, would attempt to develop in him a sense of responsibility for his fellow men in place of the glorification of power and success in our present society.[2]

Hence socialism entails a planned appropriation of the surplus product, it is its "innermost secret". Einstein pointed out, however, that this feature could not be the single characteristic of a socialist society,

> it is necessary to remember that a planned economy is not yet socialism. A planned economy as such may be accompanied by the complete enslavement of the individual. The achievement of socialism requires the solution of some extremely difficult socio-political problems: how is it possible, in view of the far-reaching centralization of political and economic power, to prevent bureaucracy from becoming all-powerful and overweening? How can the rights of the individual be protected and therewith a democratic counterweight to the power of bureaucracy be assured? ... Clarity about the aims and problems of socialism is of greatest significance in our age of transition.[3]

In order to prevent the reestablishment of a ruling class in a socialist economy the collective appropriation of the surplus product must be under popular control. The mechanisms for achieving this have yet to be developed. In summary then, the socialist project consists of changing the property relations and establishing forms economic organisation and political institutions necessary for such a collective appropriation process. But who can carry this project forward?

The structural capacity of the working class

The organisational abilities of political forces to undermine ruling-class domination, affect state policy, and advance the goals of socialism, are dependent on the economic class-positions of its mass base. The process of social reproduction places people in different economic positions with

---

[2] Albert Einstein, "Why Socialism?", *Monthly Review*, May 1949.
[3] Ibid.

different structural constraints and capacities to successfully develop and sustain organisations.

Historically, the mass base of socialist movements has never been exclusively the proletariat but has, to various degrees, also included the peasantry and sections of the professional middle class, such as teachers, lawyers and doctors. Mass movements and organisations have developed a socialist character to the extent that they have been rooted in working-class struggle. The Chinese communist movement was a case in point. Its mass base was overwhelmingly rural and dominated by the peasantry, but its organisational form and strategic outlook was initially formed in working-class struggle. Conversely, the Polish Solidarnosc started out as a militant working-class movement with demands of rights and "workers' self-management", but its leadership and strategic outlook was soon dominated by the Catholic church and liberal 'market reformers', and became a vehicle for capitalist restoration.

Class conflict is always embedded in the relations of production as a conflict over working conditions. Workers, individually or collectively, derive their bargaining power vis-a-vis their employers to the extent that they are indispensable to the production process. One can distinguish between two broad types of bargaining power:

(i) *Marketplace*, which results directly from tight labour markets. Workers with skills or credentials in relative scarcity.

(ii) *Workplace*, which results directly from the disruptive potential of halting certain units of production. Workers in a strategic location or key sector of the capitalist economy.[4]

The specific combination of these bargaining powers is what endows workers a structural capacity to advance when latent conflict over working conditions breaks out into collective class struggle with employers and the capitalist class. Their success depends on their collective ability to raise and sustain the potential costs of disrupting production relative to the cost of concessions for capitalists. From the moment the struggle goes beyond one with immediate employers and contests instead the structure of existing property relations, it involves state and class struggle becomes a political struggle.

To summarise, Marxists have maintained that an organised working-class must constitute a central component of the socialist political forces.

---

[4]Cf. Beverly Silver, *Forces of Labor: workers' movement and globalization since 1870*, Cambridge University Press, 2003.

Not because of the heroic historical struggles fought by working-class movements globally, but because of its

historically constituted nature as the exploited collective producer within the capitalist mode of production. As the *exploited* class, it is caught in a systematic clash with capital, which cannot generally and permanently satisfy its needs. As the main *producing* class, it has the power to halt – and within limits redirect – the economic apparatus of capitalism, in pursuit of its goals. And as the *collective* producer it has the objective capacity to found a new, non-exploitative mode of production. This combination of interest, power and creative capacity distinguishes the working class from every other social or political force in capitalist society, and qualifies it as the indispensable agency of socialism.[5]

Class interests and ideologies

Whilst the working class is an indispensable agent for the socialist project, it does not make its class individuals favour socialism; that requires an ideological transformation. Ideology is the 'medium' through which human beings perceive and live their lives as conscious agents. It informs them of what is desirable/undesirable; what exists/does not exist; what is possible/impossible and so on.[6] Ideologies clash and compete over which individuals they can address; they are reproduced in and through practices that affirm or sanction according to their respective postulated beliefs.

The daily practices on the commodity and labour market address human beings as abstract isolated juridical subjects (buyer/seller, employee/-employer), while the liberal parliamentary system addresses them as abstract universal citizens (equal voters and MPs representing their abstract 'will'). These practices affirm the liberal capitalist ideology by atomizing individuals: Economic processes appear as an external, uncontrollable force while politics is represented as a matter of personal preferences and public debate. Conversely, individuals that attempt go against the social order are faced with practices that sanction in accordance with liberal capitalist ideology: unemployment, legal sanctions or public ex-communication.

---

[5]Francis Mulhern, "Towards 2000, or News from You-Know-Where", *NLRI*/148,1984.

[6] Cf. Göran Therborn, *The Power of Ideology and the Ideology of Power*, Verso 1980.

Through these practices of affirmation and sanction the capitalist social order is reproduced ideologically. For those who benefit from the system, society appears as free and just, and attribute their wealth to personal success, while for those who are at the other end it appears as unequal and attribute their lack of wealth to personal failure. For the former capitalism is desirable, for the latter no alternative appears possible.

It can therefore not be expected that a wage-labourer becomes a committed socialist merely by virtue of her economic position. Furthermore, while different class-specific practices reproduce class-specific ideologies, the ideological makeup of individuals is not exhausted by them. In other words, certain practices may evolve in working-class neighbourhoods that address its inhabitants as a distinct social class. But other practices, such as reading the national newspaper, attending public school or church, address other ideological subjects than class – as nationals, religious believers etc. The relative strength of these ideologies are determined by the pertinence of the practices through which they are affirmed and sanctioned.

Since workers belong to an exploited class, class-specific practices reassert themselves periodically in the systematic conflict with capital. Because of the exploitative nature of the capital to labour relationship, these conflicts cannot generally and permanently satisfy workers' needs. It is from this fact that an objective *interest* in establishing a non-exploitative mode of production arises. Agents have an interest in some state of affairs if it enables them to achieve their wants. But it is quite another thing to be aware of this interest; that entails an ideological transformation that tells an agent how to realize its interest.[7]

In other words it is in and through socialist organisations that engage in working-class struggle that this transformation can occur. Through their victories the collective structural capacity of workers is affirmed. A necessary condition for this is that the organisations involve a wide section of the working class with a strong collective bargaining power. Through solidarity the objective interest in the socialist project is affirmed. A necessary condition for the viability of the project is the emergence of intellectuals – experts in discursive practices – within the movement that can develop, condense and disseminate ideas and programmatic options. Lacking the former condition leads to demoralising defeats, sanctions that undermine socialist ideology. Lacking the latter condition working-class struggle becomes defensive or sectional without any long-term political goals, only eternal conflict over working conditions in capitalism is perceived on the

---

[7]Cf. Alex Callinicos, *Making History*, Haymarket Books, 2005.

horizon.

Processes of transition

The socialist project advances when ruling-class power is weakened and when forms of collective appropriation expand. Both undermine the exploitative relations of production. This occurs for instance through winning workers' rights in the workplace and in society, the establishment of co-ops, a public welfare sector with universal principles of distribution, peer-produced digital libraries, participatory budgets, and so on. In these advances, the seeds of a socialist society grow, but they face immediate obstacles in the existing property relations defended by the constitution of the state apparatus. The question of transfer of state power is therefore unavoidable for socialists.

Karl Kautsky[8] argued that the working class had to gain power in society before socialists enter a parliamentary government to implement a transitional programme. Since they set out to change the property relations and establishing a collective appropriation process, the socialist government is pited against ruling-class power. At first there may be political opposition by the organised business community. When the conflict intensifies the systemic power of capital to withdraw investments sets the economy into stagnation and the tax base of the state is weakened. Pressure may increase as sanctions from the international markets and the possible collapse of production follows. Under certain conditions the socialist government may even face counter-revolutionary military force. Its fate is in other words conditioned on the organisational capacities of the socialist movement – outside the centre of the state apparatus – to defend against ruling-class reaction and sustain the productive sectors of the economy.

On the other hand, when Kautsky's strategic road to power is blocked by the state itself – e.g. in authoritarian forms of rule – the process of socialist transformation becomes conditioned on the emergence of a political revolution. Following Weber's famous formula, the state is defined by the exercise of a monopoly of legitimate use of force over a given territory. A revolution always involves a breaking of that monopoly and the emergence of 'dual power' that contests it. As Perry Anderson points out, from Weber's formula follows three possible ways in which it can arise:[9]

---

[8] A prominent German Social Democrat of the early 20th century.
[9] Perry Anderson,"Two Revolutions", *NLR*II/61, 2010.

17

★ *Legitimacy.* The monopoly of state power is broken by disjunctures, such as military defeat or fiscal collapse, that undermine the ideology of its rule especially within the armed forces and the bureaucracy. Its legitimacy is destroyed once a powerful opposition makes a counter-claim of legitimacy.

★ *Force.* A coercive apparatus of the state is overwhelmed in a quick knock-out blow of insurgent forces. This is only possible when the state has been severely weakened by war or economic dislocation. These conditions are extremely unstable, and the outcome depends on the ability of the insurgent forces to rapidly build new state structures.

★ *Territory.* The state's monopoly of power is eroded by breaking off enough territory to erect a counter-state that can defend itself as well as developing political, economic and military capacities within that overwhelm and finally defeat the state.

The French, Russian and Chinese revolutions involved different elements of these processes. Their outcomes were determined by the social composition of the political forces that contested state power and their organisational abilities to rapidly adapt under revolutionary conditions.

Which strategic paths are feasible for advancing the socialist project in the 21st century is an open question that will be answered as we enter a new period of turbulence in the global capitalist economy. Millions are joining the ranks of the industrial proletariat in the industrialising countries, while a vast service proletariat is being formed in the advanced countries. It is certain that the mass base of the socialist political forces will encompass a greater section of the population than the working class. But as we have argued here the working class constitutes an indispensable component in that force.

Written in 2011

2. 21st Century Marxism

In certain respects the situation of Marxism in the early 21st century has much in common with that in the late 19th century. In both cases Marxism is faced with a world in which the capitalist mode of production dominates. During what Hobsbawm called the 'shorter 20th century', the period from 1914 to 1990, world politics centred round the epochal struggle between capitalist and socialist economic systems, and that reality gave to Marxism a quite different character than in its first period 1848-1914. In historical terms then, we are some 17 years into the 21st century.

In each period Marxism has had to address itself to the theoretical and political challenges of the moment. The 19th century addressed two main problems:

1) The constitution of the proletariat as a class and thus as a political party (*The Manifesto of the Communist Party*, 1848)

2) The critique of bourgeois political economy and the establishment of a political economy of labour (*Capital*, 1867)

Certain questions were only touched on the form of a future communist society (*Critique of the Gotha Program*) and the political form of the rule of the working class (*The Civil War in France*).

If we look at the 20th century we see a quite different set of questions being addressed: How were communist ideas to be propagated (*What is to be Done*, 1902) ? How was the communist movement to actually take power (*The State and Revolution*, 1917)? Once the revolution had taken place how was the economy to be re-organised (*The New Economics*, 1926)? How were revolutions in societies that were not yet fully capitalist to take place (*Why is it that Red Political Power can exist in China*, 1928)? After the revolution how was the danger of counter-revolution to be combated (*Documents of the Shanghai Left*, 1967)?

In retrospect one can see that the mid-1970s represented the high water mark of the socialist tide. Whilst the Vietnamese revolutionaries were driving the US out of Saigon, and the last colonial empire in Africa, that of Portugal, was falling, the failure of the cultural revolution in China was setting the economic scene for the triumph or reaction in the 1980s and 90s. When, after the death of Mao, Deng threw open the Chinese economy to western capital investment, the balance of class forces across the whole world was upset. An immense reserve army of labour, hire-able of the lowest of wages, was thrown onto the scales. The bargaining position of capital in its struggles with its domestic working classes was, in one country after another, immensely strengthened.

So today we are faced with a whole new set of questions. The general intellectual/ideological environment is much less favourable to socialism than it was in the 20th century. This is not merely a consequence of the counter-revolutions that occurred at the end of the 20th century, but stems from a new and more vigorous assertion of the classic tenets of bourgeois political economy. This re-assertion of bourgeois political economy not only transformed economic policy in the West, but also prepared the ideological ground for counter revolutions in the East.

The theoretical preparation for the turn to the free market that occurred in the 1980s had been laid much earlier by right wing economic theorists like Hayek and Friedman. Their ideas, seen as extreme during the 1950s and 60s gained influence through the proselytising activities of organisations like the Institute for Economic Affairs and the Adam Smith Institute. These groups produced a series of books and reports advocating free market solutions to contemporary economic problems. They won the ear of prominent politicians like Margaret Thatcher, and from the 1980s were put into practice. She was given the liberty to do this by a combination of long term demographic changes and short term conjectural events. Within Britain, labour was in short supply, but across Asia it had become super abundant. Were capital free to move abroad to this plentiful supply of labour then the terms of the exchange between labour and capital in the UK would be transformed. Labour would no longer hold the stronger bargaining position. The conjunctural factor making this possible was the surplus in foreign trade generated by North Sea oil. Hitherto, the workers who produced manufactured exports had been essential to national economic survival. With the money from the North Sea, the manufacturing sector could be allowed to collapse without the fear of a balance of payments crisis. The deliberate run-down of manufacturing industry shrank the social basis of social democracy and weakened the voice of labour both economically and politically.

The success of Thatcher in attacking the working class movement in

Britain encouraged middle class aspiring politicians in the East like Klaus and presaged a situation in which Hayekian economic doctrines would become the orthodoxy. Thatcher's doctrine TINA, There Is No Alternative, (to capitalism) was generally accepted.

The theoretical dominance of free market economic ideas had by the start of the 21st century become so strong, that they were as much accepted by social democrats and self-professed communists, as they had been by Thatcher. In policy making circles they remain unchallenged to this day. They owe dominance both to class interests and to their internal coherence. The capitalist historical project took as its founding documents 'the Declaration of the Rights of Man', and Adam Smith's *Wealth of Nations*. Together these provided a coherent view of the future of Bourgeois or Civil Society, as a self regulating system of free agents operating in the furtherance of their private interests. Two centuries later when faced with the challenge of communism and social democracy, the more far-sighted representatives of the bourgeoisie returned to their roots, restated the original Capitalist Manifesto, and applied it to current conditions. The labour movement by contrast had no such coherent social narrative. Keynes's economics had addressed only technical issues of government monetary and tax policy, it did not aspire to the moral and philosophical coherence of Smith.

The external economic and demographic factors that originally favoured the turn to the market are gradually weakening. Within the next 20 years the vast labour reserves of China will have been largely utilised, absorbed into capitalist commodity production. Globally we are returning to the situation that Western Europe had reached a century ago: a maturing world capitalist economy in which labour is still highly exploited but is beginning to become a scarce resource. These were the conditions that built the social cohesion of classical social democracy, the conditions that gave rise to the IWW and then CIO in America, and led to the strength of communist parties in Western Europe countries like France, Italy and Greece post 1945. We see in South America this process in operation today.

These circumstances set 21st century Marxism a new historical project: to counter and critique the theories of market liberalism as effectively as Marx critiqued the capitalist economists of his day.

The historical project of the world's working classes can only succeed if it promulgates its own political economy, its own theory of the future of society. This new political economy must be as morally coherent as that of Smith, and must lead to economically coherent policy proposals, which if enacted would open the way to a new post-capitalist civilisation, just as those of Smith opened the way to the post feudal civilisation.

21st century Marxism can no longer push to one side the details of how the non-market economy of the future is to be organised. In Marx's day this was permissible, not now. We can not pretend that the 20th century never happened, or that it taught us nothing about socialism. In this task 20th century Western critical Marxists like Cliff, Bettleheim or Bordiga will only take us so far. Whilst they could point out weaknesses of hitherto existing socialism, it did this by comparing it to an ideal standard of what these writers thought that a socialist society should achieve. In retrospect we will see that these trends of thought were a product of the special circumstances of the cold war, a striving for a position of ideological autonomy 'neither Moscow nor Washington', rather than a programmatic contribution to Marxism. The very psychological detachment that such writers sought, deflecting from their own heads the calumnies directed at the USSR, prevented them from positively engaging with the problems faced by historically existing socialism. It is only if you envisage being faced with such problems oneself, that one would come up with practical answers:

> "It is not the critic who counts: not the man who points out how the strong man stumbles or where the doer of deeds could have done better. The credit belongs to the man who is actually in the arena, whose face is marred by dust and sweat and blood, who strives valiantly, who errs and comes up short again and again, because there is no effort without error or shortcoming, but who knows the great enthusiasms, the great devotions, who spends himself for a worthy cause; who, at the best, knows, in the end, the triumph of high achievement, and who, at the worst, if he fails, at least he fails while daring greatly, so that his place shall never be with those cold and timid souls who knew neither victory nor defeat." (Citizenship in a Republic, Roosevelt)

Instead we must recover and celebrate the advances in Marxist political economy that arose from the Russian experience: the method of material balances used in preparing the 5 year plans and systematised as Input-Output analysis by Leontief; the method of linear programming pioneered by Kantorovich; the time diaries of Strumlin.

In the 19th century Marx's Capital was a critique of the political economy that underlay British Liberalism. 21st century Marxists must perform a critique of neo-liberal political economy comparable in rigour and moral depth to Marx's 19th century critique. In particular we must engage with and defeat the ideas of the Austrian school: Boehm-Bawerk, Mises, Hayek, whose ideas now constitute the keystone of reaction. Soviet Marxism felt strong enough to ignore the then, and the response in the West came in the main from non-Marxian socialists like Lange and Dickinson. If we are to reconstitute socialism as the common-sense of the 21st century – as it was the common-sense of the mid 20th, then these are the ideas that must be confronted.

In attacking them we should not hesitate to use the advances in other sciences – statistical mechanics, information theory, computability theory. And, to re-establish Scientific Socialism there must be a definitive break with the speculative philosophical method of much of Western Marxism. We have to treat political economy and the theory of social revolution like any other science.

We must formulate testable hypotheses, which we then asses against empirical data. Where the empirical results differ from what we expected, we must modify and retest our theories.

To understand this new form of Marxist science consider the debate on the so-called 'transformation problem'. There was, in the 20th century, a huge and pointless literature attempting to rebut Boehm-Bawerk's criticism of Marx's theory of prices of production. The net result of this debate was only to detract attention from the labour theory of value and Marx's analysis of exploitation. The eventual breakthrough, in the 1980s, against this Austrian critique of Marxism came from two mathematical logicians Farjoun and Machover. Their work 'The Laws of Chaos', was to my mind the most original contribution to Marxist theory of the late 20th century. They used methods derived from statistical mechanics to show that the assumption of a uniform profit rate, shared by Marx and Boehm-Bawerk, was erroneous, and that in reality the classical labour theory of value (*Capital* vol I) operates. This was then confirmed by the empirical investigations of Shaikh and others.

This willingness to learn from other sciences and use them in the struggle against the reigning ideology can be seen in the work of Peters who brought the ideas of the computer pioneer Zuse into play in order to validate the possibility of rational socialist planning. We see again in Peters, what was evident in Shaikh and Farjoun & Machover, a re-assertion of the importance for Marxism of the labour theory of value. Whereas for

Shaikh and Farjoun & Machover its role is causal in explaining the actual dynamics of capitalism. For Peters it becomes both a moral principle and an organising concept for the future socialism.

The theoretical advances I refer to, occurred as the 20th century gave way to the 21st. Vladimir Lenin said: "Without a revolutionary theory there cannot be a revolutionary movement." This is as true today as in 1902. In the late 20th century we came to lack such a theory. Thatcher's idea that 'There is no alternative', only seemed credible because we lacked a revolutionary political economy, one which not only interpreted the world but explained how to change it, how to construct a different world.

21st century Marxism is starting out along the path to build that revolutionary political economy. Let us hasten its achievement so that when the next major restructuring crisis hits the capitalist world economy we are in a position to equip progressive movements with the ideas that they need if they are to prevail.

Written in 2007

3. How physics is validating the Labour Theory of Value

When I was a student my economics professor told us that whilst the labour theory of value had been an important historical stage in the development of economics, it was now known to be fatally flawed. 20th century economists such as Sraffa and Samuelson had shown that it was unnecessary to accord labour any special place in our understanding of prices. Instead, the structure of prices could be perfectly well understood as the result of the monetary costs faced by firms and the behaviour of profit maximising entrepreneurs. If there was in reality no such thing as labour value, it followed that Marx's theory of exploitation was an invalid incursion of moral prejudices into the 'positive science' of economics.

The professor who taught us this, Ian Steedman, was actually quite left wing, an active member of the Communist Party.

This is just an anecdote, but fact that even a prominent communist intellectual believed that the central component of Marx's theory was scientifically worthless is significant. In retrospect it gave an indication of how poorly prepared the intellectuals of the communist movement were to be, when faced with the very intense ideological attacks on socialism which unfolded in the 1980s and 1990s.

But 25 years ago help came from an unexpected source. Two mathematicians Moshe Machover and Emanuel Farjoun, wrote a book called *Laws of Chaos*. Their book gave a radically new way of looking at how capitalism worked as a chaotic and disorganised system. Farjoun and Machover had the the insight to see that physics had already developed theories to describe similar disorganised and chaotic systems.

In a market economy, hundreds of thousands of firms and individuals interact, buying and selling goods and services. This is similar to a gas in which very large numbers of molecules interact, bouncing off one another. Physics speaks of such systems as having a 'high degree of freedom', by which it means that the movements of all individual molecules are 'free' or random. But despite the individual molecules being free to move, we can still say things about them in the aggregate. We can say what their average speed will be (their temperature) and what their likely distributions in space will be.

The branch of physics which studies this is statistical mechanics or thermodynamics. Instead of making deterministic statements, it deals with probabilities and averages, but it still comes up with fundamental laws, the laws of thermodynamics, which have been found to govern the behaviour of our universe.

Now here is the surprise! When they applied the method of statistical mechanics to the capitalist economy, they found that the predictions it made coincided almost exactly with the labour theory of value as set out in volume 1 of Marx's *Das Kapital*. Statistical mechanics showed that the selling prices of goods would vary in proportion to their labour content just as Marx had assumed. Because the market is chaotic, individual prices would not be exactly equal to labour values, but they would cluster very closely around labour values. Whilst in *Das Kapital I* the labour theory of value is just taken as an empirically valid rule of thumb. Marx knew it was right, but did not say why. Here at last was a sound physical theory explaining it.

It is the job of science to uncover causal mechanisms. Once it has done this it can make predictions which can be tested. If two competing theories make different predictions about reality, we can by observation determine which theory is right. This is the normal scientific method.

Farjoun and Machover's theory made certain predictions which went directly against the predictions made by critics of Marx such as Samuelson. In particular their theory predicts that industries with a high labour to capital ratio will be more profitable. Conventional economics predicts that there will be no such systematic difference between the profit rates in different industries. When put to the test it turned out that Farjoun and Machover were right. Industries with a high labour to capital ratio are more profitable. But this is exactly what we should expect if the source of profit was the exploitation of labour rather than capital. Their theory made predictions which not only turned out to be empirically spot on, but at the same time verified Marx's theory of the exploitation of the worker.

The next big advance was made by the physicist Viktor Yakovenko, who showed in his paper 'the Statistical Mechanics of Money' that money in a market economy played the same role as energy in physics.

Just as energy is conserved in collisions between molecules, so money is conserved in the acts of buying and selling. So far so obvious!

What was not obvious was what this implies. Yakovenko showed that the laws of thermodynamics then imply that the distribution of money between people will follow the same form as the distribution of energy between molecules in a gas: the so called Gibbs-Boltzmann distribution. This sounds very scientific, but what does it actually mean?

What the Gibbs-Boltzmann distribution of money says is that a few people with end up with a lot of money and a lot of people with end up with very little money. It says that the distribution of money will be very uneven, just as we see in capitalist society. In fact Yakovenko showed that the distribution of wealth in the USA fits the Gibbs-Boltzman distribution pretty closely.

There is a tendancy to think that rich people owe their wealth to intelligence or effort, but physics tells us no. Given a market economy, then the laws of chance mean that a lot of money will end up in the hands of a few people.

In fact when we look at the USA we find that the distribution of wealth is even more uneven that we would expect from the Gibbs-Boltzmann law. If the Gibbs Boltzman law held, there would be millionaires but no billionaires. Why the disparity?

Yakovenkos original equations represented an economy that is rather like what Marx called 'simple commodity production'. It assumed only buying and selling. More recent work by Yakovenko and Wright, has shown that if you modify these equations to allow either the earning of interest on money, or the hiring of wage labour, then the equations predict a polarisation of the population into two groups. The great bulk of the population, the working class and petty bourgeois, follow a Gibbs-Boltzmann income distribution. But there is a second class, those whose income derives from capital, whose wealth with follow a different law, what is called a power-law. Again, look in detail at the distribution of wealth in and you provide exactly the distribution predicted by Yakovenko's theory. This, says Yakovenko, proves that Marx was right when he said that modern society was comprised of two distinct and opposed classes: capitalists and workers.

So modern physics has shown that not only was Marx right in his basic analysis, but he was right because his conclusions follow from the most basic laws of physics, the laws of thermodynamics.

There is also a less obvious conclusion that we can draw from physics relating to the undesirablity of Market Socialism. We can see from Yakovenko's work that a market socialist economy would also have a very uneven distribution of money. There too the Gibbs-Boltzmann law would rule. A small number of people or co-operatives would end up with a lot of money, and many such people or co-operatives would end up poverty stricken. From this capitalism would be regenerated. As Lenin wrote: "small production engenders capitalism and the bourgeoisie continuously, daily, hourly, spontaneously, and on a mass scale."

Written in 2008

4. Historical Materialism or Subjectivism

I am an engineer[1], so I was naturally pleased when the leading materialist philosopher of today, Daniel Dennet came out in defence of the significance of the engineering viewpoint to philosophy.[2] In what follows I will present some observations on the Materialism of Marx, from an engineers viewpoint – the materialism of a Watt, Shannon and Turing.

The leitmotif of these observations, is an antagonism to subjectivism and the idealist concept of the subject. The concept of the subject and of the will, have, I believe no place in the materialist world-view. Those familiar with the current state of penetration of idealism into 'Marxism', will doubtless be able to identify the schools against whom I am arguing.

Is value the 'subject' of Capital?

In Capital, the idea of the circuits of money and of capital play an important roles. In both $c - m - c$ and $m - c - m'$, value in a sense plays the role of subject. It is tempting to see the whole of the argument in Capital as an investigation into the self development of capital/subject. My grasp of Hegel is not sure enough for me to say if this view of things is actually Hegelian, but whether or not this is the case, it does suffer from drawbacks. One of them is philosophical, the other is historical.

If we see capital as a subject, then the real material subjects of the system of production are not adequately represented, or, if represented at all, appear just as instantiations of the ideal subject.

By the real material subjects, I mean abstract legal personalities or subjects of right.[3] Under capitalist systems of law, some of these legal subjects

---

[1] Both authors are.

[2] Dennet, *Darwin's Dangerous Idea*, Chap 8.

[3] A good materialist theory of the subject of right was presented by Pashukanis, in his *Allgemaine Rechtslehre und Marxismus* 1929, translated as General theory of law and Marxism, and published by Ink Links, London, 1978.

correspond to human bodies, others to bodies corporate. It is these juridical subjects that buy and sell commodities, and, reproduce themselves in the process. In this reproduction process, they are reproduced both as proprietors, and as physical processes (human metabolisms, active oil refineries, ...).

From the standpoint of the self development of capital/subject, material subjects, firms, are thought of as 'capitals', instantiations of CAPITAL. This way of looking at things is an idealist inversion.

The second problem, is that the notion of capital as a subject is tied up with the idea of capital as self-expanding value. This is what the formula *m-c-m'* is all about. Where gold is money, the formula is realistic. But even as it was written this was historically obsolete. Commercial transactions were not, carried out using gold. Capitalist trade is a balancing of accounts, either, in Marx's day, through the circulation of bills of exchange, or through the clearance of cheques.

If commerce occurs through cheque clearance, then there is no longer a circuit of value through the forms *m-c-m'*. An account with a bank, unlike a hoard, has no value. It is instead a record of entitlement to value. I think, therefore, that the use of the circuit *m-c-m'* by Marx must be seen as a pedagogic device, presenting what goes on in a simple to understand but basically anachronistic form.

When one is steeped in an old literature, one's mind become inhabited by dead social relations. Christians, today think in categories like Christ the Lord, Christ the Redeemer, concepts of a slave society with the institution of manumission, without a grip on the modern world. We Marxists have our thoughts about money shaped by a presentation, intuitive to workers in Victoria's day, to whom money was gold, without correlates in a world of debit cards.

Focus instead on material subjects and their conditions of reproduction, then money appears clearly in the form in which Smith presents it – power to command the labour of others. A bank balance is power over labour. Focus not on the self evolution of sums of value, but on how juridical subjects, firms, reproduce their despotism over labour.

Is capital the 'subject' of Capital?

Is Marx's *Capital* about the self development of the subject 'capital', or is it about capitalism. My immediate bias is to say it is about capitalism, since to say that capital was the object of investigation might imply a Hegelian

30

presumption that from the concept of capital all the concrete features of capitalism could be deduced – something which I feel to be mistaken.

Then the issue arises of whether there is one or many laws of motion of modern society, which is clearly related to the above. My first thought is that one requires several laws to have motion and dynamics – in mechanics one assumes several conservation laws plus the force laws. This would then reinforce the objection to a Hegelian deduction of the development of capitalism from a concept of capital. Then it struck me that work in cellular automata theory has demonstrated that one can derive highly complex laws of motion from a single evolution function of a cell and its neighbours. In fact as I think Margoulis has shown one can, given a universe of this type set up a configuration that is Turing machine equivalent.[4]

This indicates that it is not philosophically absurd that one law may be a sufficient foundation for the motion of a very complex system. But although this law may be a foundation for the motion of the whole system, there are other preconditions before you get something of Turing equivalent complexity: a set of boundary conditions. These initial configurations are guaranteed a certain stability by the underlying cellular evolution law, but in their turn impose other constraints on the future evolution of the system and these constraints become higher-level laws.

Thus the simple law may allow a multiplicity of different configurations to evolve and some of these different configurations would have their own, higher level laws of motion – which would not necessarily all be equivalent.

Did Marx ever clearly state *the economic law of motion of modern society*?

I think that we have to say no, not as a single clearly defined law. Can we say then, that the law of value is this foundational law? We then have the problem that he never stated this explicitly as a law either, i.e. in the sense of Hooke's law or the laws of thermodynamics. I think however, one can reconstruct the concept of law that he had beneath the texts on value.

At the level of explanation in volume 1 of *Capital*, the law would state that 'In the exchange of commodities, abstract socially necessary labour time is conserved.'

Although he does not state this explicitly, I think that it is clearly a logical presupposition of much of his argument. I would agree that he does not establish the correctness of this law, but that does not mean that it may not both be a valid law empirically, and one whose assumption allows one

---

[4] and hence capable of modelling any system of laws of motion.

to model or simulate the important features of capitalism. There is now a growing body of evidence that the law actually applies, but it is an interesting question as to just why it applies.

One could, using the same law of value, hypothesise other systems than capitalism. If we made the auxiliary hypothesis that there was a tendency for the value of labour power to be equal to the value created by labour, then you would not get capitalism but some other social system, perhaps a system of workers co-operatives.

The assumption that the value of labour power is systematically below the value-creating power of labour is, it seems to me, a boundary condition that is specifically reproduced by capitalism. In this sense, although the law of value is the underlying law of motion of modern society, it is abstractly the law of motion of more than one possible sort of modern society.

This incidentally raises the question of what we mean by abstraction.

Abstraction and abstract labour

Is it only in the process of exchange that labour become abstract?

There is a confusion here between the role of abstraction in science and the partial way in which the abstract categories discovered by science become apparent to quotidian perception.

Science must always seek the general behind the concrete, the abstract behind the particular. Thus in the development of thermodynamics one has the formation of the abstract concept of heat, which is distinguished from the forms in which it becomes apparent as warmth, temperature or thermal radiation. To measure heat, one needs to co-ordinate several distinct observations and data. If you want to measure the number of calories released by by burning 10 grams of sugar under a bomb calorimeter, one must know the starting temperature of the calorimeter, the volume of water it contains, the final temperature, the specific heat of water, etc.

Prior to the development of a coherent theory of heat, and data on the specific heat of water one might come up with regularities like 'other things being equal, the rise in temperature was proportional to the sugar burnt', but this is not a measure of abstract heat.

The similarity to exchange is clear, a capitalist can observe that, other things being equal his turnover is roughly proportional to the number of workers in his employ, but this proportionality does not yet give him a measure of abstract necessary labour time. The fact that such proportionalities exist is an indication that there is an underlying material cause for them, just as the proportionality between temperature rise and fuel burned indicates a similar abstract cause.

A scientific measurement of abstract labour needs the analogue of adjustments for different specific heats and calorimeter volumes, the fact that in a given factory the techniques of production are worse than average, will indicate that the measure of actual expended labour has to be corrected to arrive at a measure of abstract labour.

The existence of objective material causes underlying the phenomenal forms to which they give rise, is one of the basic postulates of philosophical materialism. That these causes not only exist bur are discoverable and measurable is a further necessary postulate for scientific materialism. This, it seems to me is one of the fundamental distinctions between Marxism and Hayekism, and more generally between materialism and empiricism. For Hayek, the worth of things is in principle unknowable outside of market exchange. Thus the Marxist programme of a communist society in which economic calculation transcends the market, is hopelessly utopian, scientism, the engineering fallacy etc.

I think, therefore, that it is a fundamental philosophical error, and one which, moreover can be exploited by our enemies, to say that it is only through market exchanges that abstract labour can be measured. This may be the only form in which it becomes apparent to the practical concerns of bourgeois society, but that does not exhaust the matter.

One must distinguish the scientific abstraction, abstract labour as the expression on a polymorphous human potential, from the empirical abstraction performed by the market.

An analogous polymorphous potential, one regularly used in industry is the computing machine cycle. One costs algorithms in terms of the number of machine cycles they cost. A computer is a universal machine, its computation power can be expressed in a vast variety of concrete forms, so there are different sequences of machine cycles with different concrete effects. But when one uses machine cycles as a metric of algorithmic costs, one abstracts from what these cycles are – adds, subtracts, moves etc. – and reduces them to the abstract measure of an almost infinitely plastic potential. The abstraction over labour is analogous.

We can not use wages to measure abstract labour, although for certain purposes they may be a useful statistical surrogate where other data are lacking. If we measure wages we are measuring the price of labour power not the amount of abstract labour time necessary to manufacture a use value.

To measure the latter, it has obviously to be done in natural units of time, which as such, already abstracts from the concrete form of the labour. As such its study starts with Babbage in his Economy of Machinery, proceeds with Taylor in the machine shop of the Midvale Steel Company and his successors like Charles Bedaux, whose unit of abstract labour the B was defined as 'a "B" is a fraction of a minute of work plus a fraction of a minute of rest, always aggregating to unity, but varying in proportion according to the nature of the strain'.

There is nothing impossible in principle about such measurement, indeed, the science of systematic exploitation had depended on it for years. But within the capitalist social order such computations are restricted to the factory, the comparative statistics necessary for a social calculus of labour time do not exist. But this is not to say that they could never be produced under some future social order.

James Watt, and the concept of Labour Power

At about the same time as one Adam Smith was professor of Moral Philosophy here, and was setting out a coherent formulation of the labour theory of value, Dr. Black of the department of Natural Philosophy along with a technician, one James Watt, were laying the foundations for a proper understanding of heat and temperature. These two exercises have more in common than might be imagined. Reflection upon it, brings out how concepts from engineering science, from the practice of material production, parallel and become the foundation for materialist political economy.

One might, if one were a bourgeois economist, argue that values can not be measured independently of market prices just as temperature can not be measured independently of the height of mercury on a thermometer. I think that this is basically a fair comparison. But if we rest our analysis at this level, whether in political economy or in natural philosophy, we have a pre-Smithian political economy and a pre-Watt understanding of heat.

What Smith did, drawing on others, was to show that behind relative prices there was an underlying objective cause – the labour required to produce things. "The real price of every thing, what every thing really costs to the man who wants to acquire it, is the toil or trouble of acquiring it." We will leave out for the moment that one can also measure the temperature of a body by analysing its black body radiation spectrum, and concentrate on the analogy between temperature and price. This was a great scientific advance since it related the immediately visible phenomenon – price measured in money to something behind the scenes – labour time. Both of the entities involved in the causal theory are independently observable and measurable. This contrasts with the notions of 'utility' in vulgar economics which are not objectively observable, but have to be deduced from the observed prices.

The parallel advance by Black and Watt, was the introduction of the notion of heat as something independent of temperature. A necessary component of this theory was the notions of specific and latent heats. Thus, by experiment, they were able to establish that the change in temperature of a body was proportional to the heat input divided by the specific heat of the substance concerned. This again related the observed measurement – temperature to something behind the scenes – heat. Like labour, heat was independently measurable, for instance in terms of the amount of coal burned. Later with Carnot the equation between heat and work is made. Not only does this make the analogy with value and labour even closer in terms of the then existing conceptual framework, but it opens up the way for more accurate objective measures of heat energy. By use of a dissipative calorimeter, Carnot could show that the work of a given weight falling a known distance would produce a definite rise in temperature of water. This then gives a fixed and external measure of heat energy.

Let us construct table of analogy between terms in the two domains of Moral and Natural Philosophy, with a subject matter befitting the Scottish Enlightenment.

Thus the two schools of philosophy reduce the phenomena they are concerned with to indirect manifestations of work done, Smith taking human labour as his standard, Watt taking the labour of horses.

However, in compiling this table I have shown five rows. Smith and Watt would probably only have recognised three (for Smith rows 1, 2 and 4, and Watt rows 1, 2 and 3). If, however we take Smith enhanced by Marx and Watt by Carnot, we get the five rows. Now the interesting thing about rows 3,4 and 5 is that in each case they are different ways of considering the same thing. One may measure heat in calories, but it is the same thing as energy in terms of joules, Watt, ergs, foot-pounds, horsepower hours etc. Similarly value is the same thing as labour time.

But value is not price, nor is heat temperature. To obtain a price from a value we need the intervention of gold with its own specific labour/value content per ounce. To obtain a temperature from the heat one needs the specific heat of the substance being heated.

Moral Philosophy	Natural Philosophy
1.Price in gold guineas of whisky	Temperature on an alcohol thermometer of whisky
2.Specific labour content of gold	Specific heat of whisky
3.Value of whisky	Heat content of the whiskey
4.Labour required to distill whiskey measured in hours	Thermal energy of hot whiskey. measured in foot pounds or horse-power seconds
5.Ability to work or labouring power of distillery workers	Ability to work or horse-power of the distillery engine (raising barrels?)

The polemical status of Labour Power

I am using labour in the sense of labour hours, which, to use Watt's ter-minology is Work done (horse-power hours). I think that it is pretty clear that the concept of labour-power could not have been formulated until the genius of Watt had made the concept of horse-power, or power in general part of the universal inheritance of the industrial age.

My chief concern is to defend the scientific superiority of the labour the-ory of value vis-a-vis bourgeois subjectivist ones. What makes the labour theory scientific and the others unscientific is that there is no way that one can determine whether prices do exchange in proportion to marginal util-ity, since utility has no independent measure. Labour time, by contrast, is susceptible to measurement. Its measurement, just like that of tempera-ture, presupposed a definite technology. Measurement of temperature de-pended on the invention of the thermometer, measurement of labour time depended upon the invention, with Galileo, of the pendulum escapement mechanism. In using a clock to determine the time taken to perform a task, on must of course average ones measures over a large number of runs and a large number of individual to obtain the average necessary time taken.

If labour-power is ability to perform work, then its dimension must be work-performable/per hour. Clearly if the working day is lengthened with the daily wage being the same, the wage rate per hour has declined. Whether the value of labour power has similarly declined or has remained the same is indeterminate, since we have no means of measuring the value of labour power other than the price paid for it.

I would thus argue that the concept 'value of labour power' has no scientific explanatory power and its presence in Capital must be understood as deriving from Marx's intention to perform a critique of political economy using its own categories. He thus assumes the exchange of equivalents, and assumes that workers, like other sellers get a fair price for their commodity. This necessitates that a value be imputed to labour power.

Ironic answers to a Marxist idealist

I was recently asked, what objective force led me to write a particular polemic against subjectivism. Was it not an expression of my will and thus a living reproof to my anti-subjectivist world-view?

That such questions could be raised, and raised by a Marxist, indicates a retreat towards idealism.

Force is an important concept. As a mechanical process, a depression of keys, my writing certainly involved forces exerted by muscle on bone. But the concept of force is quite limited, it relates to the ability to impart motion, to overcome mechanical inertia. Its compass does not extend to explaining the creation of a complex information structure like an article.

Here we need to explain how this particular sequence of characters was generated. This page is so astronomically improbable, its probability of arising by chance being of the order of 1 in 10 raised to the power of 4000, that its particularity demands explanation. Force, the mere overcoming of momentum, can not explain such order. So what is left?

The will and its creativity, suggests the humanist.

But is this really an explanation?

I would suggest that it is not an explanation but a place-holder, a linguistic token demanded by a set of possible sentences. This may seem a little obscure, but to illustrate the sort of thing that I am referring to, consider the sentences:

"It is raining."

"Paul is writing."

What is the it that rains? There is obviously no real it that does the raining, but English grammar demands a subject for the sentence, structurally equivalent to the Paul who writes. The it is a place holder demanded by the sentence form. We gain no understanding of the weather pattern that led to the rain by using it, but it is impermissible for us to say simply "Is raining".

The question "what led me to write", demands an answer of the form "x led me to write", with some linguistic subject x. Grammar allows the substitution of a proper name for x, as in "William led me to write", or "my Will led me to write". Instead the abstract noun 'will' can be used: "my will led me to write".

The word 'will' is then a place holding subject, analogous to the it responsible for the bad weather this last week. The 'will' is philosophically more sophisticated, than it, being one of the conventional tokens that idealist philosophy uses to translate a non-terminal symbol of a grammar into a constituent category of reality. The will is the symbolic grammatical subject in philosophical garb, the linguistic subject becomes The Subject.

An explanation of what is causing rain to fall, would go something along the lines of "an updraught of warm moist air is causing condensation as pressure falls, and this precipitates as rain". Here, instead of a place marker, we have a description, albeit abstract, of a physical process. One can give a highly abstract description of my writing in terms of my brain being a probabilistic state machine that undergoes state transitions whose probability amplitudes are functions of it current state and its current input symbols, and whose output symbols are a lagged function of current state. For my article the relevant input symbol would have been the argument that I was replying to, and my current state would be the Cartesian product of the states of my individual neurones.

It may be objected that this hopelessly abstract, as abstract almost, as talking about will. But there is an important difference. The approach of treating the brain as an automaton has engendered a productive research program. One can, as Chomsky did in the 1950s ask what class of automaton is required to recognise languages with different classes of grammars, and show that some features of natural language imply automata that are at least Turing equivalent. One can begin to look at how it is that things like visual perception can occur, as neurophysiology has done over the last 30 years, etc. In contrast, 'will' will take us nowhere. It closes of discussion.

Putting aside the question of nature, who transforms the world if not individuals, acting individually and as parts of social classes and groups?

I have a three year old daughter, and today as we sat down to supper, she pointed to the pie in the middle of the table, and asked us 'who is that?'.

We explained that this was the wrong question, she should have asked 'what is that'. A who question, demands a person as an answer.

"Who transforms the world?"

Why, the Great Helmsman, il Duce, those supermen who bestride history like colossi.

Ask instead, what transforms the world, and other answers spring up: maize, smallpox, gunpowder, the auto mobile, capitalism.

"What role do individuals have in history?"

To suffer and glorify God, for who else could have written the play and assigned them roles?

"Are individuals merely unconscious actors in a historical process?"

Ask me instead whether the laws of history are knowable, whether political parties can make calculated attempts to exploit this knowledge, and I would answer yes.

Ask me instead whether people can be made to believe that their actions contribute to diverting the river of history, and again I answer yes.

"Are their beliefs born out by events?"

For those on the winning side, yes.

Written in 1996

5. Competing theories wrong or not even wrong

Intellectual background

The cringe

From the start of the 20th century up until the end of the 1970s Marxists had great intellectual self confidence. They saw themselves as the wave of the future, not just in the development of society but also in the realm of ideas. The economic system they advocated seemed to be going from strength to strength. Increasing areas of the world were won by communist revolutionary movements. Marxism had political power, economic success and science behind it and seemed bound to triumph.

The political setbacks of the 1980s dented this self confidence. An alternative economic programme came to dominance – that of neo-liberalism. First in Chile, next in the Anglo-Saxon countries and then in Eastern Europe liberal economic policies and doctrines rose to power.

The response of some Marxists was to change sides and, with the enthusiasm of new converts, to adopt the doctrines of their former opponents.[1] Some others on the left, whilst remaining opposed to the doctrines of neo-liberalism, became skeptical about what had previously been taken to be key components of Marxian economics such as the labour theory of value.[2] The neo-liberals had laid claim both to scientificity in economics and to the best policy proposals and this caught the left on the back foot, unsure where to tread next.

Education and the scientific method

Liberal economics has been able to claim scientificity based both on the large and sophisticated mathematical apparatus of neoclassical value theory, and on a vast number of detailed econometric studies. Those who are

---

[1] See for example [Ste92] or [BL91] or [Sci95].
[2] A recent example is [NB09], an influential earlier one [Ste81].

professionally involved in the subject are expected to be mathematically literate and experienced in the analysis of statistical data. These aspects of their training means that their background has in some ways more in common with people who are trained as natural scientists than with other social scientists. There has also been a long tradition of economists borrowing conceptual structures from the natural sciences. Mirowski showed that many of the concepts used in marginalist economics were borrowed directly from classical mechanics during the late 19th century [Mir89].

But there is, I think, a significant difference between the way the natural sciences are taught and the way neo-classical economics is taught, and this difference is significant.

When a student is taught an introductory course in physics or biology, they are both taught theories and told of the crucial experiments that validated the theories. They are told of Galileo's experiment that validated what we would now see as the equivalence of gravitational and inertial mass. They learn of the Michelson-Morley experiment on the invariance of the speed of light, that inconvenient fact whose explanation required Special Relativity. Biology students hear of the experiments of Pasteur and Koch that established the germ theory of disease, etc. The function of these accounts in science education is twofold. On the one hand they emphasize to students the reasons why they should give credence to the theory being taught, on the other, these historical examples are used to teach the scientific method.

If one contrasts this with introductory courses in economics one sees that whilst theory is taught, the student gets no equivalent history of crucial economic observations in order to support the theory. This is no accident.

No history of crucial observations is taught, because there is no such history.

Failure of orthodox economics to relate to empirical data

In science an experimentum crucis serves to discriminate between competing hypotheses or to show the inadequacy of a previously dominant theory. The crucial difference between neo-classical economics and the classical school of political economy lay in their theories of value. The classical school, from Smith to Marx, had adhered to a labour theory of value which neo-classical economics replaced with marginal utility theory[3] . But one

---

[3] Of course there is more to the neo-classical theory than just marginal utility, but the introduction of this, and elision of labour as a source of value were the

would search the history of economics in vain were one to look for the crucial experiment or observation which disproved the labour theory of value. There was none.

After Koch and Pasteur, the miasma theory of disease died out. It was completely replaced by the germ theory, whose greater practical effectiveness as a guide to public health measures was no longer in doubt. But after Jevons and Menger, the labour theory of value did not by any means die out. It continued to spread and gain influence, becoming the orthodoxy in the USSR and other socialist countries in the middle of the 20th century. Where and when a particular theory dominated owed a lot to politics, a little to aesthetics and nothing to observation.

Not even wrong

I mention aesthetics because there can be little doubt that the edifice of neo-classical economics had a mathematical sophistication and elegance that the labour theory of value at first lacked. The marginal theory had calculus, homogeneous functions, and in its later versions Brower's fixed point theorem. In contrast the labour theory of value initially involved nothing much more sophisticated than the concepts of ratios or averages[4].

Maths can be seductive. The rigour and consistency of a mathematical theory can, to those who have expended the effort to understand it, give it credence. This is unproblematic where the theory is just maths. But when the maths claims to be a model of the real world, beauty can mislead. There has, for example, been recent criticism within physics of the dominance of string theory [SH08,Woi06]. Smolin alleges that the mathematical beauty of string theory has seduced a generation of physicists into an area which, lacking any experimental verification, is little more than beautiful speculation. That, he says, is why five Fields Medals given for mathematical work on String Theory but no Nobel prizes. Fields Medals are given for being smart, Nobel Prizes for being right. The problem with string theory, Smolin and Woit say, is that it gives no substantive testable

---

crucial end results of the marginalist revolution. The marginal principle was not itself new, it had been incorporated in the Ricardian and Marxian theories of rent. In the transition between the two schools it can be argued that Gossen and Jevons supported a marginal labour theory of value [Hag06, Hag10].

[4] With time, the labour theory of value became much more complicated, from Dimitriev on it acquired the full rigour of linear algebra, and by the middle of the 20th century the maths used by Marxian and Neo-classical economists tended to have rather distinctive flavours.

predictions, and in the absence of these it is neither verifiable nor falsifiable as a scientific theory.

It would be a mistake for non-specialists to express a definite opinion on this. String theorists may yet come up with some empirically testable proposition. But the basic methodological point raised by its critics is surely valid. To be scientific, a theory must tell us something different about the world. It has to tell us something we would not have known without it. If the theory is true, then reality must be discernibly different from the way it would be if a rival theory was true.

A hypothesis can be scientific and turn out eventually to be wrong. It may make predictions about observations, and when these observations are made, some of them may turn out different from what was predicted. Such a theory was at least a scientific hypothesis, albeit a finally falsified one. But the charge is that string theory is not even wrong, because it says nothing about the universe that can be empirically tested.

If we go from physics to economics we can ask, what sort of theory is the labour theory of value?

Is it a validated scientific theory, a falsified theory, or one that is not even wrong?

Well it is clear that, in its strongest and simplest form, the labour theory of value does say something testable. It says that expended labour is the source of monetary value added. One can, in principle, add up hours of labour that are directly and indirectly used up in producing the outputs of different industries and then compare this with the monetary value added. If the hours of labour turn out to be uncorrelated or rather poorly correlated with the monetary value added then the theory would have been falsified.

One can often guard a theory against falsification by auxiliary hypotheses. The most famous of these were the Greek epicycle and deferent adjustments to models of planetary motion. These allowed the hypothesis that all planetary motion could be decomposed into uniform circular components to be reconciled with the at times visibly retrograde motion of the planets. In more recent theory, one may suspect that the hypothesized dark matter and dark energy, used to explain galactic orbits and accelerated cosmic expansion, play a role that is philosophically analogous to Ptolemaic epicycles.

In economics one can formulate weaker versions of the labour theory of value in which monetary value added is proportional not to observed labour, but to social necessary labour. If one so defines socially necessary labour, that its necessity is only revealed by by the movement of market prices, then one does indeed end up with a theory so weak as to be not even wrong. There is an ambiguity in the usage of the term socially necessary labour. On the one hand it may be used to mean using no more labour to produce say a loaf of bread than is necessary under the prevailing state of technology, on the other it may mean using no more labour in the baking industry than is necessary given the level of demand for bread. The first interpretation of 'socially necessary' still leaves us with a testable hypothesis, the second insulates the hypothesis from test. There has been a regrettable tendency by some authors[5] to formulate the labour theory of value in this weak unfalsifiable form.

The strong form of the labour theory of value, however, is not only testable but has actually been tested and verified by empirical studies, [Sha98], [MCC95], [Zac06], [TM02] among others. These studies show typically show correlations of around 95% or more between the monetary value of industries' outputs and the labour required to produce that output.[6]

It is interesting to contrast this strong result for the simple labour theory of value, with its main competitor – the marginalist theory of value. This is based on the idea that prices evolve to levels at which marginal utilities per $ are equalised across different products. This is an unfalsifiable proposition. Since subjective utilities are unobservable, it is impossible to do the sort of correlation studies comparing the price structure of a country with utilities that have been done for the labour theory of value. Any price structure that one observes could be said to reflect subjective utilities. This part of marginalist theory is unscientific and falls into the 'not even wrong' category.

The other part of marginalist theory – that prices will be set equal to marginal productivities is potentially falsifiable. It deals with things that are in principle observable and measurable. It is falsifiable, and has already been falsified [Hal88].

The marginalist theory of value melds the wrong to the not even wrong.

---

[5] I am thinking here of advocates of 'value form theory' such as Williams and Reuten.

[6] It is worth mentioning in the light of criticism by Bichler and Nitzan, that these high correlations are obtained whether labour inputs are measured directly in person years as was done in Zachariah's work on Sweden, or estimated indirectly from wage bills as was done in other studies. The Swedish government data has the advantage of giving direct person-year figures for the labour used in each industry.

The relevance of probabilistic models

The labour theory of value is empirically testable, and the evidence for it is empirically strong. The marginalist theory is in large part untestable, and testable parts have been falsified, but it retains enormously more influence than its old rival. Why?

There are obviously sociological reasons why the labour theory of value might be unpopular and it also takes time for results published in relatively little read journals to percolate. But even among those sympathetic to classical or Marxian political economy who are aware of the published results there has been less than universal acceptance of them. This, I think, is because whilst the labour theory of value is empirically supported, it has historically lacked any obvious mechanism. It remained at the level of a stable empirical relationship but the causal process behind it was unclear. Why should prices be determined by the work necessary to make things?

Farjoun and Machover's theory

> In that early and rude state of society which precedes both the accumulation of stock and the appropriation of land, the proportion between the quantities of labour necessary for acquiring different objects, seems to be the only circumstance which can afford any rule for exchanging them for one another. If among a nation of hunters, for example, it usually costs twice the labour to kill a beaver which it does to kill a deer, one beaver should naturally exchange for or be worth two deer. It is natural that what is usually the produce of two days or two hours labour, should be worth double of what is usually the produce of one day's or one hour's labour.([Smi74] Chapter 6)

Well, a skeptical neo-classical might say, that was all very well in an early and rude state of society, but why should the same principle apply today when Smith's original mechanism no longer operates?

The first really coherent reason why was given by Farjoun and Machover [FM83] back in the 1980s. They point out that for any commodity it is in principle possible to work out how much wage expenditure was directly or indirectly incurred in its production. So a particular model of Ford would have wage expenditure at the Ford factory, wage expenditure at the tyre factory, at the power station that supplied the factory etc. In principle one

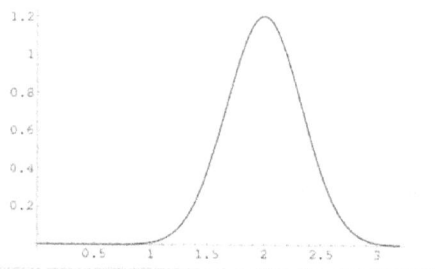

Figure 5.1.: Only a very small proportion of products will sell for less than their aggregated wage content. The horizontal axis shows the selling price in $ of the commodity per $ spent on direct and indirect wages. The vertical axis shows the relative frequency with which this is likely to occur. The exact mean and standard deviation of the normal distribution are chosen for illustrative purposes.

might have to trace this back through many layers of the economy, but the further back you go, the less difference it starts to make. In practice one obtains reasonably stable estimates if one goes back through about 8 or 10 layers of indirect inputs. These wage costs are called 'vertically integrated labour costs'.

A Ford selling for $20,000 might have an ultimate wage cost of let us say $12,000. From this you can get a figure for the value added per $ spent on wages: in this example 20,000/12,000=5/3=1.66. For different commodity sales the ratio of selling price to vertically integrated labour costs will vary in a random fashion. The actual ratio for any given product will be the result of a huge multiplicity of adventitious causes. It will depend on wage rates and the prices of inputs which are themselves randomly varying in terms of labour cost. Statistical theory says that a random sum of things which are themselves random can be described by the Normal distribution, the familiar Bell Curve shown in Figure 5.1.

A normal distribution can be characterized by only two numbers:

1. The mean or average of the distribution

2. The width or standard deviation of the distribution

What can we deduce about bell curves for value added per vertically integrated $ of wages, like that shown in Figure 5.1?

Farjoun and Machover point out that wages tended to make up around 50% of value added in developed capitalist countries[7] , which implies that the mean value added per $ of wages will tend to be around 2 as shown in the diagram. We can also say something about the width of the distribution. They point out that only a very small proportion of commodities will sell for less than their vertically aggregated wage costs. Were they to do this not only would the firms making them be failing to meet their wage costs, but there would be no room for profit income in the raw materials supplied. They suggest that only about 1/1000 of sales of commodities will be at prices this low.

By consulting a table of the normal distribution, one finds that the probability of events 3 standard deviations away from the mean is about 1/1000, so for a mean of 2, then the standard deviation must equal 1/3. How do these predictions stack up against real data?

Using data for the United Kingdom in 1984, the year after their book was published, we calculated [CC98] that the bell curve for the UK could be pretty well approximated by a normal distribution with a mean 1.46 and standard deviation of 0.151. They had underestimated the wage share in UK income, but they had got the share of output selling below its aggregated wage cost about right: for the UK the standard deviation was 1/3 the distance between 1 and the mean.

What are the implications of this?

If the standard deviation in the ratio of the selling price to vertically integrated labour costs has to be small, the consequence is that real selling prices have to be closely clustered around Marxian labour values.

In other words the simple labour theory of must hold. The strong correlation[8] observed between labour content and monetary value of output is a necessary or emergent result of the statistically random process of price formation.

The form of argument used by Farjoun and Machover is rather alien to the tradition of political economy. The later has tended, from its in-

---

[7] This was roughly right when they were writing.
[8] We use the term correlation here, but other statistical measures of the closeness between labour content and monetary value such as the coefficient of variation or the cosine metric could be used. They all show a close relationship as predicted by Farjoun and Machover's theory.

ception, to look for explanations in terms of the actions of rational profit-maximising individuals directing the economy towards some sort of equilibrium. Instead Farjoun and Machover, who were mathematicians not economists, imported the form of reasoning that had been used in thermodynamics or statistical mechanics. This branch of physics deals with the behaviour of large complex systems with huge numbers of degrees of freedom. The classical example of this type of system is gas composed of huge numbers of randomly moving molecules.

In such a system it is fruitless to try and form a deterministic and microscopic picture of the interaction of individual molecules. But you can make a number of useful deductions about the statistical properties of the whole collection of molecules. It was from the statistical properties of such collections that Boltzmann was able to derive the laws of thermodynamics [Bol95].

What Farjoun and Machover did was apply this form of reasoning to another chaotic system with a large number of degrees of freedom: the market economy. In doing this they initiated a new discipline of study: econophysics. This, in a very radical way, views the economy as a process without a subject. It assumes nothing about knowing subjects, instead it attempts to apply the principle of parsimony. It assumes nothing about the individual economic actors. Instead it theorises the aggregate constraints and and statistical distributions of the system that arise from the assumption of maximal disorder. A such this approach is anathema to the subjectivist Austrian school.[9]

Yakovenko's model

The econophysics approach was further developed by Yakovenko who at the time did not know of Farjoun and Machover's earlier work.

Thermodynamics predicts that systems tend to settle into a state of maximum entropy. The conservation laws specify that whilst this randomization occurs energy must be conserved. Boltzmann and Gibbs showed that this implies that the probability distribution of energies that meets these two criteria is one like that shown in Figure 5.2.

Yakovenko [CMC+09, DY02] has argued that since money is conserved in the buying and selling of commodities it is analogous to energy. If

---

[9] Given their Catholic problematic, the Austrian school find it is inconceivable for economics to dispense with the category of subject; see the debate on this issue at the Mises Organisation.

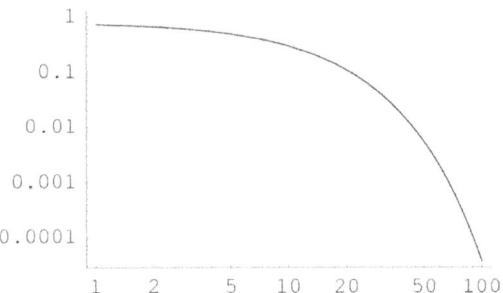

Figure 5.2.: The Gibbs Boltzmann form of distribution. Logarithm of energy on the horizontal axis, logarithm of probability density on the vertical one.

the system settles into a maximum entropy state then monetary wealth will come to follow a Gibbs Boltzmann distribution. He is able to show (see Figure 5.3) that the observed income distribution for 97% of the US population is well explained by a negative exponential distribution of the Gibbs form.

There remains a super-thermal tail of income (the top 3%) whose income is not conformant with maximal entropy but follows a power law distribution.

The fact that income distribution consists of two distinct parts reveals the two-class structure of the American society. Coexistence of the exponential and power-law distributions is also known in plasma physics and astrophysics, where they are called the thermal and super-thermal parts . The boundary between the lower and upper classes can be defined as the intersection point of the exponential and power-law fits in Fig.[5.3]. For 1997, the annual income separating the two classes was about 120 k$. About 3% of the population belonged to the upper class, and 97% belonged to the lower class. [YRJ09]

The thermal distribution arises from the application of the conservation

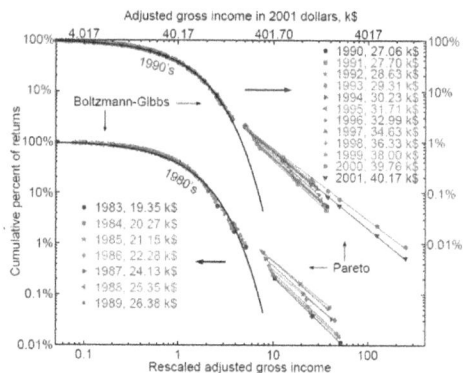

Figure 5.3.: The results of Yakovenko and Rosser [YRJ09] for the actual distribution of money income in the US, showing a good fit to the Gibbs Boltzmann distribution for the majority of the population. There exist a population of very wealthy people that do not fit on the curve and whose wealth must arise from a different process.

law plus randomness. The non thermal distribution from the violation of conservation law. Yakovenko says that the non thermal group rely on income from capital and the stock market. This is consistent with Marx's analysis that profit in general can not arise within a conservative system, but from something outside of the conservative system production of surplus value. The initial analysis of the exchange of commodities by Marx in Capital can be read as describing the laws governing the conservation of value in exchange.

The subject of income and wealth distributions and social inequality was very popular at the turn of another century and is associated with the names of Pareto, Lorenz, Gini, Gibrat, and Champernowne, among others. Following the work by Pareto, attention of researchers was primarily focused on the power laws. However, when physicists took a fresh look at the empirical data, they found a different, exponential law for the lower part of the distribution. Demonstration of the ubiquitous nature of the exponential distribution for money, wealth, and income is one of the new contributions produced by econophysics. The motivation, of course, came from the Boltzmann-Gibbs distribution in physics. Further studies revealed a more detailed picture of the two-class distribution in a society. Although social classes have been known in political economy since Karl Marx, realization that they are described by simple mathematical distributions is quite new. Very interesting work was done by the computer scientist Ian Wright [Wri05, Wri08], who demonstrated emergence of two classes in an agent-based simulation of initially equal agents. [YRJ09]

Wright has shown, in the work that Rosser and Yakovenko cite, that random exchange models generate combined Gibbs plus power law distributions as soon as you allow the hiring of labour. This is again consistent with Marxs old analysis.

In conclusion we can say that recent work has gone a long way to reestablishing the scientific credentials of Marxian economics. It has done so by taking literally his aphorism about discovering the 'laws of motion' of the capitalist system.

Written in 2011

References

BL91 W. Brus and K. Laski, From Marx to the market: Socialism in search of an economic system, Oxford University Press, USA, 1991.

Bol95 L. Boltzmann, Lectures on gas theory, Dover Pubns, 1995.

CC98 Paul Cockshott and Allin Cottrell, Does Marx need to transform?, Marxian Economics: A Reappraisal (R. Bellofiore, ed.), vol. 2, Basingstoke, 1998, pp. 70-85.

CMC+09 W.P. Cockshott, GJ Michaelson, A. Cottrell, I. Wright, and V. Yakovenko, Classical econophysics, Routledge, 2009.

DY02 A. Dragulescu and V. M. Yakovenko, Statistical mechanics of money, income and wealth: a short survey, 2002, http://arXiv.org/abs/cond-mat/0211175.

FM83 Emmanuel Farjoun and Moshe Machover, Laws of chaos, a probabilistic approach to political economy, Verso, London, 1983.

Hag06 K. Hagendorf, A Note on Ronald Meek's' Studies in the Labour Theory of Value', 2006.

Hag10 _____, A Critique of Gossen's Fundamental Theorem of the Theory of Pleasure, 2010.

Hal88 R.E. Hall, The Relation between Price and Marginal Cost in US Industry, Journal of Political Economy 96 (1988), no. 5.

MCC95 G. Michaelson, W. P. Cockshott, and A. F. Cottrell, Testing Marx: some new results from UK data, Capital and Class (1995), 103-129.

Mir89 P. Mirowski, More Heat Than Light: Economics as Social Physics, physics as Nature's Economics, Cambridge University Press, 1989.

NB09 J. Nitzan and S. Bichler, Capital as power: a study of order and creorder, Routledge, 2009.

Sci95 C.M. Sciabarra, Marx, Hayek, and utopia, State Univ of New York Pr, 1995.

SH08 L. Smolin and J. Harnad, The trouble with physics: the rise of string theory, the fall of a science, and what comes next, The Mathematical Intelligencer 30 (2008), no. 3, 66-69.

Sha98 A. M. Shaikh, The empirical strength of the labour theory of value, Marxian Economics: A Reappraisal (R. Bellofiore, ed.), vol. 2, Macmillan, 1998, pp. 225-251.

Smi74 Adam Smith, The Wealth of Nations, 1974.

Ste81 Ian Steedman, Marx after Sraffa, Verso, London, 1981.

Ste92 D.R. Steele, From Marx to Mises: Post-capitalist society and the challenge of economic calculation, Open Court, 1992.

TM02 L. Tsoulfidis and T. Maniatis, Values, prices of production and market prices: some more evidence fro the Greek economy, Cambridge Journal of Economics 26 (2002), 359-369.

Woi06 P. Woit, Not even wrong: the failure of string theory and the search for unity in physical law, Basic Books, 2006.

Wri05 I. Wright, The social architecture of capitalism, Physica A: Statistical Mechanics and its Applications 346 (2005), no. 3-4, 589-620.

Wri08 _____, Implicit microfoundations for macroeconomics, Economics Discussion Papers (2008).

YRJ09 V.M. Yakovenko and J.B. Rosser Jr, Colloquium: Statistical mechanics of money, wealth, and income, Reviews of Modern Physics 81 (2009), no. 4, 1703-1725.

Zac06 David Zachariah, Labour value and equalisation of profit rates, Indian Development Review 4 (2006), no. 1, 1-21.

Part II.

Agitation

6. Against Nationalism

Nationalism is a form of state-supporting ideology specific to capitalist society. Nationalism is an idea. Its function is to persuade people to be loyal to a state or to a government. Nationalism is the idea that makes people who live in a state think of themselves as citizens of that state.

French nationalism makes people who live in the French state think that they are French. The function of French nationalism is therefore to make people who live there loyal to the French state. The function of British nationalism is to make people loyal to the British government. People who are loyal to a government do what the government tells them.

To win people's support the state uses all sorts of symbols and myths. These are called national symbols or national tradition. For instance a state will have its own cloth design. This is called a national flag. On ritual occasions people will wave these pieces of cloth in the air or tie them onto poles or buildings. In some states, America for instance, people look at these cloths and then touch their foreheads with their hands. They call this saluting the flag. Sometimes on such occasions, they will sing a special song which says how great and good their nation is. Whenever they hear this song people are supposed to stand up straight.

National Myths

An example of a national myth is the legend of Joan of Arc. She was a poor peasant girl who is said to have heard the voice of god telling her take up arms and drive the English out of France. She was burned at the stake by the English for her pains. This makes her a national martyr.

Governments need nationalism to make people obey them. They use nationalism to make people think that they are not just obeying a particular group of men – the government. It tries to persuade them that they are doing something more important. This important thing is called the person's 'duty' to the nation.

Duty

Duty has to be made out to be a very, very important thing because it often turns out to be dangerous or unpleasant. In the early years of this century the government decided that it was our grandfathers duty to go and kill people who came from Germany. This involved putting on brown clothes which were called the national uniform. Next our grandfathers were told that it was their duty to obey certain men from the upper classes called officers. Next these officers told them that it was their duty to walk in front of machine guns which men in grey uniforms were going to aim at them. Most of them did as they were told and got shot.

Afterwards their bodies were lined up in neat rows and white stones were put on top of them. Their bodies were then given a new name. They were called 'our glorious dead'.

The nationalist idea became common in last two hundred years. It went along with the development of capitalism. In feudal times people were less nationalistic. Instead of singing anthems and saluting flags, they swore allegiance to a particular person. This person was called a sovereign. People promised to obey him and fight for him. In less orderly places people swore to obey local clan chiefs or various types of lords.

Causes

The reason that nationalism has become common since the start of capitalism is that the capitalist classes in different parts of the world wanted to protect their home market. To do this they needed to set up capitalist governments. These governments would then put up customs barriers that would protect them from foreign competition and pass various other laws to help the development of industry. These governments would be made up of business men and other professional men such as lawyers.

Kings used to claim that they must be obeyed because they were acting as God's representative on earth. In other words they claimed a divine right to rule. In modern times this idea became less and less plausible. If people would no longer believe the myth that the king was God's representative, they were even less likely to believe that a government made up of bankers and industrialists had been sent by God. This is why the nationalist idea became necessary. People were to be taught that obedience to the government was their duty to the nation. By the use of songs and symbols and ceremonies, the nation was made to seem some supernatural entity, just as god had been in the past.

This is why from a socialist standpoint nationalism is – always – an illusion. There are no good and bad nationalism, it is as De Leon called it, the falsest of all false paths.

In this it is like religion, it is false, but lots of people believe in it and one can not reliably make them dis-believe it by oppression. Oppression of a religion or a nationalist ideology by another religion or nationalism only reinforces peoples sense of identity with it. It was for this reason and this alone that Lenin defended the right of nations to self determination – because any attempt to deny it merely reinforced nationalist ideology.

Written in 1991

Postscript 2011

At a recent meeting in Berlin I got into conversation with Sabine Wils an MSP for Die Linke. In the course of the conversation I was trying to persuade her that the Left should aim for a strong and democratic European republic with the power of the existing nation states much reduced. I made no progress with my attempt. She said that whilst Die Linke were in favour of a more democratic and socialist Europe, they were also in favour of devolving as much as possible to the nation states.

The appeal of the idea of devolution to the nation states is understandable given the obvious democratic deficits in the current EU constitution, but I am convinced that it is short sighted. It would be far better for the Left parties in the EU to unite into a single Europe wide socialist party that would stand in elections accross the continent as the European Socialist Party rather than as separate national parties.

The economy of Europe is no longer organised on national grounds, and in consequence, were a socialist government to come to power in one EU state, even in a big state like France, they would be unable to carry through a socialist programme. Current EU treaties place so many restrictions on public intervention in the economy that a socialist government would have to chose between staying in the EU or abandoning its socialist programme. This proved to be the case even for the mildly socialist government of Mitterand back in the late 20th century. If a Left government choses to stay in the EU then it has to accomodate to the existing economic structure, but if it choses to leave the EU it will face the loss of its major markets and the potential loss of major suppliers. The disruptive economic effects that can follow the breakdown of a previously unified economy were made all to evident in the terrible economic retrogression that followed the breakup

of the USSR into distinct national economies in the 1990s.
Faced with this alternative, Left governments in individual countries are likely to see compromise with the existing order as the lesser evil. The nation states do have some significant elements of economic autonomy left to them – the most important being the ability to set their own tax rates, but in the context of a competitive capitalist market, this fiscal autonomy helps capital more than labour. As I write, the SNP government in Scotland is busy demanding fiscal autonomy from London. I think that there is little doubt that the SNP are the most left wing of the UK political parties. They have remained old style Social Democrats and Anti-Imperialists long after the Labour Party has become Social Liberal and Liberal Imperialist.

But what is the SNP's main reason for seeking fiscal autonomy? In order to emulate the Irish and reduce corporation tax!

Their aim is to bribe firms into investing in Scotland rather than England. So even a Left party is tempted by social dumping. From a short term parochial viewpoint, cutting corporation tax might seem a smart move, but it is a race to the bottom that can only aggravate the chronic financial problems in Europe caused by the systematic under-taxation of profit incomes.

The main way that the existing social order is maintained is via ideology, via the ideological machinery of the state.[1] The nation states and the organisation of political parties around these remain a unity of repressive an ideological state apparatuses in Europe. The upper classes lack EU wide ideological apparattu. They have it is true international ideological machinery: the catholic church of course, and some news agencies that operate trans nationally, but these are less effective than the nationally or-

---

[1] "I shall call Ideological State Apparatuses a certain number of realities which present themselves to the immediate observer in the form of distinct and specialized institutions. I propose an empirical list of these which will obviously have to be examined in detail, tested, corrected and re-organized. With all the reservations implied by this requirement, we can for the moment regard the following institutions as Ideological State Apparatuses (the order in which I have listed them has no particular significance):– the religious ISA (the system of the different Churches),– the educational ISA (the system of the different public andprivate 'Schools'),– the family ISA,[8]– the legal ISA,[9]– the political ISA (the political system, including thedifferent Parties),– the trade-union ISA,– the communications ISA (press, radio and television, etc.),– the cultural ISA (Literature, the Arts, sports, etc.).... But now for what is essential. What distinguishes the ISAs from the (Repressive) State Apparatus is the followingbasic difference: the Repressive State Apparatus functions 'by violence', whereas the Ideological State Apparatuses' function 'by ideology '."(Althusser, "Ideology and State Ideological Apparatuses", in *Lenin and Philosophy*, Monthly Review Press 1971, page 144.)

ganised ideological apparatuses of the political parties, law, and national media.

As currently constituted the EU structure constantly reinforces the process of national identification. Political parties are national. Negotiations in the Council of Ministers are between representatives of the national state machines, with ministers claiming to represent the Greek, German or French. etc. interests. Since the EU has no tax collection machinery of its own, its revenues appear as something 'given' to it by the nation states. All this reinforces self identification with and loyalty to the national states.

Some comrades said to me whilst in Germany, yes ideally we would like to see international socialist organisation, but you can not get away from the reality of nations or people's attachment to national cultures. Europe is not the US they say, we have different languages and thus different nations.

I believe this is the wrong way to look at things. The nationalism is consequence of todays political structure not the cause of it. In many cases nationalism is a recent historical product, manufactured by nationalist movements seeking their own state machine to control. Today one can witness how the nationalist party in Scotland is manufacturing such identification: it paints the trains, bus passes and government stationary with the national flag, it constantly raises political issues in national us versus them terms. This process was carried out on a grand scale in the 20th century – with the dissolution of Austro-Hungary, in the lead up to and aftermath of world war II, and again after the fall of the Soviet Block.

Europe has many languages. But we can see that different languages do not necessarily lead to nationalism. India is a federal state with many languages, but its politics are mainly organised around all India political parties and movements, and people's primary identification is with India as a federation rather than with the federal states. This is because the federation has a strong center, with a parliament that has tax raising and legislative powers.

In Europe economic crises are settled by haggling between the leaders of the nation states, with the big states like France and Germany inevitably dominating. But in a US context that would be like the governors of California or New York having summits to determine the fate of the Union. It just does not happen, nor does it happen in India, because these countries have a proper federal state.

Today there are three great forces in Europe that are undermining nationalism. The first is the internet – by means of which the recent protest movements have organised. The second is movement of people to work and to study. In Scotland today, with a population of about 5 million we have had 600,000 coming to work from Poland alone. A multinational working population is being created. And finally there is the economic logic of monetary union which is making the old EU constitutional structure unviable.

The Left needs now, more than ever, to break with nationalism's web of maya.

7. Beyond anti-imperialism

For socialists, the recent attempt by the US state apparatus to bring back large-scale occupations on the world scene revived the relevance of anti-imperialism as a stance from which to oppose the havoc and carnage inflicted on masses of Iraq and Afghanistan. It also renewed an interest in the theory of imperialism since the US occupations marked a break in the trend after 1945, when the advanced capitalist states shifted their mode of operation.

For some socialists operating in a 'Marxist-Leninist' discourse, however, 'imperialism' has always been a central element of its understanding of contemporary capitalism. This view is theoretically rooted in the classic texts of Hobson, Hilferding and Lenin written in what Hobsbawm called an Age of Empire, from 1875 to World War I. Lenin's short pamphlet from 1916, beyond some dubious economics[1] , had the undoubted political virtue of providing both an explanation of the World War and a moral standpoint for root and branch opposition to it. To him imperialism was the key to revolutionary strategy, arguing that a war between empires to redivide the world lead to revolutions. Imperialism, as the age of war and revolution, provided the justification for and strategy of the new communist international. The prediction was that another imperialist war would not be long in coming, and that this would allow revolution to spread. The Comintern were right on both these counts, as World War II and its crop of revolutions bore witness.

The mechanisms of imperialism in the era of capitalist states

The general concept of 'imperial power' goes back to pre-capitalist historical empires, such as the Holy Roman Empire and Empire of the Great Qing. What distinguished them from other polities and states of the time is commonly taken to be features of 'imperial power' rather than simply 'state power'. The key feature was their use of *extra-economic coercion*

---

[1]The late Bill Warren, one of the CPGB's most capable theorists pointed many of these out in *Imperialism pioneer of capitalism*, Verso 1980

to incorporate other regions and polities into subordinate economic relations. As such imperialism has a transient aspect; the process of incorporation by extra-economic means is limited in time whereas the maintenance of subordination by such means may or may not persist.

The specifically capitalist form of imperialism resulted from the convergence of the competitive interests of states with the interests of competing capitals. In medieval Europe inter-state competition for territory and resources arose from the tendency towards 'political accumulation' inherent to feudal relations of production. When other states entered into competition with the English state whose productive capitalist form of agriculture allowed it to extract more surplus, these other states either pursued capitalist modernisation or succumbed through warfare.

The capitalist imperative on the other hand had its origins, as Luxemburg had argued, in the fact that commerce could not penetrate non-commodity producing societies by purely economic means. Extra-economic coercion was required to separate the producers from their means of production, tax them, and force them into the market economy. That demanded gunboats, armies and Governor Generals in plumed hats.[2]

In the era of capitalist states, imperial power has operated through three primary mechanisms:

1. Direct colonial expansion and control.

2. Indirect control by threat of military violence and use of coercion.

3. Coordination between the repressive state apparatuses of the advanced and developing country.

The first and second mechanisms were crucial for the process of incorporating non-capitalist regions into subordinate economic relations. Colonial expansion was actively pursued in Africa and South and South-East Asia, and gunboat diplomacy in South America and East Asia. The third mechanism was put into operation when resistance by states was too powerful or costly to defeat, but local ruling class interests could be coordinated with the ruling class of the centre. After WWII this mechanism was central for the US state apparatus in its struggle against the Soviet-socialist bloc

---

[2] As Ellen Meiksins Wood puts it, "The history of early agrarian capitalism – the process of domestic 'colonization', the removal of land from the 'waste', its 'improvement', enclosure and new conceptions of property rights – was reproduced in the theory and practice of empire". *Empire of Capital*, p. 78, Verso, 2003.

as well as securing the supply of oil – the main energy source in modern industrialised capitalism, highly concentrated in West Asia.

The first mechanism was at its peak during a phase that Lenin assumed to be the 'highest stage of capitalism', but after the Yalta conference it was in terminal decline. One by one each mechanism was either weakened or in a process of destruction on a global scale. To cope with the dramatic shifts in global capitalism, subsequent 'Marxist-Leninist' theories of imperialism shifted focus to concepts such as 'neo-colonialism', 'unequal exchange' and 'labour aristocracy'. We argue that this understanding of the world since 1945 is theoretically and empirically ill-founded, drawing as it were on certain transient aspects of imperialism. Moreover, the politics that flows from the theory has unintended reactionary consequences.

Epicycles: Neo-colonialism, unequal exchange and labour aristocracy

Neo-colonialism 'Neo-colonialism', for instance, is in part a concoction cooked up by Khruschovite revisionism and bourgeois nationalists during the 1950s and 60s, and once served a purpose: to justify a diplomatic alliance between the USSR and new bourgeois leaders like Nasser and Nkrumah. As a policy it was terrible. Anti-imperialist alliances with the national bourgeoisies in Egypt, Iraq etc., did the working classes of those countries no good at all. And the Soviet alliance tended to be dumped by the bourgeoisies once they established themselves. Politically, it never offered any perspective of independent working-class politics.

The notion 'neo-colonialism' implies the persistence of relative underdevelopment in the global South, even after formal colonial rule has been overthrown and independent states have been formed. Processes of underdevelopment may indeed continue through (i) the class structures of the pre-industrial economies impeding productive reinvestment of the surplus product and (ii) competition on the world market pursued through a low wage, primary-sector strategy. But (i) and (ii) operate differently in regions subject to colonial rule from regions with independent capitalist states.

Consequently the political strategies to weaken and destroy the mechanisms of inequities are fundamentally different in colonialism and independent capitalist states subject to competition. By obscuring the difference between them one also downplays the tremendous efforts and struggle by anti-imperialist movements to end the first mechanism of imperial power:

direct colonial expansion and control.

Unequal exchange   The theory of 'unequal exchange' is even more anti-working class than 'neo-colonialism', designed to destroy the confidence of the workers in capitalist countries by portraying them as exploiters of the Third World. It has nothing in common with Marx's economic writings, which go on at great length to show that capitalist profit can not arise through inequality in *exchange*. He argued that it arose instead, in the process of capitalist *production*.

Trade did play an important part in the operation of the British empire by regulating the appropriation of surplus products across regions. At the height of European imperialism, Britain established a particular global pattern of trade and credit flows, in which it ran a persistent trade surplus with India, China and Japan that enabled it to finance a substantial part of its deficit with the advanced capitalist countries in North America and Europe.[3] In other words, the South and East Asian masses were drawn into debt by British net exports, and this helped finance the empire's appropriation of the surplus product produced by workers in the advanced capitalist economies. But since the collapse of empires there is nothing comparable to this historically specific parasitical mechanism. By contrast, the most advanced capitalist economy of today, the USA, has for a long time run a persistent *deficit* with China, Japan and oil producing countries in West Asia, sinking deeper into debt to these less developed capitalist economies.

Unequal exchange theory, however, rests on the medieval Thomist doctrines of 'just price' and is a regression from scientific political economy. True enough, if a worker in the US buys a shirt made in Mexico, it will contain more labour than one made in the US, and is likely to be cheaper into the bargain. Does this turn the US worker into an exploiter of Mexican labour?

The unequal exchange theorists will say yes. Since the terms of trade are 'unequal'. Goods requiring 100 hours of US labour, when exported to Mexico exchange for goods requiring perhaps 400 hours of Mexican labour. Thus even allowing for the fact that she only gets back in wages about half the labour she puts in, worker in the US can obtain for an hours work goods that took a couple of hours labour by Mexican workers.

But the labour that contributes to value is *socially necessary* labour.

You will recall that I used the word "*Social* labour", and

---

[3]Mike Davis, *Late Victorian Holocausts*, Verso, 2002.

that many points are involved in the qualification *"Social"*. In saying that the value of a commodity is determined by the *quantity of labour* worked up or crystallised in it, we mean *the quantity of labour necessary* for its production in a given state of society, under certain social average conditions of production, with a given social average intensity, and average skill of the labour employed. When in England, the power loom came to compete with the hand-loom, only one-half the former time of labour was wanted to convert a given amount of yarn into cotton cloth. The poor hand-loom weaver now worked seventeen or eighteen hours daily, instead of the nine or ten hours that he worked before. Still the product of twenty hours of his labour represented now only ten social hours of labour, or ten hours of labour socially necessary for the conversion of a certain amount of yarn into textile stuffs. His product of twenty hours had, therefore, no more value than his former product of ten hours. (Karl Marx, *Wages Price and Profit*, p. 28, Moscow 1981)

As economies with lower productivity of labour are opened up to competition with advanced ones, this process repeats itself. Labour performed in pre-state of the art conditions, is devalued as the social labour necessary to produce commodities fall. But this is an inevitable effect of the exchange process. For in exchange, the social status of private labours, is established by equating use values, and this presupposes self-identity. Thus the equality

$$1 \text{ kilo of maize} = 1 \text{ kilo of maize}$$

must hold. So as the Mexican maize market is opened up to the products of US agriculture, 1 kilo of maize produced by a peasant in Chiapas becomes equivalent to 1 kilo of US maize that might require only a 10th or a 20th as much labour, and with this the labour of the peasant is further devalued. An consequently the livelihoods of direct producers in less developed economies are threatened. But all this is due not to a law of inequality, but of equality. "The sphere of circulation or commodity exchange ... is in fact a very Eden of the innate rights of man. It is the exclusive realm of Freedom, Equality, Property and Bentham."[4] According to Marx it is in production not circulation that exploitation arises. Marx's economic

---

[4]Karl Marx, *Capital I*, p. 280, Penguin edition

writings are one long polemic against the sort of moralising socialism that demanded the installation of a regime of 'fair exchange'. Capitalism, he said, rests on just such exchange.

Average wages are fundamentally constrained by labour productivity. Not even the most well-organised workers' movement could raise incomes above the value added. But what accounts for the gap of the industrialising economies to the advanced capitalist ones? The historical roots of relative stagnation in productivity lie in a combination of (i) unevenly distributed environmental conditions that enabled intensified economic development and warfare, (ii) the laws of motion of pre-capitalist relations of production, which lacked a structural dynamic to reinvest the surplus products in developing the means of production to enhance productive capacity. The devastating effects of imperialism *aggravated and perpetuated this productivity gap* in the formation of the 'modern world' pioneered by capitalist England.

Labour aristocracy   Rather than providing a well-grounded materialist explanation of the episodic and discontinuous organisation and militancy of the working-class movement, the 'Marxist-Leninist' theories attempted to use 'imperialism' to fill the theoretical void left when expectations of ever-growing class consciousness and organisation failed to be realised. The idea was that by the upper-classes deriving net incomes from their subordinate regions, a fraction was transferred through capitalist firms in imperialist countries to a section of the working class in order to 'buy them off'. This would lead to quiescence and even support by the working class to imperial power abroad.

Leaving aside the empirical validity of such a mechanism, its theoretical status is dubious. First, if it a small section is supposed to be bought off, it is questionable why they would be capable to wield such extraordinary powerful and persistent influence over the entire working class. Secondly, if it is a large section that is bought off it could hardly be done by net incomes flowing from the less developed economies since they could barely sustain more than a tiny fraction of the wage bill.[5] Even so, since the bulk of the workforce is employed in firms that are not directly involved

---

[5]Charlie Post reports that for US firms, total profits earned abroad constituted a mere 6% of the total US wage bill in 2003. Given that the bulk of incomes that flow to advanced capitalist countries are derived from other advanced countries, the percentage from the global South would be still smaller. C. Post, "The Labor Aristocracy Myth", *Against the Current* 123, July, 2006.

in extraction of such incomes, it is less obvious how the distributed profits to them would generate support for imperialist policies. Finally, higher wages are as such not an index of working-class quiescence but rather the marketplace and workplace bargaining power of workers in different professions and sectors. Skilled workers organised in sectors that are critical points in capitalist production – e.g. requiring large amounts of fixed capital or are central to the supply/demand chain – can win concessions and advance their position collectively. Hence it is no surprise that better paid sections of the working class have often been the vanguard of the movement; its most militant and best organised activists from Petrograd to Paris to Seoul.

Banks based in Tokyo, London and New York extract billions in interest payments on sovereign debt each month. But this does not mean that Japan, Britain etc., exploit Third World countries. That is to abandon all class analysis. The *capitalist classes* of Japan and Britain participate in the exploitation of workers and peasants in the Third World – but the working classes of the Old Industrialised Countries gain nothing from this. Far from being a bribed labour aristocracy, their own subjugation to capital becomes more complete, threatened as they are, with their jobs being moved to the Newly Industrialised Countries.

The decline of imperialism

With the end of WWII Stalin thought he would strike it three times lucky. In 1951 he was predicting the imminence of new imperialist wars.[6] Britain and France, he said, would soon be at war with America defending their empires.[7] With 20-20 hindsight we can assess the acuity of his foresight. Far from fighting to extend their empires, the imperial powers found them

---

[6]*Economic Problems of Socialism*, Chapter 6.
[7]He obviously had some difficulty in persuading others in the Soviet government of this view, this is evident from his references to 'some comrades' who doubted the inevitability of new inter imperialist wars. For a discussion see *How the Soviet Union is governed,* Jerry F. Hough, Merle Fainsod, Harvard University Press, 1979 page 185. The communist movement had during the inter war years anticipated a war between the USA and UK for world domination, and whilst the US armed forces had detailed plans for the invasion of Canada as late as 1935 (see *Critical areas of Canada and approaches thereto,* Prepared by: Subcommittee No. 3, Major Charles H. Jones, Infantry, Chairman. Lt. Col. H.W. Crawford, Engineers. Declassified 1974, available from http://www.glasnost.de/hist/usa/1935invasion.html) there was never any political commitment towards this on either side of the Atlantic.

unsustainable. Holland first, then Britain, France and eventually Portugal gave them up. In Britain the Labour Party dissolved the Empire in India at its first opportunity. In other cases it took defeat in guerrilla struggles to produce the same effect.

But the ultimate cause – beyond such immediate factors as the opposition of the workers' movements to imperialism and the aid of the USSR to anti-imperialist movements – was the development of the capitalist world economy. One by one the mechanisms of imperialism were weakened or destroyed across the world due to three factors:

* The rise of capitalism results in the rise of militarily viable states across the global South and the formation of popular classes that are capable of creating and extracting the resources to defend themselves in more powerful ways. This raises the *economic cost* of imperial aggression by the advanced states on the developing ones.

* The process of democratisation and growth of labour movements in the advanced world. This raises the domestic *political cost* of imperial aggression, either through resistance or by budgetary demands of social-democratic policies.[8]

* Once pre-capitalist economies are destroyed and the market set in their place, the extra-economic coercion of imperialism becomes obsolete; capitalist relations of production and the normal process of capital accumulation can continue without it. This weakens the *capitalist imperative* for imperial aggression.

The economic costs were a central reason why states adopted the first strategy of imperialism, colonial expansion and rule, instead of other means of extra-economic coercion in certain regions. E.g. while the West African states were of marginal importance to the British empire compared to non-colonized Latin America and China, they were much weaker and had consequently lower costs of colonisation. This strategy had its last spurt during the 1930s with the Italian invasion of Ethiopia and the Japanese colonisation of Manchuria and China. Due to the economic costs these proved much harder for the new imperial powers than the earlier British and French expansions. The second strategy, control by threat of military

---

[8]The dynamics arising from the economic and political costs of imperial aggression has been laid out by Vivek Chibber, *The Global Crisis and Hegemonic Dilemmas*, Lecture in New Delhi, 2010.

violence and use of coercion, was in decline after WWII due to economic and political costs. By the end of the Suez crisis in 1956 the former British and French empires had to abandon such means.

In the 1950s the US was quick to step up to the role left by the declining imperial powers. It was capable of doing so because the political costs were lower there than in most other advanced states, where the demands of national labour movements impinged on state policy. The economic costs of imperial aggression were however on the rise and at the same time the capitalist imperative was weaker, for the end of WWII had also brought the end of the transient dynamics of imperialism as an enabler of capitalism.

The central concern for state policy was now to maintain capitalist relations of production and prevent autonomous economic regions, not subject to the world market. Under this combination of costs and priorities US strategy relied primarily on extra-economic coercion through coordination between repressive state apparatuses across the world, constructing a vast network of military bases. In doing so it pursued points of convergence with local ruling classes wherever it was possible, from South Vietnam to Indonesia. Where it was not possible, efficient military violence and coercion was attempted provided the economic costs could be contained. The debacle of the invasions of Iraq and Afghanistan has seriously weakened the ability of the US to threaten similar incursions elsewhere. A fundamental reorientation of the US state policy in the near future would, however, require raising the political costs of imperial aggression by demands of changes in the composition of state expenditure. Unfortunately, the peculiar settler-state trajectory of the US has blocked the formation of a powerful national labour movement to impose such demands.

The limits of anti-imperialism

It is 2011 not 1911 and the new world order is global capitalism not imperialism. An Engels or a Zola would find nothing unfamiliar in the degradation and exploitation of today's Djakarta, Shanghai or Mexico. The new Manchesters share the industrial dynamism, sweatshops, oppulence and pauperism of the old. To advance anti-imperialist rather than simply anti-capitalist slogans now is meaningless at best: The only courses of economic development open are integration into the world market or socialism. Anti-imperialist phraseology obscures this by implying that there exists some third way short of socialism.

Any advocate of a specifically anti-imperialist political strategy would have to answer the following questions:

* ★ If wars leading to revolution are not imminent, on what do you base your strategy for socialism?

* ★ What is the political and economic content of 'anti-imperialism', i.e., what changes in economic or state structure do you struggle for other than those implied by an anti-capitalist strategy?

* ★ What extra allies does an anti-imperialist strategy bring to the struggle for socialism that a simple anti-capitalist strategy would not?

Written in 2011

8. Against Republicanism

New-speak

For his dystopia 1984, Orwell posited a dialect of English, New-speak that was so conceptually impoverished that subversion became literally unthinkable. New-speak led one to believe that war is peace, freedom is slavery etc. Writing in 1948 he was both prescient and subtle.

Prescient in that wars have now routinely become peacekeeping operations, and resumption of war can be greeted with the assertion that 'this must not stop the peace process'. Subtle in that we already speak and think a New-speak – the language of capitalism. Invented, not by a ministry of truth, but by the generations of half forgotten philosophers, economists and constitutional theorists, it binds our thoughts before it binds our actions. It redefines some words so radically that they take on almost the obverse of their original import, and in the process, it renders the converse, these words original meanings unspeakable and inconceivable.

Most affected are 'power words', like Democracy or Republic. At the heart of the incomprehension with which Dave Craig has greeted my criticisms, is the fact that he uses New-speak, and use these words in their older original meaning. Before universal suffrage, before newspapers, when political discourse was restricted to an aristocratic elite, such debate was free from euphemism and hypocrisy. All politically educated men knew that democracy was dangerous, probably the worst fate that could befall a state. It meant rule by the mob, the plebs, the villains, or if you knew your Aristotle 'rule by the poor'. It was the tyranny of the majority, rule by mass meetings that could ride roughshod over the law, where neither person nor property was safe.

A Republic stood, by contrast, for sound government. Rome, the original Republic, renown for martial prowess and sagacious laws remained its lasting epitome. The ideal constitution it secured for the wealthy the enjoyment of their estates, secure from the depredations of tyranny or the rapine of the mob. To the plebs it gave citizenship, the right to elect their tribunes, and above all the right to bear arms and fight for the glory of the

Republic. Legislation and executive power, in contrast, were the preserve of a political elite – the Senate.

When the slave-holders and bourgeois of the American Colonies rebelled against the Crown, relying as they did on an army of free citizens, and being at the same time desirous of securing their properties they settled upon the republican form of government, that had so well served their ancient forebears. By this act they formed the die from which modern republics and republicanism have been cast. Its keystone was election, both of the legislature and the magistracy – presidents, governors, judges. Until the early 19th century, the idea of a 'democratic republic' was a self-evident contradiction. A republic was the means by which the state could be secured against the danger of democracy. For democracy, it was understood, used not elections but the chaotic and almost anarchic institutions of the mass assembly or selection of officials and legislatures by lot.

Pre-bourgeois political theorists, from Aristotle to Machiavelli knew its function – to give the masses the illusion of power, whilst ensuring that it remained, in reality, in the hands of the upper classes. Any person has the right to stand for election, but if a poor tradesman stands in election against a sophisticated and urbane lawyer, nine times out of ten the lawyer wins. Freely elected legislatures are almost devoid of poor men, and totally devoid of poor women. But bourgeois theorists could not be so frank. They thus retained the republican form of government, whilst telling the people 'this is democracy'. There is no such thing as bourgeois democracy. What they call democracy is nothing of the sort – it is oligarchy, rule by the few, rule by the rich.

The real meaning of democracy was thus forgotten, and for over a century, those believing themselves to be democratic radicals like Craig, have struggled for its practical antithesis – the republic. The depth of the incomprehension to which this has given rise, is illustrated by Craig's thinking that I was advocating the election of juries. On the contrary, I was advocating sovereign juries, drawn, as in the past, by lot. From Aristotle to Mill, it was recognised that with sovereign juries, the people controlled the law. To Craig, it is a matter of detail as to whether one should demand elected juries or elected judges. But the election of juries is a totally reactionary demand. It would remove the only remaining relic of primitive democracy in the constitution. To whom would you rather entrust your liberty – a jury of your peers or a group of full-time, politically elected jurors. It does not take much think who would stand for and get elected to such posts – the same sort of retired conservative busybodies who become magistrates today.

Let's Hear it Again For...

Those who do not study history are supposedly doomed to repeat it. Those, whose knowledge of history is focused on the Russian Revolution, can, it seems, dream of nothing more than its repetition. But if Marx's aphorism is anything to go by, when history repeats itself, first comes tragedy then farce.

There was, tragedy enough in 1917 and its aftermath, triggered as it was by three years of a war whose privations can scarcely be imagined in our generation, a movement which precipitated a hundred million half starved peasants against a brutal landowning class and it police state. A revolutionary war and terror besides which that of the Jacobins pales, are to be put on a level with the pathetic scandal of the Windsors?

Craig imagines that this will involve a constituent assembly and a provisional government. Such institutions have, it is true, been thrown up in some countries at the dawn of bourgeois rule, but, given the past history of English revolutions we know that they are an irrelevance here. In a country that has never had a sovereign parliament or free elections, they may be necessary steps in the establishment of a stable civil society, but how would such an assembly differ from the existing parliament?

It would be elected on the same franchise, peopled by the same set of politicians, have no powers that parliament does not already have. It would, in short, have no cause to exist. When necessary parliament can, and has, dispensed with dynasties. A constituent assembly would if anything, be a reactionary step, seeking to 'bind its successors' with a written constitution that would enshrine the rights of liberty and property. These aspirations for a constituent assembly ill suit a pretended Leninist, given the master's forthright way of dealing with the Russian one.

Nowhereland?

The conservatism and historical narrowness of vision of the RDG[1] are astounding. Just as for the economists, economics is the economics of bourgeois society, for Craig, history is the history of the bourgeois epoch. Craig accuses me of drawing my advocacy of direct popular rule from Nowhereland, i.e., from Erehwon or Utopia.

---

[1] Revolutionary Democratic Group, a split from the SWP.

Exactly the same objection can be levelled at the very idea of Communism: it is utopian, where has it been tried before?

Marxism has a double answer. First, communism, the abolition of classes, private property and the state, is posited as the dialectical negation of civil, burgerlich, society: the resolution of its inner contradictions. Second it is, in historical terms the negation of the negation: the upswing of the cycle from primitive communism through class society to the communism of the future. Similarly direct rule by the masses is posited firstly as the antithesis of the political forms of burgerlich society: 'just as the representative system, the constitutional state or the representative republic of the type that exists in North America constitutes the pure, precise political instrument of the bourgeoisie, so direct legislation through the people constitutes the best political instrument of the toiling masses, and in particular of the organized proletariat' (Karl Burkli, *Vorwarts*, 12 Oct 1892) Secondly, it represents the negation of the negation, where primitive democracy is the thesis, oligarchic class state the antithesis, and New Democracy the synthesis. Just as we study primitive communism to get a glimpse at the society of the future, primitive, ancient democracy shows us the political form of the rule of the masses. Just as republicanism and the civil code of law were the conscious bourgeois re-creation of Rome, the European workers movement must recall the political forms thrown up by the demos, working masses poor, of the ancient East Mediterranean in their struggle against the rising class of big landowners and slave magnates.

The mass citizen assembly is echoed in the mass strike meetings of the modern proletariat. The dicasteria, the sovereign mass jury of Greece, is echoed in the mass people's courts that tried landlords and reactionaries in the Great Chinese Revolution, and today strike terror into the hearts of the reactionaries in the liberated zones of Peru.

The communist political revolution can no more base itself upon the outdated bourgeois ideology of republicanism than the economic revolution base itself upon the notion a just wage.

Stages

Craig is right, I do envisage revolution as a staged process, but the stages will not be the old Russian ones. That sort of dual power situation only arises when a dictatorship or absolute monarchy is defeated in war. Only that provides the soviets of workers and soldiers deputies needed to contest state power with the republic. In the absence of military cataclysms like

1870, 1905, or 1917, in a normal peacetime civil society, such an alternative focus of state power does not arise. Since political power grows out of the barrels of guns, the only remaining path is people's war.

But to create a revolution one must first create revolutionary public opinion. It is just not credible that people should take up arms to replace one form of elected government by another. One has to pose a goal of a quite different moral order – the final overthrow of class rule, of oligarchy, the rule of the many by the few. Only this, democracy in its original sense, provides the moral legitimization for the rejection and overthrow of elected government.

In revolution one must unite all who can be united against the principal enemy – the bourgeois representative state. Thus 'the first step in the workers revolution, making the proletariat the ruling class, is the conquest, in battle, of democracy', since it is only in fighting for unrestricted democracy that the proletariat can win the support of other sections of the people. Democracy is not overt proletarian dictatorship, non-proletarians retain citizenship, but it is in the words of the Manifesto, 'die Erhebung des Proletariats zur Herrschenden Klasse', it raises the proletariat to the status of ruling class. Why?

For the reason that Aristotle characterised democracy the rule of the poor – 'the poor are everywhere many, but the rich are few.'

The development of the class struggle will then lead the democracy to make 'despotic inroads' upon bourgeois property rights. Should the democracy be threatened with subversion and wrecking by the old upper classes, the struggle will then lead it to take on a more openly dictatorial form with expropriations and denials of citizenship rights to class enemies.

I am not a republican, but a Democrat, an advocate with Engels of 'die Erkampfung der Democratie'. 'Without state power, all is illusion. Storm the heavens with gunfire.'

Written in 1989

9. Democracy without Politicians

A classical proposal

This article argues for a far more representative form of government than modern parliamentary systems, one that can better address the issues of common citizens. To cut the argument short, the proposal is:

1. A direct assembly of citizens, made possible by modern communication technology.

2. Citizen councils with appointees chosen at random.

These ideas are by no means new. They are based on ancient insights put in practice as early as the 5th century B.C.

Some ancient insights from Athens

Most modern parliamentary states have a set of democratic rights (such as freedom of speech and assembly, etc.) won through important popular struggles in the late-19th and 20th century. But as a form of government, these states are quite distinct from classical democracy that existed in the Greek city-state of Athens for more than 200 years: None of its central institutions had any elected officials!

Athenian democracy rested on three main institutions: *The Assembly*, which made decrees and legislated. Any citizen could attend it, to make speeches and vote. *The Council of 500*, served as the full-time government but merely enacted the policies of the Assembly. It consisted of 500 citizens randomly chosen by lot. A new selection was made each year and a citizen could at most serve on the council twice in their lifetime. The legal system rested on *The People's Court*. Its juries were also made up of representatives drawn by lot. In sum, election of officials was an exception, confined mainly to generals, since commanding the military required expert knowledge and experience.

Of course, in ancient Athens citizenship excluded slaves and women and we have no reason to follow them on this. Nonetheless, poor peasants and artisans had an equal right in decision making as wealthy land and slave owners. The power, property and privileges of no person was safe from the sovereignty held by the citizens.

Parliamentarism and unrepresentative representatives

In modern parliamentary states political parties compete through elections to control state power. When parties are based on mass movements, it ensures a degree of popular control on party representatives. However, the right to vote is not the same as the right to exercise power and sooner or later the oligarchic nature of parliamentarism becomes apparent in the lack of:

* *Accountability*. It may take years before the people can vote unpopular politicians out of power. Politicians seeking careers and privileges will not support any proposals that threaten their interests. If they collectively decide to raise their salaries, paid by the citizens, who is going to stop them?

* *Representation*. Have a look at the politicians in your national parliament. Do they reflect the citizens in terms of age, gender, ethnicity or class? Do full-time politicians act in accordance with the same experiences and interests as common people? Patronage and nepotism worsen the representation further.

* *Participation*. How often do you have a say in the decisions that affect you and your family's lives? Some politicians sit and debate in parliament for decades, while other people's issues and concerns are never even considered. When faced with demands for referendums, politicians often reveal their contempt for the will of the people they claim to serve.

This is an inevitable result of elected decision makers. No matter how well intentions political parties and candidates have initially, their primary goal is to win and maintain power, in worst case for privilege. Democracy, as originally understood, is the rule of the common people; Parliamentarism, on the other hand, is the rule of professional politicians.

A brief elaboration of the proposal

The guiding principle here is that those affected by a decision should have an opportunity to make it.

Each year citizens could collectively decide on a few major issues, such as: the level of taxation; changes in the share of the budget going to education, health care, infrastructure, national defence; war or peace. These issues could be debated by randomly drawn citizens and experts on national television and then voted electronically by the viewers. Public internet servers could be set up to channelise public opinion; issues are brought up, if they gather sufficient signatures they are subject to referendums. This would be a modern Assembly.

Naturally there is only a limited number of issues that can be brought to public vote each year. Appointees in national councils must run the daily decision making, coordinating and allocating resources to local councils. For example a local council administering a hospital could be made up by a random sample of local residents and workers at the hospital. The appointees in the national health care council could be drawn by the same principle or by a random sample from a pool of candidates elected by the local councils. In any case, their term of service is limited. They are economically compensated for loss of work and subject to recall.

Some common objections to neoclassical democracy

1. Ordinary people are incompetent.

   Reply: No more incompetent than the average politician who lacks technical knowledge in specific matters. Moreover, the citizen councils outlined above ensure that expertise is combined with the political judgement of citizens who act on the basis of interests shared with others.

2. They have no experience in direct democracy.

   Reply: That is a matter of practice. The general principles are not only found in ancient Athens or the Althing assembly in Iceland in the Middle Ages, but also in the jury system, the modern Swiss cantons and recently in the Canadian province of British Colombia that set up a Citizens' Assembly on Electoral Reform in which members were chosen at random.

3. The reforms are too radical.

Reply: They need not to be imposed all at once but can begin gradually on the local level. Online referendums and citizen councils can easily replace the functions of a local administration.

4. No politician will support such reforms.

Reply: Therefore the first step is to build mass opinion for neoclassical democracy. Faced with pressure of reform it will become evident which politicians are democrats and which are not.

Written in 2007

Further reading

Blackwell, C., 2003. 'Athenian Democracy: a brief overview'. Available at: http://www.stoa.org/projects/demos/home

Burnheim, J., 1985. *Is Democracy Possible?*, University of California Press.

Cockshott, P., 2006. 'Electronic and Athenian Democracy', given at Workshop on e-Voting and e-Government in the UK.

Finley, M.I., 1985. *Democracy Ancient & Modern*. Revised edition. Rutgers University Press.

Part III.

Strategic paths

10. Limits of social-democratic politics

Introduction

How did social-democracy turn from being one of the most successful political mass movements in history into a series of national parties in political crises and deep ideological disarray during the course of one hundred years since the formation of the Second International in 1889? The thesis in this article is that the crisis of social-democracy is a long-term result of the fundamental problems that the reformist strategy of any workers' movement invariably encounters in relation to the state and the economy. They have yet to be solved.

These problems will increasingly bring the question to the fore: is the goal of social-democracy to be a party in government or an organization for social transformation? Whilst this may at one point have been synonymous to its members, it will be argued why it necessarily ceases to be so with the passage of time.

Conceptions of the state

The struggle of early social-democracy for the modern democratic rights, and universal suffrage in particular, rested on an impulse that went back to antiquity, best summarised by Aristotle's observations of ancient Athens:

> A democracy exists whenever those who are free and are not well off, being in a majority, are in sovereign control of the government, an oligarchy when control lies in the hands of the rich and better born, these being few.[1]

---

[1] Aristotle and Saunders (1981, p.245).

It was this class aspect that formed the basis of the struggle by the upper classes to prevent or undermine democracy throughout centuries. Bourgeois thinkers, such as the liberal John Stuart Mill, worried about the "danger of class legislation on the part of the numerical majority, these being all composed of the same class"[2] and could therefore not accept equal votes.

The struggle for democratic rights by the workers' movement was a precondition for it to become a strong mass movement with a base in the industrial working class in the advanced capitalist countries. As long as organizing was illegal this strategy for social transformation would remain impossible. The struggle for universal suffrage was thus an element of the strategy. The spectacular membership growth of social-democratic organizations strengthened the belief that seizure of state power through the parliamentary road was inevitable. State power would be used for progressive reforms with the long-term goal to "transform the organization of bourgeois society and liberate the subjugated classes, to the insurance and development of intellectual and material culture".[3]

The split of the workers' movement after the outbreak of World War I and the October revolution also implied a theoretical split in the conception of the state and thus different political strategies. In the social-democratic conception, the existing state was an instrument that could be conquered by the workers' movement, while the followers of the Bolsheviks contended that the state always was an instrument for the ruling classes to uphold their domination.

The gains made by European social-democracy would eventually show that the communist parties' conception of the state in capitalist economies was mistaken. The altered political balance of forces after World War II brought social-democracy to governments in several countries, in which it could implement a series of important working-class reforms. Even in a country like the United Kingdom, whose parliamentary system was long considered to have kept the state safe from the workers' movement, the Labour party could implement a series of nationalizations of industry and the country's most important reform during the 20th century: the introduction of a National Health System that provided the population with health care according to socialist principles.

At the same time it became increasingly evident for the Western European communist parties, for instance the large Italian PCI and French

---

[2]Mill (1862, ch.7,§.1).
[3]Party programme of the Swedish Social-Democratic party (SAP) from 1911 (§.1).

PCF, which had grown through their instrumental role in the anti-fascist struggle, that the revolutionary strategy based on the Comintern model was fruitless in societies with a stable capitalist economy and working parliamentary state with universal suffrage; unable to find an alternative they all eventually gravitated towards a reformist position during the post-war period. Only in parts of Asia, Africa and South America, where such social conditions did not pertain, did the original strategy still have relevance.

The blind spots of social-democracy

But the social-democratic conception of the state would also prove to be simplistic.

Firstly, the workers' movement's struggle for universal suffrage was not based on the classical theory of democracy as a form of government. None of the central institutions of Athenian democracy had elected representatives, instead they were drawn randomly among the citizens. Elected representatives were considered to be an 'aristocratic' principle for choosing 'the best' in terms of status and education. This method was used almost exclusively for electing the ten generals of the city. Only candidates chosen by lot could guarantee that poor farmers and artisans held political power. A look at the national parliaments in the modern world in terms of class, gender and ethnicity shows that the Athenian insight was correct; they are populated by representatives that are not statistically representative. For mass parties the formation of professional politicians, whose social background differs from the movement, leads to long-term problems since there is increasing risk that they cease to share the same perspectives and priorities. The risk is further increased when the primary goal is to win parliamentary elections and when the professional politicians can secure economic privileges.

Secondly, even if the state is a juridical subject, and can at times act unitarily, it is a hierarchy of state apparatuses that do not always act in concert. The most extreme example is Chile during 1970-3 when the class bias within the military establishment made it perceive the government of Allende as a threat to the order and decided to end it in blood. In the unlikely scenario that the armed forces would turn against an elected government in the advanced capitalist countries today, it would not be hard to guess which political direction the state would take. More plausible examples, however, are the Ministries of Finance or Central Banks, which can limit a government's scope for economic policy and therefore influence its direction.

Thirdly, the power of the state apparatuses flow from the monopoly of use of force. No decisions taken within the state, no executive orders by ministries, no laws passed by parliament, would be effective without the possibility to sanction those whom do not follow them. To the extent that this power is used to reproduce the capitalist mode of organizing social production the state is effectively capitalist by nature regardless of what party or intentions are in government.

Fourthly, and most significantly, is the *structural dependence between the state apparatuses and the capitalist sector*. This is the central problem of the reformists' instrumental conception of the state and needs to be elaborated at greater length below.[4]

The state in a capitalist economy

The total labour performed in the capitalist sector results in a product that is distributed among the agents in the figure below. People who administer the state hold a position in the economy that gives them opportunities to privileges, wealth and power through its capacity to levy taxes. The state provides the capitalist sector with a juridical system and laws without which it could not operate, but at the same time the state is dependent on tax revenues from the incomes in the sector and credits in order to act in the world economy.

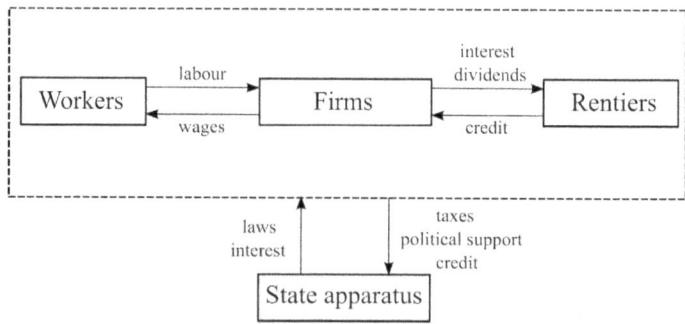

This dependency forces state managers to be concerned about maintaining the economic activity, irrespectively of whether they are bureaucrats

---

[4]The following analysis is based on Block (1980) which was a response to a debate initiated by Nicos Poulantzas (1969) and Ralph Miliband (1970, 1983) in *New Left Review*.

or elected professional politicians; regardless of whether their goals are to build military capacity or implement social reforms. At the same time they have to assume an economy-wide perspective in order to keep the destructive effects of the capitalist sector – e.g. crises and unemployment – in check, or else the state rapidly risks losing political support from other sections of the population on which it is dependent to various degrees.

Economic activity is highly dependent on the level of investments in the economy. This fact endows individual capitals a collective veto over policy: Firms make productive investments and rentiers provide credit depending on how they perceive profitability and the political-economic climate, i.e. if society is stable; if the economy is expanding; of the workers' movement is kept under control; if the level of taxes do not rise, and so on. If the business confidence of capitalists falls, the level of economic activity and hence the scope for state policy does too. This occurs in the context of rivalling states, that historically pre-dates capitalism, which act in a world economy. An investment strike is followed by capital flight to other states and mounting difficulties in obtaining credits for foreign exchange.

Under stable conditions, this structural mechanism disciplines individual states to implement policies that do not harm the confidence of owners of capital and, on the contrary, act to maintain a stable development of the entire capitalist sector.

Economic growth and scope for social-democratic reform

During certain historical periods – wars, international crises, reconstruction, mass mobilization – the balance of forces between the agents in the economy is altered and the confidence of individual capitalists carry less weight. This increases the scope for the state to conduct an alternative set of policies depending on the other forces in society.

But as the situation stabilises, the weight is shifted back to the dependence on the incomes in the capitalist economy. This creates sooner or later insuperable problems for the reformist strategy. The only way to reduce the dependence then is to increase the non-capitalist sector's share of production from which it is possible to redistribute resources in order to implement progressive reforms. Within the early workers' movement it was clear that this meant some form of common ownership but it did not have a worked-out theory and political strategy for how to organise and run the economy.[5] The policies that social-democracy mainly applied

---

[5]See for instance SAP:s first 'general thesis' up to 1990 or the British Labour

85

was nationalization of industries, measures that had grown out of a period of national production processes and mobilization for war and economic catastrophe 1914-1950.

The question of the structure of the political economy was, however, not central to the reformist strategy that was established immediately after WWII, when the nation-states prioritised reconstruction and industrial development. The balance of forces in the economy shifted to the benefit of industrial capital and workers at the expense of the rentier capital; whose movement and ability to extract interests and dividends were restricted to maintain high levels of investment. Under these circumstances social-democracy in power could be a progressive force without having to challenge the economic order.

The high levels of investment contributed to an enormous growth of wealth and facilitated full employment in Western Europe while avoiding to severely damage the confidence of industrial capital. The dependence on the incomes in the capitalist sector did not appear to be an obstacle, on the contrary the scope for social-democratic reform was wide. The capacity that the workers' movement had built since the days of the foundation of Second International in 1889 finally yielded political dividends on a scale that was impossible before 1945.

Obstacles on the parliamentary road

But high levels of investment imply huge consequences for the development of a capitalist economy. When the size of the workforce stabilises and the growth rate of productivity in large-scale industries cannot be pushed further upwards, high investment levels will lower average profitability of invested capital.[6]

At the same time workers are concentrated in industries that strengthen their bargaining power since union actions there affect a large part of the

---

party's *Clause IV* from 1918 to 1995: "To secure for the workers by hand or by brain the full fruits of their industry and the most equitable distribution thereof that may be possible upon the basis of the *common ownership* of the means of production, distribution and exchange, and the best obtainable system of popular administration and control of each industry or service." (Emphasis added.)

[6] The average rate of profit rate follows a dynamic equilibrium, $R^* = (g_l + g_p + d)/i$ where g_l and g_p are the relative growthrates of labour and productivity, respectively; d is the rate of depreciation of the capital stock and i is the ratio of gross investments to profits. Cf. Cottrell & Cockshott (2006), Zachariah (2009).

86

entire economy.[7] The Polish economist Michal Kalecki predicted already in 1943 that the maintenance of full employment would create social and political changes that would destroy the confidence of industrial capital:

> Indeed, under a regime of permanent full employment, the 'sack' would cease to play its role as a disciplinary measure. The social position of the boss would be undermined, and the self-assurance and class-consciousness of the working class would grow. Strikes for wage increases and improvements in conditions of work would create political tension.[8]

Furthermore, industrial capitals would try to compensate wage demands and taxes by raising prices, i.e. inflation, which damages the interests of the rentiers.

In other words, it was precisely the high levels of investment, which had facilitated the scope for progressive reforms, that generated two separate processes (i) a declining rate of return on invested capital and (ii) the rising strength of the workers' movement. These processes resulted in a crisis of profitability and business confidence in the advanced capitalist economies during the mid-1970s. In general, social-democracy did not have a strategy to fall back upon, other than the same Keynesian policies. The attempts to formulate a new path either did not result in worked-out political programmes and strategies or they arrived too late.[9]

The most ambitious plans within the Western European workers' movement was the Swedish 'wage-earners funds' proposal of 1976 in which a share of the value-added from highly productive firms would be transferred into funds controlled by the movement in order to transform the structure of ownership in the economy. This would have reduced the dependence on the capitalist sector in the long-term, increased the scope for reform and control of development. But the proposal arrived too late for it to be developed into a political strategy in the international context of the 1980s, and was further weakened by an influential section of the Social-Democratic party that stubbornly maintained a non-confrontational reformist strategy whose possibilities were exhausted.[10]

---

[7] See Silver (2003).

[8] Kalecki (1943, p.351). This prediction originated in Marx's theory of a 'reserve army' of unemployed.

[9] For instance the Labour party attempted to formulate plans to nationalise parts of the manufacturing industry and subject the economy to a public planning framework, but did not advance beyond this. Cf. Glyn (2006).

[10] See Olsson och Ekdahl (2002).

In an attempt to embark a path of its own, a parliamentary coalition led by the French Socialist party conducted a series of nationalizations of industry and finance in 1981, as part of a package of reforms. But despite generous compensations such policies were at this point met with falling business confidence, capital flight and hence macroeconomic problems. The scope for policy actions by the state was further limited by the rules of the European Monetary System. The government chose to turn policy around completely by 1983, as predicted by the theory of the capitalist state outlined above.

Instead of the workers' movement it was the representatives of the rentier interest which took the initiative during the crisis and shifted the balance of forces in the global economy during the 1980s: Capital mobility was opened up, as well as new markets and labour reserves in the East; full employment was abandoned in favour of low inflation and high interest rates[11] ; privatizations and slashing of publicly financed welfare services followed. This also implied the end of the successful reformist period of European social-democracy. But instead of trying to deal with the cause of the decreasing scope for progressive reforms, in other words, the structural dependence on the capitalist sector, social-democracy moved away from the issue altogether and towards the so-called 'Third Way'.

Nation-based social-democratic parties continued to pursue the same goals they were set up to achieve, namely winning elections in national parliaments but now with an internationally weakened workers' movement, a decreasing scope for reform and abandonment of the issue of an alternative political economy. What remained then was nothing but their role as administrators of the state. In practice, therefore, they had fewer alternatives to offer other than "budget cuts with a human face". The crisis and ideological disarray of social-democracy that exists to varying degrees throughout Europe is the result of this development. It has also left the field open for the extreme Right to win support among a part of the population that has conservative social values but who support progressive economic policies and therefore had a reason to vote for social-democracy in the past.[12]

In the past expansive welfare policies relied on economic growth in order to redistribute resources and facilitate progressive reforms without threatening incomes. Hence such policies are becoming increasingly problematic when the national product per capita must be restricted in order not

---

[11]In the countries in which full employment was an institutionalised commitment it took longer time to break down those policies. Cf. Therborn (1985).
[12]Cf. Svallfors (2004).

to accelerate the growth of greenhouse gas emissions and the use of limited natural resources. This will restrict the scope for social-democratic reforms even more. Returning to expansive state policies would require a return to curbing the rentier interest and maintaining high investment levels, which would eventually reproduce the same crisis tendency that followed the post-war boom.

Furthermore, welfare services cannot be rationalised in the same way as in industry, which implies that a growing share of total labour must perform them. But in order to conduct welfare policies this implies that the tax-financed public sector's share of the economy must increase as well, making such policies ever more conflict-ridden and increases the need for political support (see the figure above). However, such support cannot be won through election propaganda or even agitation but through practical politics.

The future of social-democracy

In order to strengthen the support for the public sector among its workers and the citizens in general it must be organised in a way that is superior to the capitalist sector. The primary way of doing so among state enterprises would be to raise workers' control to a level that is impossible to achieve in the capitalist sector. That would furthermore contribute to a practical training in self-management and possibilities to explore new innovations in organization, technology and coordination of common resources.

At the same time the Athenian insights about the representative institutions of the state cannot be ignored; if social-democratic parties want to win in this arena, the institutions should be populated by people from its social base. That requires their reorganization according to classical democratic principles.[13] To prevent the non-representative state apparatuses from undermining the policies of the workers' movement when in power, the movement must activate and educate members within these parts of the state, preferably through independent trade-unions.

None of this will by itself, however, reduce the dependence on the incomes in the capitalist sectors which becomes increasingly problematic for the reformist strategy, especially since the public sector primarily produces tax-financed welfare services and hence cannot be a decisive source for economic scope for action. What possibilities remain then for the original social-democratic goals of a thorough social transformation through

---

[13]Cf. Burnheim (1985) for a discussion about such institutions.

the parliamentary road?

It should be clear that the structure of the political economy can no longer be ignored, but must be, in practice and not mere theory, a central issue. One can only speculate how European development would have turned out if social-democracy had succeeded in implementing reforms analogous to wage-earner funds as early as the 1950s, but in any case it would have given the workers' movement a completely different position at the onset of an economic crisis. The relevance of this issue reemerges, however, irrespective of the workers' movement since the growing ecological constraints on economic expansion demands some form of macroeconomic coordination and planning.

The French example illustrates the potential obstacles for changing the structure of the political economy through the parliamentary road and that *the possibilities to circumvent them depend on the capacity of the workers' movement to organise itself outside the national parliaments*: If social-democracy had continued implementing its programme it would have required abandoning the rules of the European Monetary System or changing them through political pressure from an internationally coordinated movement. Even if that would have succeeded, the problems of inflation and balance of trade would have required price and import controls, which would have accelerated the crisis of business confidence of the capitalists and their capital flight. At that point it would have been crucial to sustain the activity of the productive sectors of the economy by its workers and to maintain cross-national trade relations which in the long-term would have depended on an international political context that favoured the workers' movement.

This, however, is a scenario for which the nation-centric reformist strategy has remained entirely unprepared. Therefore every parliamentary advance must be used to strengthen the extra-parliamentary capacity of workers' movement – to organise people, articulate coherent political programmes from its vantage point and control parts of the economy – which history shows takes decades to build. But it is imperative if successful, progressive reforms should not be destroyed by a simple change of government.

The crisis of social-democracy is a long-term result of its goal of winning parliamentary elections while lacking a coherent strategy to circumvent the obstacles on the parliamentary road to social transformation. Instead it has responded by abdicating on the so-called 'Third Way' – towards the abyss.

If the primary goal of social-democracy no longer is to conduct social

transformation but to be a ruling party then nothing remains but its role as an administrator of the state and it will be locked in a structural necessity to reproduce capitalist relations of production and hence preserve a class-divided society. Then it has exhausted its historically progressive role.
Written in 2010

References

Aristotle och T.J. Saunders (ed.). 1981. The Politics, Penguin Classics.

Block, Fred. 1980. "Beyond relative autonomy: state managers as historical subjects." *The Socialist Register*, vol. 17 (1980), sid. 227-41.

Burnheim, John. 1985. *Is Democracy Possible?*, University of California Press.

Cottrell, Allin. and Cockshott, Paul. (2006). "Demography and the Falling Rate of Profit". *Indian Development Review*, Vol.4, No.1, June 2006.

Glyn, Andrew. 2006. *Capitalism Unleashed—Finance, Globalization and Welfare*, Oxford University Press.

Kalecki, Michal. 1943. "Political Aspects of Full Employment." *Political Quarterly*, vol.14, no.4.

Miliband, Ralph. 1970. "The Capitalist State—Reply to N. Poulantzas." *New Left Review* I/59, Jan-Feb. 1970, sid. 53-60.

Miliband, Ralph. 1983. "State Power and Class Interests." *New Left Review* I/138, Mar-Apr. 1983, sid. 57-68.

Mill, John Stuart. 1862. *Considerations on Representative Government*, Harper & Brothers. Available at http://www.gutenberg.org/etext/5669

Olsson, Lars and Lars Ekdahl. 2002. *Klass i rörelse—Arbetarrörelsen i svensk samhällsomvandling*, Arbetarrörelsens Arkiv och Bibliotek, Arbetarnas Kulturhistoriska Sällskap.

Poultanzas, Nicos. 1969. "The Problem of the Capitalist State." *New Left Review* I/58, Nov-Dec. 1969, sid. 67-78.

Programme of the Social-Democratic Workers' Party of Sweden. 1911. Available at Arbetarrörelsens Arkiv och Bibliotek, http://www.arbark.se

Sachs, Jeffrey och Charles Wyplosz. 1986. "The economic consequences of President Mitterand." *Economic Policy*, vol. 1, no. 2, Apr. 1986, sid. 262-322.

Silver, Beverly J. 2003. *Forces of Labor. Workers' Movements and Globalization since 1870*, Cambridge University Press.

Svallfors, Stefan. 2004. *Klassamhällets kollektiva medvetande*, Borea.

Therborn, Göran. 1985. *Nationernas ofärd—Arbetslösheten i den internationella krisen*, Arkiv förlag.

Zachariah, Dave. 2009. "Determinants of the Average Profit Rate and the Trajectory of Capitalist Economies." *Bulletin of Political Economy*, vol. 3, no. 1.

11. Six theses on the problems of the communist movement

Open Polemic has provided a valuable service to the movement by creating a forum in which the basic questions underlying the crisis in the socialist movement can be thrashed out.

One of the most striking features of this crisis is that we no longer know what we stand for. We know what we are against, but not what we are fighting for. If you listen to left polemic you hear a roaring portentous silence when it comes to socialism. It seems we no longer dare to define it.

I have taken the liberty of submitting a list of theses, which, starting with a diagnosis of the crisis, lead on to, perhaps controversial, programmatic conclusions.

Part I: Assertions

Thesis 1 The crisis of world socialism is due primarily to economic failure.

Thesis 2 The collapse of previously existing socialism is due to identifiable causes embedded in its economic mechanism, but which are not inherent in all possible socialisms.

Thesis 3 The political failures of the left in this situation stem from the lack of a programmatic conception of how a socialist economy should be operated.

Thesis 4 Marxist economic theory, in conjunction with information technology provide the basis on which a viable socialist economic program can be advanced.

Thesis 5 The communist movement has never developed a correct constitutional program. In particular it has accepted the misconception that elections are a democratic form.

Thesis 6 The content of a communist program should differ radically from what the British Left presently proposes.

Part II: Arguments

1. Argument for thesis

The crisis of world socialism is due primarily to economic failure.

Bourgeois opinion is unanimous on this but it is not universally accepted on the left. An alternative view is that the crisis was primarily political. According to the latter conception it was basically the lack of democracy combined with a corrupt and exploiting bureaucracy that brought about the system's failure.

In asserting the primacy of economics I am not denying the existence of a corrupt bureaucracy, a new bourgeois class wishing to establish capitalism or conjunctural features like the rise of Gorbachov. I am asserting that these only became critical once the system had failed economically.

Proposition 1. *Political corruption or oppression will not cause a thriving economic system to be overthrown.*

Whilst an economic system is still capable of rapidly developing the forces of production it can tolerate a very high level of political oppression without the economic system itself being destabilised.

As an example of this consider the Stalin period in the USSR and Eastern Europe. Then, the bourgeoisie and petty bourgeoisie were cruelly suppressed. But, contrary to what one might expect, this repression did not discredit the system politically at the time. On the contrary the Communist Parties in general and Stalin personally were at the height of their popularity when at their most ruthless. The intelligentsia whose offspring are now so hostile to communism, responded at the time by prostrating themselves before the Communist Parties and participated with every apparent enthusiasm in socialist construction. Mere trepidation could not explain such abnegation; its underlying reason was the outstanding rates of economic growth produced by stalinism.

An organisation that is powerful and economically successful provokes not only fear but respect.

One can see this phenomenon, inverted and reduced in form, in that supine fear tinged with admiration which Thatcher induced in sections of our left intelligentsia. If we look to the east we see more substantial capitalist success stories, like Taiwan and South Korea, which have combined stark authoritarianism, crony-ism and corruption with rapid economic growth.

When such an economically successful dictatorship 'loosens up', what happens is a political liberalisation that leaves the economic foundations intact. The USSR under Khrushchev or recent events in Korea are evidence of this. It is only if political liberalisation occurs in conditions of economic failure, that the crisis grows out of control to economic revolution.

Proposition 2. *Political repression persisted because of economic weakness.*

The official justification for the Berlin wall was that it was an anti-fascist defence wall.

There was an element of truth in this, as the immediate influx of Nazi organisations which took place into the former DDR as soon as the wall came down showed. But as everybody knows, the wall also functioned to stop emigration to the BRD. The more fundamental question is: why was it the DDR rather than the BRD that had to build a wall?

Historically the answer is clear: it happened because it was the DDR that was losing population to the West. Although its fugitives might cite love of liberty as motive, liberty must it seems, be gilded to be loved. Whatever political gloss was given it, money was what was at stake. India has been 'free and democratic' since the start of the cold war, but for some reason Soviet and East European citizens have not clamoured for the right to emigrate there.

To return to Central Europe; in the 1950s both German republics were actively suppressing their political enemies. The Communist Party was outlawed in the BRD as a threat to the state, just as actively pro-capitalist parties were in the DDR. But by the 1970s the rulers in the West were confident enough to legalize the CP whilst the East remained a besieged fortress. The differences in politics flowed from relative economic performances.

Had the economy of the DDR been forging ahead of the BRD, then people would have been jumping the wall in the other direction. It would, in the end, have been the East Berlin government that was imposing unification terms on the West.

2. Elaboration of thesis

The collapse of previously existing socialism is due to identifiable causes embedded in its economic mechanism, but which are not inherent in all possible socialisms.

I will examine some of the well known contradictions within the economics of previously existing socialism. The argument that these are not inherent in any socialism will be advanced in section 4, below.

Elaboration 1. *The mechanism for the extraction of a surplus product progressively collapsed resulting in inadequate investment.*

Marxist economics views the method of extracting a surplus product as being the distinguishing feature of a mode of production.

> The specific economic form, in which unpaid surplus labour is pumped out of the direct producers determines the relationship of rulers and ruled, as it grows directly out of production itself and, in turn, reacts upon it as a determining element. Upon this, however, is founded the entire formation of the economic community which grows up out of the production relations themselves, thereby simultaneously its specific political form. It is always the direct relationship of the owners of the conditions of production to the direct producers – a relation naturally corresponding to a definite stage in the development of the methods of labour and thereby its social productivity, – which reveals the innermost secret, the hidden basis of the entire social structure, and with it the political form of the relation of sovereignty and dependence, in short, the corresponding specific form of state. See [6],p 791

In a socialist economy the extraction of a surplus product takes place by means of a politically determined division of the material product between consumer goods and other products in the state plan. This is socialism's "innermost secret, the hidden basis of the entire social structure".

Its system of extracting a surplus is quite different from under capitalism in the following respects:

96

The division of the product is determined directly in material terms rather then indirectly as a result of exchange relations.

The division is determined centrally rather than through numerous local bargains over the price of labour power, hours worked etc.

The actual level of money wages is irrelevant because the supplies of consumer goods are predetermined in the plan. Higher money wages do not necessarily result in increased real wages. Besides which a large part of the real wage is in the form of free or subsidised goods.

This form of extraction rises out of the highly integrated and socialised character of production under socialism. From it is developed the absolute necessity of individual factories being subordinated to the centre, and the comparative irrelevance of their individual profitability. Following on it determines the centralised character of the state and the impossibility of local authorities having an autonomous disposition over resources. All these are invariant characteristics of socialism.

This innermost secret determines the relationship of rulers and ruled as follows; consider two possibilities, either the rulers and the ruled are distinct groups, or they are one and the same.

If, as in hitherto existing socialism, they are distinct, then whoever controls the planning authority is both the effective owner of the means of production, and a ruler. These rulers (in practice have the central committee of the communist party), though often venal, can not fulfil their social function by the shameless bourgeois pursuit of self interest. They are compelled instead, to take on the highly social and public role, of so organising the political and ideological life of the society, as to ensure compliance with the plan. One of the most effective ways of doing this is through the cult of a charismatic leader, backed to a greater or lesser extent by state terror.

Personality cults, in which the leader is presented as the General Will incarnate are no accident, but an efficient adaptation to the contradictory demands of a socialist mode of production (which dictates the dominance of political over civil society), combined with institutions of representative government.

Some readers may protest at this point: it is bad enough that I unblushingly characterize the Leninist system as socialist, but how can I say that it had a representative government?

Representative government selects certain humans, commonly called politicians, to stand in for, or represent, others in the process of political decision making. This is just what the Leninist party does in power. It acts as a representative of the working class and takes political decisions on its behalf. As such it is no less representative a form of government than parliamentary government, there are differences over who is represented and how they are represented, but the representative principle remains the same: decisions are not taken by those affected but are monopolized by a group of professional rulers, whose edicts are legitimated in terms of some representative function. Selection of such rulers by multiple party elections can not diminish their representative character nor abolish the distinction between rulers and ruled.

The contradictory character of socialist representative government is banally evident. The representatives of the proletariat, through their control of the plan, and thus the method by which unpaid surplus labour is pumped out of the direct producers, become effective controllers, pro-tem, of the means of production. As such their individual class position is transformed and their ability to go on representing the proletariat, compromised.

Only if the distinction between ruler and ruled is abolished, when the masses themselves decide all major questions through institutions of participatory democracy does the totalitarian inner secret at the heart of socialism cease to be contradictory. Only when the masses in referenda decide the disposition of their collective social labour: how much is to go on defence, how much on health, how much on consumer goods etc., can the political life of socialism cease to be a fraud. But to return to the question of surplus extraction. Under socialism this is an inherently totalitarian process, a subordination of the parts to the whole, the factory to the plan, the individual to the collective. Production is not for private gain but for the totality of society. Under a system of participatory democracy, this totalitarian conformism might take on a Swiss democratic rather than German fascist air, but it would be no less real.

Gorbachov undermined the whole surplus extraction process by attacking the totalitarian principle. One of his first measures was to allow factories to retain the greater part of their profit. At a stroke, he introduced an antagonistic bourgeois principle of surplus extraction: the pursuit of profit by individual enterprises. He threw the whole system into chaos.

The government, deprived of its main form of revenue, resorted to the printing press. The result was hyperinflation.

The factories had extra money, but, since the division of the social product was still determined by the plan, could not act as private firms would and convert this new money into productive capital. The socialist system of surplus extraction was sabotaged without a bourgeois one to replace it, and the economy spiralled into an inflationary decline.

Elaboration 2. *Previously existing socialism was limited by a deficient system of economic calculation.*

This point is made by all right wing critics. They point out, with justification, that the price system operating in the USSR made rational economic calculation impossible. Numerous anecdotes tell of this:

> Here is one of many examples. Some time ago it was decided to adjust the prices of cotton and grain in the interests of cotton growing, to establish more accurate prices for grain sold to the cotton growers, and to raise the prices of cotton delivered to the state. Our business executives and planners submitted a proposal on this score which could not but astound members of the Central Committee, since it suggested fixing the price of a ton of grain at practically the same level as a ton of cotton, and, moreover, the price of a ton of grain was taken as equivalent to that of a ton of baked bread. In reply to the remarks of the members of the Central Committee that the price of a ton of bread must be much higher than that of a ton of grain, because of the additional expense of milling and baking, and that cotton was generally much dearer than grain was also borne out by their prices in the world market, the authors of the proposal could find nothing coherent to say.

So wrote Stalin in April 1952 [9], but some 40 years later, pricing policy had improved so little that Gorbachov could cite the example of pigs being fed bread by collective farmers, because the price of bread was lower than that of grain.

When the relative prices of things differs systematically from their relative costs of production, it becomes impossible for people to chose cost effective methods of production. This produces a general decline in economic efficiency.

Elaboration 3. *Unlike capitalism, previously existing socialism lacked an inbuilt mechanism to economise on the use of labour, and thus to raise its productivity.*

The fundamental economic justification of any new production technology has to be its ability to produce things with less effort than before. Only by the constant application of such inventions throughout the economy can we gain more free time to devote either to leisure or to the satisfaction of new and more sophisticated tastes. This implies that in socialist production workers must seek always to economise on time. Time is, as Adam Smith said, our original currency by which we purchase from nature all our wants and necessities, a moment of it needlessly squandered is lost for ever. A socialist system will only be historically superior to capitalism if it proves better at husbanding time.

The wealth of capitalist societies is of course unevenly divided, but its inbuilt tendency to advance the productivity of labour underpins the continuing progressive role of capitalist economic relations. Had capitalism lost this potential, as some Marxists believed in the 1930's then it would long ago have lost out in competition with the Soviet block.

In a capitalist economy, manufacturers are driven by the desire for profit to try to minimise costs. These costs include wages. Firms often introduce new technology in order to cut the workforce and reduce labour costs. Although this use of technology is frequently against the direct interest of workers, who loose their jobs, it is to the ultimate benefit of society. For it is through these economies in labour that the living standards of the society is raised. The benefits of technical change are unevenly spread, the employer stands to gain more than the employee, but in the end, it is upon its ability to foster technological improvements that capitalism's claim to be a progressive system is based. The need to accept new labour saving technology is generally recognised within the Trades Unions, who seek only to regulate the terms of its introduction so that their members share in the gains.

It is a very naive form of socialism that criticises technical change under the pretext that it causes unemployment. The real criticism that can be levied at capitalist economies in this regard is that they are too slow to adopt labour saving devices because labour is artificially cheap.

A good example of this could be seen in the computer industry. In the 1950s IBM developed highly automated machinery to construct the core memories for their computers. As demand grew their factories became more and more automatic. In 1965 they even had to open an entire new production line just to make the machines that would make the computers. Still they could not keep up with demand.

> The situation was becoming desperate. Then a newly appointed manger at Kingston who had spent several years in Japan, proposed that workers in the Orient could be found with sufficient manual dexterity and patience to wire core planes

by hand. Taking bags of cores, rolls of wire, and core frames to Japan, he returned ten days later with hand wired core planes as good as those that had been wired by automatic wire feeders at the Kingston plant. It was slow and tedious work but the cost of labour in the Orient was so low that production costs were actually lower than with full automation in Kingston. See [8], p.209

But in this respect the USSR was even worse.

The USSR subsidised food, rent, children's clothes and other necessities. The subsidy on basic goods compensated for low money wages. But subsidies, and social services had to be paid for out of the profits of nationalised industries (which formerly met most of the Soviet budget). For these to make a profit, wages had to be kept low, and low wages meant that the subsidies had to be retained!

The worst aspect of all this was that enterprises were encouraged by the cheapness of labour to be profligate with it. Why introduce modern automated machinery if labour was so cheap? Besides, it created work and prevented unemployment: real voodoo economics. True enough, any socialism worthy of the name must prevent unemployment, but that is not the same as creating unnecessary work. Its better to automate as fast as possible whilst reducing the working week.

Elaboration 4. *Nationalised ownership of industry held back international economic cooperation in comparison to the capitalist world.*

Modern capitalist industry is dominated by big multinational firms. Only these have the resources and size of market to reap economies of scale and meet the heavy research costs demanded by competition. The nationalised enterprises of Eastern Europe and to a lesser extent the USSR were just too small to gain such benefits.

3. Argument for thesis

The political failures of the left in this situation stem from the lack of a programmatic conception of how a socialist economy should be operated.

The bourgeoisie internationally entered the current crisis of socialism with a well developed critique of the failings of the socialist economies. Alongside this critique went a program of economic measures to solve the crisis. Political leaders in the socialist block were at first unwilling to recognise that the societies that they controlled were fundamentally sick. Those most ready to point this out, both East and West were the intellectual and political right. They saw the chance to seize power and impose their own cure on the patient. By the time modernizing wings arose in the Communist and Social Democratic movement, their modernism consisted of little more than the adoption of some vulgarized form of right wing neoclassical economics. As Keynes said back in 1935

> ... the ideas of economists and political philosophers, both when they are right and when they are wrong, are more powerful than is commonly understood. Indeed the world is ruled by little else. Practical men, who believe themselves to be quite exempt from any intellectual influences are usually the slaves of some defunct economist. Madmen in authority, who hear voices in the air, are distilling their frenzy from some academic scribbler of a few years back.

So Gorbachov in his great role and Gould in his lesser one echo pro-market economists like Lieberman, Sik, Nove and ultimately Von Mises. The radical movements of the '60s and '70s, whether workers and students in the West or red guards in the East were too far from real centres of power and to diffuse in their aims to pose a practical alternative.

4. Argument for thesis

Marxist economic theory, in conjunction with information technology provide the basis on which a viable socialist economic program can be advanced.

This is obviously a complex case to make out, and I can only give a few key points here.

Proposition 3. *Using modern computers it is possible to efficiently plan an economy in terms of natural units without recourse to the intermediary of money or markets.*

Bourgeois writers such as Nove [7] have argued that the vast number of different products in a modern industrial economy (perhaps 10 million) makes detailed planning impossible. Planners, he asserts, are forced to work in terms of aggregates. They can only specify general targets like 'we need 500 million screws', but they fail to say how many 5mm screws, 10mm screws etc., are needed. As a result the wrong mix of screws gets produced.

It is impossible, they assert to do planning in terms of use values or natural units. In consequence, they say, money and markets have to be brought in.

This assertion is false. The technical mathematics of the argument is complex, but Allin Cottrell and I have demonstrated [3], [2] that modern supercomputers are capable of solving the millions of equations the equations necessary for a complete plan in a matter of minutes.

What would have been an impossibly complex problem to solve by the old bureaucratic means, has become an eminently practical proposition using modern information technology. Such a computerised planning system could respond to events far faster than any market could hope to do, thus undermining the main objection raised by bourgeois economists as to the unwieldy nature of socialist planning.

Proposition 4. *Socialism requires the abolition of money and its replacement by a system of remuneration based on labour time. This is the key to promoting both equity and technological advance.*

It is clear both from a reading of Marx's own work, and from the whole tenor of 19th century socialism, that it was a common assumption that socialism would involve the abolition of money and the introduction of a system of payment based on labour vouchers.

> ... the individual producer receives back from society – after the deductions have been made – exactly what he gives to it. What he has given to it is his individual quantum of labour. For example, the social working day consists of the sum of the individual hours of work; the individual labour time of the individual producer is the part of the social working day contributed by him, his share in it. He receives a certificate from society that he has furnished such and such a an amount of labour (after deducting his labour for the common funds), and with this certificate he draws from the social stock of consumption as much as the same amount of labour costs. The same amount of labour which he has given to society in one form he receives back in another. See [5].

Marx qualified this as being only a first step towards greater equality, but it is far more radically egalitarian than anything achieved by hitherto existing socialism. The principle of payment in labour time recognizes only two sources of inequality in income: that some people may work longer than others, or, in a piece work system, some may work faster. It eliminates all other income inequalities based upon class, race, sex, grade or professional qualification.

Also, by forcing workplaces to pay workers the the full value created by their labour, it eliminates the squandering of labour brought about by low pay, and encourages the introduction of labour saving innovation. It provides, moreover, a rational and scientifically well founded basis for economic calculation. If goods are labelled with the labour required to make them, the arbitrary and irrational character of the old Soviet price system is avoided.

Proposition 5. *Consumer goods prices should be set at market clearing levels and the discrepancies between these prices and the values of goods used to determine the optimal levels of production.*

Given that supplies of and demand for goods is never exactly equal, it is only average prices that should equal labour values. Individual items in short supply would sell at a premium, balanced by those in oversupply selling at a discount. These premiums and discounts can them guide the planning authorities to decide which goods to produce more of, and which to produce less off.

Note that this does not in anyway presuppose the existence of private trade.

Proposition 6. *The funding of the surplus product should come from taxes on income, approved by referendum.*

In any society a certain proportion of the social product must be set aside for investment and to support those unable to work etc. In a socialism based on labour values, this would be expressed as a deduction of so many hours work a week that had to be performed for the community. If the phrase had not been purloined, one might call it the community charge.

In the countries of hitherto existing socialism the decision as to how the social working day was to be divided between necessary and surplus labour time was taken by the government. As, over time, the government became alienated from the working classes, the process became exploitative. The state as an alien power was depriving the workers of the fruits of their labour.

To prevent this, it is essential, that the division of the working day between social and necessary labour, be decided by the working class itself; rather than by a government which claims to act in its interests. There should be an annual vote by the working population to decide on the level of the 'community charge'. A multiple choice ballot could allow the people to decide between more public services or more consumption. Only when the surplus product is provided voluntarily does it cease to be exploitation.

5. Explanation of thesis

The communist movement has never developed a correct constitutional program. In particular it has accepted the misconception that elections are a democratic form.

Proposition 7. *Soviets and elections on universal suffrage are both ultimately aristocratic forms of government.*

Aristocracy means rule by the best.

In a feudal society, landowners are self evidently the best, most honourable, most noble elements of society. But this does not limit aristocracy as a principle to feudalism. Aristocracy simply means an elitist system of government.

Aristotle argued that any political system based upon elections was an aristocracy. (See [1] pp 286). It introduces the deliberate element of choice, of selection of the best, the aristoi, in place of government by all of the people. What he implies, as would be evident to any Marxist, is that the 'best' people in a class society will be the better off. The poor, the scum and the riff-raff are of course 'unsuitable' candidates for election. Wealth and respectability go together.

In a bourgeois parliamentary system this aristoi is comprised in the main of men of high social status: lawyers, business men etc. In a soviet system the aristoi who get elected onto the local soviets, and still more those who get promoted from the local to the supreme soviets, are initially the elite of the working class. They are the politically active, the class conscious, the self-confident, in short, activists of the Communist Party.

The leading role of the Communist Party, translates it, in an electoral mechanism with a purely proletarian constituency, into the aristocracy of labour. As such it becomes prey to the characteristic corruptions of aristocracy. Soviets, based as they are on the electoral principle, transform themselves from instruments of proletarian democracy into their opposite.

This degeneration is not accidental, not to be explained away by historical contingencies, but inevitable.

Elaboration 5. *Democracy is an ancient term for a type of popular rule based upon mass assemblies and selection of officials by lot. What has come to be termed democracy in the 20th century has almost nothing in common with this original meaning.*

The political systems that currently label themselves democracies are all oligarchies. The fact that they can still get away with calling themselves democracies is one of the most remarkable confidence tricks in history. (See [4]).

In his dsytopian novel *1984* Orwell makes ironic reference to Newspeak, a dialect of English so corrupted that phrases like 'freedom is slavery' or 'war is peace' could pass unremarked. What he was alluding to is the power of language to control our thoughts. When those in authority can redefine the meanings of words they make subversion literally unthinkable. The phrase 'parliamentary democracy' is an example of new-speak: a contradiction in disguise. Go back to the Greek origins of the word democracy. The second half of the word means 'power' or 'rule'. Hence we have autocracy; rule by one man; aristocracy, rule by the aristoi the best people, the elite; democracy meant rule by the demos. Most commentators translate this a rule by the people, but the word demos had a more specific meaning. It meant rule by the common people or rule by the poor. Aristotle, describing the democracies of his day was quite explicit about the fact that democracy meant rule by the poor. Countering the argument that democracies simply meant rule by the majority he gave the following example:

> Suppose a total of 1,300; 1,000 of these are rich, and they give no share in office to the 300 poor, who are also free men and in other respects like them; no one would say that these 1300 lived under a democracy(*Politics*, 1290).

But he says this is an artificial case, "due to the fact that the rich are everywhere few, and the poor numerous." As a specific definition he gives:

> A democracy exists whenever those who are free and are not well off, being in a majority, are in sovereign control of

the government, an oligarchy when control lies in the hands of the rich and better born, these being few.

In the original meanings of the words what exists even in countries that are termed parliamentary democracies is oligarchy not democracy. In its origins, 'democracy' meant rule by the working poor. In modern language: workers power or proletarian rule (the proles being the Latin equivalent of the Greek demos). We can see how far a parliamentary system is from a democracy in practice by looking at the actual institutions of the demokratia.

Institutions of classical democracy

The first and most characteristic feature of demokratia was rule by the majority vote of all citizens. This was generally by a show of hands at a sovereign assembly or eklesia. The sovereignty of the demos was not delegated to an elected chamber of professional politicians as in the bourgeois system. Instead the ordinary working people, in those days the peasantry and traders, gathered together en masse to discuss, debate and vote on the issues concerning them. The similarity between the eklesia and those spontaneous organisations of modern workers democracy: the mass strike meetings that are so hated by the bourgeois world, is immediately apparent.

The second important institution were the peoples law courts or dikasteria. These courts had no judges, instead the dicasts acted as both judge and jury. The dicasts were chosen by lot from the citizen body, using a sophisticated procedure of voters tickets and allotment machines, and once in court decisions were taken by ballot and could not be appealed against. It was regarded by Aristotle that control of the courts gave the demos control of the constitution.

There was no government as such, instead the day to day running of the state was entrusted to a council of officials drawn by lot. The council had no legislative powers and was responsible merely for enacting the policies decided upon by the people.

Participation in the state was restricted to citizens. This excluded women, slaves and metics or in modern terms resident aliens.

Only where skill was essential, as with military commanders, was election considered safe. The contrast with our political and military system could not be more striking.

Written in 1994

References

1. Aristotle, *The politics*, English translation by T. A. Sinclair, Penguin, London, 1962, (Original circa 330 BC).

2. Cockshott, W. P., Application of artificial intelligence techniques to economic planning, *Journal of Future Computer Systems*, 1990.

3. Cottrell, A, Cockshott, P., Labour value and socialist economic calculation, *Economy and Society*, Volume 18, Feb 1989.

4. Finley, M., *Democracy Ancient and Modern*, Hogarth Press, London, 1985.

5. Marx, K, *Critique of the Gotha Programme*, People's Publishing House Peking, 1972 (written 1875).

6. Marx, K, *Capital*, A Critique of Political Economy , Volume III, Progress Publishers, Moscow, 1971 (first published 1894).

7. Nove, A., *The Economics of Feasible Socialism*, George Allen and Unwin, London, 1983.

8. Pugh, W, et al, *IBM's 360 and Early 370 Systems*, MIT Press, Massachusetts Institute of Technology, Cambridge, 1991.

9. Stalin, J.,V., *Economic Problems of Socialism in the USSR*, People's Publishing House Peking, 1972.

12. Reform and revolution in Leninist Politics

In the aftermath of the collapse of the USSR there is a strong pressure on the left to abandon Marxism-Leninism. Various anarchist and libertarian views on the left and social democratic ones on the right, have come into greater prominence. I wish to argue that, although Marxism-Leninism may have serious weaknesses when it comes to how to organise a socialist society, it still stands head and shoulders above any alternative on how to conduct political class struggle for socialism.

Marxism-Leninism is the application of rational science to politics, in the service of communism. It is the political method of communist parties. These parties have as their aim the creation of a classless society, which they call communism. Marxist Leninists are not the only people who say they want a classless society. Most socialists and anarchists would also share this aim. What makes a Leninist strategy different is the way it combines rational economic analysis with agitation, propaganda, organization and military leadership to achieve its ends.

Marxist Analysis of Society

The purpose of Marxist-Leninist theory is to allow communists to analyze economic and political conditions in sufficient detail to provide the basis for an effective political line. An effective political line is one which produces the maximum gains possible in the current situation.

Politics is the struggle to control or influence state power.

Political class struggle always takes place within a particular state, and since economic and political conditions differ from country to country, Marxist-Leninist analysis must focus on the specific conditions within the party's home state.

In the past it has been straight-forward to identify which is the home state. With the process of European Union it is getting harder. We currently live under a dual system of state power, in which the EC is still the weaker element. Once a single currency and European military command system are established, the EC will have become the dominant element. At that point, the establishment of an all-Europe communist party will be necessary.

A communist party must have an analysis of economy and class structure of the state that it operates in if it is to have an effective political strategy. Classic examples of this type of analysis are Lenin's The Development of Capitalism in Russia, (Collected Works Vol 3), and Mao's Analysis of the Classes in Chinese Society, (Selected Works Vol 1). The purpose of this analysis is, in Mao's words, to answer the question: 'Who are our enemies? Who are our friends?'.

This analysis can not be arrived at by a-priori reasoning. It requires an investigation. It requires the application of Marxist political economy to contemporary economic conditions. This analysis seeks to answer several questions:

i) What are the systems of exploitation in this country? Who exploits whom? Who suffers from exploitation and who benefits from it?

It is not enough to answer these questions in a general fashion, to say simply that workers are exploited by capitalists. For a start, there will be other. non-capitalist forms of exploitation. In China the exploitation of peasants by landlords was more important than capitalist exploitation. Here one has to take into account exploitation through rent and debt and the exploitation of women by their husbands and sons.

ii) Which economic systems are growing and which are shrinking?

In Lenin's time it was a matter of arguing that communal peasant agriculture was being replaced by capitalist agriculture, and thus that the populist demand to return to communal agriculture was unrealistic. This could only be proven by detailed examination of government statistics. We need to know which categories of activity are growing and which are shrinking in terms of things like: local government work, bank employees, sales employees, security guards, factory work, the self employed.

iii) What are the contradictions inherent in the economy that may cause a crisis?

110

iv) Which classes are our friends and which classes are our enemies? What are the just demands that unite our friends and isolate our enemies?

Once we know the answers to these questions, then we have to work out what are the possible courses of development of our society.

There is no point to politics unless there is more than one future open to us. We have to identify, in general terms, what futures are possible so that we can fight for the one that is in the interests of the working class.

Marxist-Leninist Politics in Stable Periods

Changes in society are due chiefly to the development of the internal contradictions in society, that is, the contradiction between the productive forces and the relations of production, the contradiction between classes, and the contradiction between the old and the new; it is the development of these contradictions that pushes society forward and gives the impetus for the supersession of the old society by the new. (Mao, *On Contradiction*, Selected works Vol I)

Capitalism is often stable for quite long periods. There are always contradictions in capitalism, but when exploitation and the accumulation of capital are proceeding smoothly, then class antagonisms remain latent rather than explosive and are not manifest in open social conflict. Exploitation of wage labour always leads to struggles over wages and working conditions, but at most times only a tiny minority of workers are engaged in strikes, work-to-rules etc. This background noise of class struggle in no way threatens the social order.

In stable periods the existing form of state, laws of property and system of ideology correspond with the needs of the economic base. They allow capital to accumulate and the economy to go on developing. Examples of such periods in Britain were the late Victorian period and the 1950s and '60s.

Stable periods greatly restrict the activities of revolutionary parties. Since there is not objective social need for them, they can all too easily degenerate into sectarian irrelevance. Although unable to intervene in national politics, the communists should still engage in political activity. It may not at these times be able to wield mass influence but it must prepare theoretically, politically and organizationally for the time when it can.

It must deepen its understanding of society so that it can identify the contradictions that may come to the fore in a time of crisis.

It must educate workers in Marxist theory so that they have the knowledge and skill required to analyze a crisis situation when it arises.

It must aid such mass struggles as do occur, and by its practical assistance gain the reputation of being selflessly committed to the interests of the working-class as a whole.

It must fight for such reforms as would improve the immediate conditions of life of the masses.

Restructuring Crises

Relative stability is the normal condition of capitalism, revolutionary crises are very rare. This is why overtly revolutionary parties rarely have a mass following. Since revolutionary situations may occur only once in a century, there would be little scope for communist politics were it not for the fact that lesser, restructuring crises occur more frequently.

The development of capitalism goes through phases. During the stable periods, the superstructure corresponds well to the needs of the base. The economy establishes a pattern of growth and capital accumulates. But as it does so, the process of gradual quantitative development eventually produces qualitative changes. Gradual changes in property ownership and in the sizes of different social classes undermine the original conditions favorable to growth and lead to economic difficulties. This is very abstract. A couple of historical examples will make this clearer.

a) Period leading up to World War I In the 19th century the expansion of capitalism in Britain had rested on the foundations of a growing working class and international free trade. The application of capitalism to agriculture along with a high birth rate ensured a constant flow of population from the countryside into the cities. This provided a pool of unemployed who could be hired at low wages, and the instability of the working population hindered the formation of trades unions except in skilled trades. At the same time the head start that British capitalism had over other countries meant that international trade provided a ready market for the ever growing output of British industry.

However, the profitable export of machinery from Britain promoted industrialisation of other countries thus creating rivals on the world market.

112

The process of urbanization eventually drained the reserve army of labour from the countryside.

Table 12.1.: Percentage of Population Classified as Urban

year	1801	1851	1901	1951
% urban	25	50	75	79

As a result two of the essential preconditions of the period of stability were removed. Internationally, competition with other capitalist powers led to militarism. Domestically the stabilization of the proletariat led to increasing trades union membership, strikes of ever increasing militancy.

British capitalism could not go on as before. From about 1910 onwards it entered a restructuring crisis, which, through wars and recessions was not eventually resolved until the reforms of the 1945 government laid the basis for a new period of stable growth.

b) The period from 1950 to 1979   The period from 1950 till the mid-1970's saw rapid and stable economic growth. Capital accumulated rapidly and there were big increases in real wages, in stark contrast to the early years of this century. For the first 50 years of the century there was effectively no growth in real wages. What workers gained in good years they lost in the bad. At the same time the bourgeoisie devoted a trivial proportion of their profits to capital accumulation, consuming the rest in a parasitic fashion.

After 1950 the picture changed. In the next 25 years real wages almost doubled, whilst accumulation either took up the greater part of profits or even exceeded them.

These changes were the effect of the progressive restructuring of capitalism that had taken place after the war: nationalization of major industries, exchange controls and Keynesian full employment policies. These changes restricted the role of the free market and introduced an element of conscious planning of economic activity. As such they were steps, albeit small and limited ones towards socialism. It was called at the time a mixed economy, since it mixed elements of state capitalism with private capitalism. The objectively progressive nature of state capitalism compared to private capitalism meant that both the productive forces and the working class benefited.

Table 12.2.: Accumulation and wage levels in the UK

Year	Index of real wages	Capital accumulation as % profit
1900	100	18
1910	94.3	4
1920	100.6	14
1930	104.2	3
1940	98	
1950	101.6	68
1960	123.3	72
1970	144.3	262
1976	193.7	

Dialectics claims that there are contradictions in everything. The Keynesian/Social Democratic solutions to the problems of the first half of the century, created new contradictions which, by the 1970's came to a head. There were a whole complex of contradictions:

1. A long period of full employment hand allowed strong trades union organisation to develop. It was this which enabled workers to improve their real wages.

2. The rapid accumulation of capital meant that more capital equipment was employed per worker. Since surplus value could only be made from the exploitation of living labour, this meant that only a diminishing portion of the capital stock was contributing to the production of surplus value. In consequence the rate of profit fell.

3. The enlargement of the state employment – armed forces, civil service, NHS and local government work diminished the number of workers directly exploited by the capital. Since only workers employed out of capital produce surplus value this further diminished the rate of profit.

4. As real wages improved, and more workers won pension schemes, savings by wage and salary earners increased. This encouraged the flooding of high streets with banks, building societies and insurance companies; all of which were basically unproductive activities. The absorption of capital and labour in these parasitic activities undermined the rate of profit.

5. High levels of saving meant a smaller portion of wages being spent on consumption. The consequent under-consumption created ever stronger recessionary tendencies and at the same time expanded the money supply in the hands of the banks. The result was a combination of unemployment and inflation, stagflation as it was called, that had never been seen before.

The result was a new restructuring crisis: a period of economic stagnation and intensified class struggle similar to that of the first decades of the century. The contradictions meant that a restructuring of production relations were an objective necessity. Two types of restructuring were possible: a reactionary one carried out under bourgeois pressure, or a progressive one carried out under working class pressure. We now know, all too well, which one took place.

Responsibility of Left

The Left, who are very willing to debate what went wrong in Russia, are a lot less willing to ask what mistakes in their own strategy contributed to that victory of Thatcherism which proved such a disaster to the working-class. None of the Left had a clear Marxist analysis or Leninist strategy for the situation. That they have not faced up to their mistakes in the last crisis bodes ill for the next.

The several strands of thinking which influenced the Left did not correspond precisely with organizational divisions. One strand was Trotskyist catastrophism, most clearly embodied in the WRP[1] , but shared at times by others. According to this Britain was in an immediately pre-revolutionary period, which, by means of a general strike could be turned into an actual revolution. This view, which involved a strong dose of wishful thinking, was not widely held.

A more common attitude was syndicalist economism, according to which the key task was to encourage and support trades union militancy. To fight for structural reforms was stigmatized as a reformist distraction from the reality of the class struggle. The key thing was to preserve the independence of the trades unions, defend free collective bargaining and oppose incomes policies. This view was widely held, from the WRP, through the SWP[2] to the trades union base of the CP.

---

[1] Worker's Revolutionary Party
[2] Socialist Woreker's Party

The only view with any economic analysis to support it, was taken by the Bennite Left and the CP leadership who put forward the alternative economic strategy. This was the only politically serious response.

The ultimately decisive response was that of the Labour government who, with no strategy for structural reform sought and ad-hoc social compact with the TUC to swap wage restraint for a full employment. Neither party to the negotiations was capable of delivering its side of the bargain.

With the benefit of hindsight it is possible to see that the best communist strategy would have had more in common with the Bennite/CP position than any of the others. It would have concede that, the situation was not revolutionary: the state retained a monopoly of armed force, the army was loyal and the proletariat completely disarmed. The key objective thus had to be to win the most radical and progressive reforms. Genuinely progressive reforms would not only resolve the immediate economic crisis, but would strengthen the social position of the working class, as those of 1945-50 had done.

What was required was a decisive shift of the economy towards fully fledged state capitalism. A rough idea of what would have been required can be gained from reading Lenin's pamphlet 'The impending catastrophe and how to combat it', (Collected Works Vol 25). The key measures would have been:

* bringing the financial institutions under state control;

* state direction of investment to ensure that profits and savings were productively invested;

* a prices and incomes policy regulated by a 'house of labour' made up of shop stewards delegates. (During the panic of the mid 70s this was actually proposed by the Economist magazine. It would have been an act analogous to Louis XVI's calling of the estates general.);

* introduction of workers control, with a majority on company boards being trades union delegates;

* replacement of the professional army with a Swiss style defence system to guard against the danger of military coups.

These are obviously not revolutionary socialist measures. They would have been radical state capitalist ones designed to resolve the crisis on terms favorable to the workers movement. Had such gains been won, then the next restructuring crisis, occurring perhaps in the early years of the next century would have posed the question of a transition from state capitalism to socialism.

Since restructuring was objectively needed, and since the workers movement had no coherent policy for it, the way was open for the reactionary restructuring of Thatcher to be presented under the totalitarian banner that 'There Is No Alternative'.

Revolutionary Crises

A revolutionary crisis is one in which there is a real possibility of state power passing from the hands of the ruling class. In all such conjunctures the immediately decisive element is military force. Political power grows out of the barrel of a gun; at least in a crisis it does.

That force is decisive, does not imply it must be used. What is important is that the ruling class should no longer be able to call on effective violence to impose its will.

This may be the result of defeat in an earlier war. In Poland for instance, the combined effect of the German invasion, the execution of the officer class by the Soviets at Katyn, and the suppression of the Warsaw uprising, left the bourgeoisie with no effective armed forces.

It may be the result of war weariness in the army; which refuses to obey orders. Examples of this are the February 1917 revolution in Russia or the 1975 revolution in Portugal.

It may be possible for power to be transfered peacefully; due to the collapse of the executive organs of the state and a consequent lack of co-ordination in the army, e.g., the initial establishment of the Paris Commune after the collapse of the imperial government.

The highest form of class struggle is revolutionary civil war. In this, the armed forces of the reactionaries are crushed and the former rulers forced to flee. Examples of this are the wars led by Cromwell, Toussaint L'Overture, Lincoln, Trotsky, Mao, Castro, Ho Chi Min and Giap.

The importance of the military factor in revolutions is so obvious that it scarcely needs to be emphasized. Even where, as in the Paris Commune, the initial transfer of power is peaceful, it has to be followed by the construction of a revolutionary army. 'Without a peoples army the people have nothing.'

It is sheer adventurism to advance revolutionary objectives in a period when military factors make the transfer of power impossible. Against every democratic and constitutional prejudice it has to be emphasized that the military situation determines where effective state power lies in a revolutionary conjuncture. Repeated experience has shown that a well disciplined army under decisive centralised command can suppress any threat to state power other than a superior army. An army can not be defeated by trades unions or other peaceful organisations of the working class.

To say that the military question is decisive in revolutionary situations, does not mean that the revolution reduces to a question of military organisation. A revolutionary war is a war of the masses and can be waged only by mobilizing the masses and relying on them. This requires that the party have a correct policy of forming a revolutionary alliance of all the oppressed; the policy of uniting all who can be united against the principle enemy. The fact that the struggle has taken an extreme form, war, does not imply that the immediate program of the CP should be extreme. The social aims of the people's war in China, were a comparatively moderate program of land reform. It aimed to unite the rural proletariat and peasantry as a whole against the landowners. Specifically socialist objectives: the formation of co-operatives and communes; were delayed until after the victory of the peoples war.

Revolutionary struggle in developed countries

What should be the attitude of communists in Britain to the military question. It is not enough to effectively ignore it by asserting that the troops, who are from working class backgrounds, would not consent to be used against workers. This is wishful thinking. There are four other approaches which at least deserve to be taken seriously:

i) Turning imperialist war into class war

This is what Lenin advocated during the first world war. The strategy worked in Russia. The preconditions for this are:

a. The existence of an imperialist war.

b. That it is prolonged.

c. That it is not an all out nuclear war.

d. That there is little prospect of 'our side' winning.

The cold war and nuclear deterrence prevented imperialist wars, and made this strategy irrelevant for its duration. If imperialist war re-emerges as a danger, this would again be an appropriate strategy.

ii) Reforming the armed forces

This strategy was advocated by Peter Tatchell and others on the Left of the Labour Party. They aimed to replace a professional army with one based on a short period of conscription with general military training similar to the Swiss or former Jugoslav models. Along with this would go an attempt to change the class composition of the officer corps. This approach has a precedent in the classical social democratic program which called for a replacement of the standing army by an armed populace. Some support for it can be found in Engels article The Prussian Military Question and the German Worker's Party (The Pelican Marx Library, Political Writings, Vol 3). In this Engels argued that a conscript army with a short period of service, which depended for its effectiveness on a general mobilization, was an unsuitable instrument for the execution of a military-coup.

Whether this such reforms would be sufficient to prevent a military coup in a time of social crisis can not be said for sure, but in comparison with Britain's current mercenary army, they would certainly be a democratic advance. There is a strong case for the workers' movement to demand such reforms from a Labour government.

iii) Urban guerilla warfare

The Maoist strategy of people's war has been successfully applied in several colonial or semi-colonial countries. This involves using the countryside to surround the towns; building up red base areas and through protracted struggle, going from guerilla war to a general offensive. No attempt to apply this in an urban context has yet resulted in victory. The nearest to an example was probably the Algerian war of independence, but this was primarily a war of national rather than social liberation.

This has led most Marxists to conclude that urban guerilla struggle is inappropriate in developed capitalist countries. It is pointed out that the nature of guerilla struggle inevitably leads to the guerillas going underground and becoming isolated from the class. European experience seems to bear this out. The attempts by the Red Army Faction and the Red Brigades, though sustained for several years never rose above isolated terrorism and have ceased to be a danger to the state. But it would be a mistake to conclude that this is inevitably the case.

An apparent counter example is close to home in Ireland. There, a guerilla war has been going on for more than 20 years. It has not become isolated from the population, indeed, a significant share of the working class vote goes to candidates who openly espouse the armed struggle. The fact that it has not long since been victorious is attributable not to military but to political factors: the political program of the IRA limits its appeal to around 25% of the population. Without a political program capable of broadening their base they are unable to break out of the stalemate.

Unlike the RAF and the Red Brigades, whose impetus came at first from the student movement, the nucleus of the IRA came from a section of the working class. It is this which enables them to move through the population like Mao's fish through water. It is their strong ties with the working class catholic population that prevents their eradication by the state. It thus remains possible that a genuinely working-class organisation, with a well thought out political program, could pursue the strategy of guerilla war to a successful conclusion.

iv) Formation of worker's defence guards

Trotsky raised the slogan of trades union defence guards that would go over from defending pickets to form the nucleus of a red army. In the USA there has been a strong tradition of strikers forming armed guards to defend picket lines against scabs. This is doubtless helped by the US constitution which secures the liberty to carry and bear arms. Such workers guards were successfully deployed in the 1948 communist revolution in Prague. In Britain nascent workers guards existed in the hit squads formed during the miner's strike. It is however, hard to see how such forces could go on to challenge state power in this country, where the general populace is completely disarmed.

Document dates from about 1992.

120

13. Review of Mike Macnair's *Revolutionary Strategy*

Mike Macnair of the Communist Party of Great Britain has recently written a book whose avowed aim is to reformulate left strategy along Kautskyan lines. One might say: surely this is a retrograde step politically. But in a sense a movement towards Kautskyism would be an advance for the 'official communist' movement.

Macnair distinguishes between the Kautskyan trend and the right wing in social democracy. Besides, recalling how much of orthodox Leninism is actually Kautskyism second hand, Macnair makes the very accurate observation that:

"The coalitionist policy of the right wing of the Second International has been, since 1945, the policy of Second International socialists and 'official communists' alike. The substantive difference between them, before first Euro-communism and then the fall of the USSR, was that 'official communists' proposed for each country a socialist-liberal coalition that would commit to geopolitical formal neutrality, combined with friendly relations with the Soviet bloc. With the Soviet sheet anchor gone, the majority of the former 'official communists' are at best disoriented, and at worst form the right wing of governing coalitions (as is the case with the ex-communists and ex-fellow-travellers within the Labour Party in Britain)."

A key discriminating feature of the Kautskyan tendency was its opposition to coalitions with bourgeois parties and an insistence that it would only enter into government when it had the requisite majority to rule unaided. In this sense then, a move to Kautskyism would amount to a considerable radicalisation of the communists in Europe.

So the book is significant. I will argue, however, that it is marked by a failure to go beyond certain fatal limits of classical social democracy, and also by a failure to have any positive theory of socialism.

This lack of a theory of socialism is first evident in the non-treatment of the history of the USSR and China, and later in a failure to spell out what sort of economy the socialist movement should be fighting for.

On the first point Macnair writes: "Under the Soviet-style bureaucratic regimes there was no objective tendency towards independent self-organisation of the working class. Rather, there were episodic explosions; but to the extent that the bureaucracy did not succeed in putting a political cap on these, they tended towards a pro-capitalist development. The strategic line of a worker revolution against the bureaucracy – whether it was called 'political revolution', as it was by the orthodox Trotskyists, or 'social revolution' by state-capitalism and bureaucratic-collectivism theorists – lacked a material basis."

He extends the argument to apply to orthodox Stalinists, who have to explain why the real Stalinists were not able to organise opposition to the restoration of capitalism. This is an interesting observation, but it has two drawbacks:

1. Its focus is exclusively on the USSR and eastern Europe post-World War II. It ignores the experience of China during the cultural revolution and, if Getty and others are to be believed[1] , the experience of the great purges. There was working class participation there. Did this arise from an "objective tendency"?

2. It could be a council of despair. The abolition of private capitalism is bound to remove the old class struggle between labour and capital over profits. If such trade union struggle is a precondition of class-consciousness, then socialism is bound to remove that class-consciousness – whether it is bureaucratic socialism or not. What then is to be the social basis of resistance to capitalist restoration?

Macnair argues with respect to the USSR: "What happened instead was to render concrete the 1850s warnings of Marx and Engels against the premature seizure of power in Germany, which formed the basis of Kautsky's caution in the 1890s and 1900s. By choosing to represent the peasantry and other petty proprietors (especially state bureaucrats), the workers' party disabled itself from representing the working class, but instead became a sort of collective Bonaparte.

"The Bolshevik leaders could see and feel it happening to themselves, and in 1919-23 the Commintern flailed around with a succession of short-lived strategic concepts, each of which would – it was hoped – break the isolation of the revolution. These strategic concepts are not simply rendered obsolete by the collapse of the USSR in 1991. The fate of the other socialist countries also proves them to be a strategic blind alley. This was,

---

[1] JA Getty, *Origins of the great purges: the Soviet Communist Party reconsidered*, 1933-1938. Cambridge 1985.

of course, like the argument of Kautsky during the 20s. Is it valid to say that the CPs represented petty proprietors when in power?"

Well, there is some truth in it to the extent that, so long as petty peasant production existed, it created wings within the CPs which defended its interest: Bukharin, Gomulka, Deng. But these were just one wing, and in most cases they did not come out on top. In the USSR private peasant agriculture was largely eliminated by collectivisation. And during the 1950s and 60s, state farms expanded at the expense even of collectives. In Poland after 1956 the pro-petty proprietor wing did come out on top, but that was not generally the case. In the German Democratic Republic, Czechoslovakia and Bulgaria, state or collective agriculture was the rule. The crisis of the socialist system, Poland aside, was not generally precipitated by the demands of petty proprietors in agriculture and the identification of state bureaucrats with petty proprietors is an unconvincing throwaway phrase, not justified by any argument.

Coalition

Macnair writes: "The policy of reform through coalition governments thus entails (a) the displacement of the down swing of the business cycle onto the weaker states and their firms and populations; and (b) the displacement of the social polarisation which capitalism produces onto polarisation between nations. On the one hand, this gives the reformists' negative claims their credibility: reforms are actually achieved and social polarisation is reduced in the successful states. On the other, the reformists necessarily commit themselves to sustaining and managing an imperial military force."

This may be true of Germany, the UK or USA, but what of Sweden? It is an unsafe generalisation.

Macnair continues: "At the point of global war between the great powers, the illusory character of the policy of reform through coalition government becomes transparent. All that maintains the reformists are mass fear of the consequences of military defeat and direct support from the state in the form of repression of their left opponents. Thus both 1914-18 and 1939-45 produced major weakening of the reform policy within the workers' movement and the growth of alternatives. In the event, after 1945 the destruction of British world hegemony enabled a new long phase of growth, and reformism was able to revive. We are now on the road to another collapse of reformist politics ... but what is lacking is a strategically plausible alternative."

While the point above is sound, Macnair then attacks the slogan, 'All power to the soviets': "But 'All power to the soviets' was also illusory in another sense. Even before they withered away into mere fronts for the Russian Communist Party, the soviets did not function like parliaments or governments – or even the Paris Commune – in continuous session. They met discontinuously, with executive committees managing their affairs. Though the Bolsheviks took power in the name of the soviets, in reality the central all-Russia coordination of the soviets was provided by the political parties – Mensheviks and SRs, and later Bolsheviks. It was Sovnarkom, the government formed by the Bolsheviks and initially including some of their allies, and its ability to reach out through the Bolshevik Party as a national organisation, which solved the crisis of authority affecting Russia in 1917.

"The point is simply that the problem of decision-making authority is not solved by the creation of workers' councils arising out of a mass strike movement. Hence, the problem of institutional forms which will make authority answerable to the masses needs to be addressed in some way other than fetishism of the mass strike and the workers' councils."

Macnair says that the Kautskyan centre opposed the left on the grounds that if the workers' party already had a majority then a mass strike would be pointless, whereas taking power after a strike whilst in a minority would be elitist and minoritarian. Against the right they argued that taking part in a coalition would saddle the workers party with responsibility for the measures taken by their middle class allies, which, like as not, would be hostile to the working class. He sums up the strategy of the centre as:

"When we have a majority, we will form a government and implement the whole minimum programme; if necessary, the possession of a majority will give us legitimacy to coerce the capitalist/pro-capitalist and petty bourgeois minority. Implementing the whole minimum programme will prevent the state in the future serving as an instrument of the capitalist class and allow the class struggle to progress on terrain more favourable to the working class."

The state

He criticises the positions of the late Engels on the state as insufficient. Engels had argued that one had to fight for a democratic republic in order for a peaceful transition to socialism by electoral means to be possible – giving the UK and USA as examples of where this might occur. Macnair

argues that Engels missed the essence of the bourgeois state form:
"The inner secret of the capitalist state form is not bourgeois democracy.
Rather, it has three elements: 1. the rule of law – i.e., the judicial power;
2. the deficit financing of the state through organised financial markets;
and 3. the fact that capital rules, not through a single state, but through an
international state system, of which each national state is merely a part."

This seems a little idiosyncratic, particularly point 2. True, states often
do use deficit financing, and indeed one can argue that the growth in the
money supply necessary for the circuit M-C-M' can often occur this way.
But why is deficit finance the key? Surely the power to tax is more important than that, and in particular, the power to levy taxes in money rather
than in kind. Along with this goes the right to issue money.

The acceptability of state-issued money, and the ability to raise deficit
finance, both in the end depend upon the power to tax. Without tax revenues, there would be no way to pay the interest on the national debt, and
without the obligation to pay taxes in domestic currency, there would be
not ability to issue money that was generally acceptable.

Why too does he miss out the monopoly of armed force held by the
state, the existence of a standing army, and salaried police? Why does
he not mention the parliamentary state as the characteristic constitutional
form of civil society?

Macnair presents an interesting critique of residual nationalist traits in
the writings of Marx and Engels. These are, of course, particularly marked
in the late Engels, where certain Jacobin patriotic themes exist, which at a
later date could provide a cover for the SPD voting to support World War
I. Macnair argues plausibly that these derive in the end from the theme of
the Communist manifesto that the proletariat of each country must first of
all settle matters with its own bourgeoisie.

Macnair summarises Lenin's line on revolutionary defeatism, but argues
that it was the specific character of the Great War that made it an effective
strategy. Had it been a quick German victory like 1870, it would have
had no purchase; and indeed, had Germany been fighting a defensive war
on German soil, then Engels' advocacy of a defencist policy would have
been vindicated. He also argues that the defeatist policy could never have
made headway or been appropriate in the conditions of World War II. The
defeatist strategy could only work if it was applied generally in all the
belligerent powers. This presupposed an international and the possibility
of a generalised revolutionary crisis.

Although this did not occur, Macnair believes that the defeatist strategy was right because it was based on an important truth about the state. The key point was that the power of the state rests on the coherence of the army. An unjust and terrible war offers the chance that, by defeatist propaganda in the armed forces, one may disrupt the main coercive power of the state and thus overthrow the rule of the old dominant class.

Macnair argues that it was a mistake of the old Second International not to have taken seriously Engels' advocacy of democratic republican measures like universal military training, a militia and the right to bear arms. They should also have argued that the army ranks should have freedom of political speech and the right to organise in political parties and trade unions. This would have created conditions favourable to opposition to an imperialist war and, although Macnair does not mention this, it would also have created conditions favourable to preventing military putsches.

Democratic republic

Mike Macnair writes: "The key is to replace the illusory idea of 'All power to the soviets' and the empty one of 'All power to the Communist Party' with the original Marxist idea of the undiluted democratic republic, or extreme democracy, as the form of the dictatorship of the proletariat ... The present task of communists/socialists is therefore not to fight for an alternative government. It is to fight to build an alternative opposition: one which commits itself unambiguously to self-emancipation of the working class through extreme democracy, as opposed to all the loyalist parties."

This is superficially correct – certainly in impetus it goes in the right direction. But it contains real ambiguities which only become evident when he lists his demands. When he does, then Macnair makes a complete hash of it and shows that his conceptions of political democracy have completely failed to break free from bourgeois republicanism.

But I am going to quibble here and argue that the phrase 'democratic republic' is wrong from the start. It couples two quite different ancient models – those of Athens and those of Rome; state forms which are radically distinct in terms of the degree of popular power that they permitted. The republic is Rome reborn; it is senatorial power; it is presidential power (the first magistrate), the political form of the dominant imperial state. It is no accident that the slave-owning classes of the USA adopted a republican constitution which took Rome as its model. The social-democratic movement should, in republics like the USA, Germany and France, be seeking to overthrow the republican constitution and replace it with democracy. In bourgeois monarchies like Britain, Sweden or Holland to raise the slogan of republicanism rather than going straight for democracy, places you no further left than radical liberals.

What does Macnair give as the political measures necessary to achieve this "extreme democracy"?

* ★ universal military training and service, democratic political and trade union rights within the military and the right to keep and bear arms;

* ★ election and recallability of all public officials; public officials to be on an average skilled worker's wage;

* ★ abolition of official secrecy laws and of private rights of copyright and confidentiality;

* ★ self-government in the localities: i.e., the removal of powers of central government control and patronage and abolition of judicial review of the decisions of elected bodies;

* ★ abolition of constitutional guarantees of the rights of private property and freedom of trade.

What is striking about this is what it omits. How are political decisions to be reached in this "extreme democracy"?

Since Macnair says nothing new about this, he accepts the pretensions of parliamentary government to be democratic. But, once he does that, he has sold the pass. He is accepting the basic structure of the bourgeois state designed by Hamilton and Madison in which the people do not rule, but are given at least the illusion of influence by being able to choose which of their betters will rule over them. The federalists knew their classical political theory and they understood that in establishing a state of this form in the USA they were not establishing a democracy, but a republic. They had read their Aristotle and understood well enough that election was an anti-democratic principle:

> "There is a third mode, in which something is borrowed from the oligarchical and something from the democratic principle. For example, the appointment of magistrates by lot is thought to be democratical, and the election of them oligarchical; democratical again when there is no property qualification, oligarchical when there is. In the aristocratical or constitutional state, one element will be taken from each – from

oligarchy the principle of electing to offices, from democracy the disregard of qualification. Such are the various modes of combination."[2]

The federalists aimed at this "aristocratical" or constitutional state, which was oligarchic in essence but had certain trappings of democracy. In practice, of course, the removal of the property qualification came later, but the key issue was election. Initially bourgeois states had property qualifications for voting and these could later be relaxed, but the principle of election was retained.

It was quite clear from classical political theory that election was an oligarchic or aristocratic principle. It involved the deliberate selection of the 'best' people, the *aristoi*, to high office. And who are our 'betters' but the upper classes, the more educated, the more wealthy, etc. Any system of election is inherently biased against the lower classes and favours the upper classes. Elections are inherently oligarchic and elitist.

Aristotle also writes: "... as an oligarchy is said to be a government of men of family, fortune and education; so, on the contrary, a democracy is a government in the hands of men of no birth, indigent circumstances, and mechanical employments."[3]

Look at the USA, the UK or Germany. Do they have government by those of indigent circumstance and mechanical employment? Clearly not. Or do they have government made up of those of family, fortune and education? Clearly they do. So they, like all bourgeois states, are oligarchies, not democracies.

The relabelling of the ancient oligarchic state form as 'democracy', was the single greatest intellectual counterfeit of the bourgeois epoch. Both Kautsky and Macnair have unquestioningly accepted the counterfeit at face value. They end up supporting oligarchy rather than democracy.

In contrast to the oligarchic form of government, Aristotle summarised the essential components of democracy:

★ that all the magistrates should be chosen out of all the people, and all to command each, and each in his turn all;

★ that all the magistrates should be chosen by lot, except to those offices only which required some particular knowledge and skill;

---

[2]My emphasis, Aristotle, *Politics* book 4, part 9.
[3]Aristotle, *Politics* book 6, part 2.

⋆ that no census[4] , or a very small one, should be required to qualify a man for any office;

⋆ that none should be in the same employment twice[5] , or very few, and very seldom, except in the army;

⋆ that all their appointments should be limited to a very short time, or at least as many as possible;

⋆ that the whole community should be qualified to judge in all causes whatsoever, let the object be ever so extensive, ever so interesting, or of ever so high a nature; as at Athens, where the people at large judge the magistrates when they come out of office, and decide concerning public affairs as well as private contracts;

⋆ that the supreme power should be in the public assembly; and that no magistrate should be allowed any discretionary power but in a few instances, and of no consequence to public business.[6]

Aristotle was by no means an advocate of democracy, but he attempted to provide a relatively objective description of the then available constitutional forms. His *Politics* provided the menu from which the classically educated founders of the US constitution placed their orders. What Aristotle was describing above is not "extreme democracy". No. He was listing the minimal conditions for a state to be called a democracy at all.

The key principle is that, instead of being elected, public officials are chosen from the general public like a jury. Aristotle argues that in democracies the best form of magistracy, or executive, is a council. If magistrates are chosen by lot, they will be untrained and lack specialist knowledge of government, but if there is a group of them, they will collectively be wiser and more competent than any one individual. There is a wisdom in crowds, for the collective will contain people with many different skills and experiences.[7]

In a modern oligarchy like France, Britain or the USA, what Aristotle called the magistracy is elected. In these elections those with education and money have a huge advantage. The election process is expensive –

---

[4]This means property qualification.
[5]This means public office. Nobody should hold the same public office twice.
[6]Aristotle, *Politics* book 6, part 2.
[7] See J Surowiecki, MP Silverman et al 'The wisdom of crowds' *American Journal of Physics* 75: 190, 2007.

there are the costs of advertising and campaigning. Historically, in Europe at least, workers' parties have been able to partly get round this by collecting dues from hundreds of thousands or millions of members. But when standing candidates they usually face the hostility of the privately owned mass media, which is hard to offset.

They are also under pressure to present candidates who are far from being "of indigent circumstances and mechanical employments". Their first generation of leaders may be of that sort: Ramsay MacDonald or Lula. But later they attempt to present candidates who are educated and polished: Obamas and Blairs. In consequence the elected representatives of popular parties tend to be from higher classes than their supporters. They tend, in consequence, to be markedly cautious in implementing the full rigour of a socialist programme when in office.

Democratic selection by lot suffers none of these disadvantages. It guarantees that the assembly will be dominated by the working classes. It guarantees that the assembly will be balanced in terms of sex, age, ethnic origin, etc. As such it would constitute the most favourable possible grounds for achieving a majority for socialism. If Macnair really wanted to follow the logic of the working class party being the most consistent advocate of democracy, what he should be demanding is:

⋆ the replacement of all parliaments, councils, assemblies and quangos by juries drawn randomly from the population;

⋆ the right of initiative and referendum, with taxes and the budget to be submitted to popular vote;[8] declarations of war only by popular vote;

⋆ full political rights, including the right to elect officers in the armed forces;

⋆ abolition of the judiciary and magistracy; juries to be supreme in courts; no loss of liberty without jury trial.

---

[8]It is notable that when the right of initiative was advocated by the left in the SPD in the 1890s Kautsky opposed it: see the account in M Salvadori *Karl Kautsky and the socialist revolution, 1880-1938*London 1990. Now, popular votes can be easily and securely organised using telephones (see WP Cockshott, K Renaud, 'HandiVote: simple, anonymous and auditable electronic voting' *Journal of Information Technology and Politics*6 (1): 60-80, 2009.

Infuriating

One of the most interesting parts of Macnair's book is his treatment of the history of internationalism. He is a strong advocate of the need for an international, but is very critical of the Third and Fourth.

The Third International is criticised for its bureaucratic military command structure, which, he claims, would only have been justified in the event of a general revolutionary civil war across Europe in the 1920s. Failing that, it suppressed local initiative and the horizontal links that real internationalism required. Macnair devotes a perhaps excessive critical attention to the Trotskyite international, in view of the latter's limited influence.

He still sees the need for a new international but cautions: "It should be apparent that the objective political conditions do not yet exist for such a struggle. But they do exist for continental united struggles for political power, which fight for continental unification: a Communist Party of Europe, a Pan-African Communist Party, and so on. A dynamic towards the continental unification of politics is already visible in bourgeois politics, not just in Europe, and in the Latin American Chavista Bolivarians. It is even present in an utterly deformed and reactionary manner in the Islamist movement in the Middle East."

In general what is infuriating about reading Macnair, is that, although his heart and impulses are in the right place, he remains dogmatically hidebound by a particular set of historical exemplars. It is clear that his programmatic repertoire is drawn almost exclusively from the Erfurt Programme and the first programmes of the RSDLP. So, although he advocates the struggle for democracy and although he says that we must oppose parliamentary constitutionalism, the only significant constitutional measure he proposes – the right of recall, is far too feeble for the task. People will not make democratic revolution if the main objective is just the right to recall MPs.[9]

If you want a democratic revolution, you would have to be intransigently opposed to the underlying elitist principle on which the existing system is based.

You would have to constantly challenge the legitimacy of an elected parliament. Your victorious candidates would have to follow the example of Irish republicans in refusing to attend and thus add legitimacy to

---

[9]Indeed Gordon Brown is reportedly planning to introduce the right of recall of MPs either before the next election or as an election pledge. It will be of some use in challenging obviously corrupt or incompetent MPs, but will hardly change the character of the political system.

the elected parliament. You might consider the Irish republican policy of combining legal with illegal struggle.

You would have to organise mass civil disobedience to unjust laws, as we in Scotland did to Thatcher's poll tax.

You would have to oppose the will of parliaments to the will of the peoples by using tactics like the local referendum that we used to block the Tory attempt to privatise water in Scotland.

You would have to look to the Chartists or Covenanters' organisation of monster petitions for change. But they should be claims of right, not petitions, since the latter concede legitimacy to those from whom one is petitioning.

You should be demanding a constitutional convention drawn by lot from the population to redefine the state structure.

You should be educating party members in the goals of revolutionary democracy, so that if such bodies drawn by lot come into existence, then any party members who randomly find themselves allotted can come to play a leading role in the citizens' jury. The party members would have to be prepared to argue intransigently in a constitutional convention for the most radical and egalitarian structures.

You would have to be prepared, at time of major crisis or political scandal, for the people themselves to take the initiative in forming such a convention drawn by lot.

You would have to argue in the trade union movement that only by raising labour's goals above the economic to the political could labour be free.

Within the labour movement you would have to be arguing for the abolition of the wages system in concrete practical terms, explaining the relatively simple steps that a democratic assembly could take to achieve these goals. The struggle over wages and conditions is not enough, but to abolish the wages system we must first win the battle of democracy.

Written in 2010

14. Ideas of Leadership and Democracy

Talk given at the Worker's Educational Association, Stockholm, transcribed by Joonas Laine.

Hi, I'm a computer scientists and an economist from Scotland, and about 17 years ago me and another colleague wrote a book which in English was called *Towards a New Socialism* and which was translated about nine years ago into Swedish. Since then a number of translations have appeared in other languages as well.

At the time we wrote that book we were concerned with the crisis in the Soviet Union, because the book was written maybe from 1989 to 1990 and we were concerned with the crisis associated with perestroika, and wanted to say how could an economy like the Soviet Union get out of the crisis in was in. So it was a book about how could a fully developed socialist economy work better. Now, obviously the Soviet Union collapsed and there aren't these fully developed socialist economies in the world today, with the possible exception of Cuba. The question started to be asked by people who were translating the book into other languages like in Czech and things, what are the steps to get to that sort of economy that we were talking about now. So [in] the talk I'm giving today I'm trying to combine two different things, because there was two talks I was originally asked to give, and I'm now trying to squash them both into one talk.

I was asked to give a talk about ideas of leadership and democracy. I was also asked to give a talk about a transition program towards socialism in the European Union that was published in Berlin in March of this year [2010]. So the latter part is the ideas that were put forward in this at the Rosa Luxembourg Institute in Berlin this year.

The background. I'm going to talk about what are the ideas that the socialist and social-democratic movement had had about what democracy is and about the nature of leadership since the start of the Communist manifesto written 150-160 years ago. And then I'm going to look at how can we deal with how to have a transition from the current economy we have to a socialist economy, immediate measures to change the economy. So let's look at the ideas that were in the Manifesto of the Communist party.

When you read that now, it seems at once familiar and at the same time, slightly strange in some of its parts because in particular when you read these phrases here, "the communists don't set up a separate party" that appears quite contrary to what happened in the 20th century when communists definitely set up separate parties. Now, in the program we put forward in Berlin we're trying to say that essentially the differences between those who call themselves communists and those who call themselves social-democrats are temporary historical phenomena of the mid-20th century, and that one should take a long historical view of the development of socialist thought which doesn't stick just to the political boundaries that seemed so relevant at one time. And that is very much the spirit in which the Communist Manifesto was written. Now, it's often said, that the idea of the avant garde, an avant garde party came into the socialist movement with Lenin, but it's clearly not the case, because if you read this section of the Communist Manifesto, it's quite clear that the idea of the communists forming an avant garde was already there in 1848. That is definitely a statement of the avant garde principle.

And if we look at what was set as the immediate goals of communism, the first is actually the constitution of the working class as a class, the constitution of the proletariat as a class. Now, that is the idea that the proletariat didn't exist as a class, except through political action. What existed was a large number of people in the same economic and social circumstance, but only becomes the class to the extent that it engages in politics, that it engages in politics with a common interest. So they're talking about the constitution of the proletariat as a class and thus as a political party, and a political party in the sense of a section of the body politic that contends for power. the first step of the revolution of the working class is to raise the proletariat to the position of the ruling class and to win the battle for democracy. Now, we have to ask what is meant by that, "winning the battle for democracy", and I think there's been a historical re-writing of what is meant by that, where people have forgotten a part of the original meaning.

The language in which Marx and Engels wrote is steeped in classical terminology. You cannot understand the way Marx wrote except by realising that he was a classical scholar. He knew his ancient Greek and Roman sources. The term 'proletariat' is a Latin term, the term 'democracy' is a Greek term, and the meaning that the word 'democracy' has now, in common bourgeois usage, is quite different from the meaning that the word 'democracy' had 160 years ago. 160 years ago the general view of what democracy meant was that it was mob rule. If you look at the sources on which this is based, if you look at the Greek sources, what does Aristotle define democracy as? He says democracy is not rule of the majority. Democracy is rule of the poor. Aristotle says it's just a coincidence in one sense that because the poor are everywhere numerous and the rich are few, democracy is also rule of the majority. But the essence of democracy is that it is rule by the poor. And in the original sense of democracy, the sense that the ancient Greeks used, the sense that Marx was familiar with – it's meaning is much closer to Lenin's term, or the later Marxist term, 'dictatorship of the proletariat'.

Now let's look at how this idea developed as we move in from the Communist party to the first social-democratic parties, and we look at the Erfurt program of German social democracy and how that understood democracy. It makes up two of the key demands in the Erfurt program, so they're saying, "direct legislation through the people by means of proposal and rejection". In other words they're not talking about a parliamentary republic, they're talking about a state where the people directly rule themselves by means of all laws being put to the people, being proposed by the people, not by politicians, and being passed by the people in a general vote. So the idea of democracy that early social-democracy had is still that of ancient Greek democracy, of direct rule by the people, not rule by parliament. The only point where they're saying that parliament and election have a role is elections of magistrates and the settlement of questions of peace and war – emergency questions like that might have to be settled by an elected assembly. Taxes and laws were to be settled by the people as a whole. There are some points where this is less radical than ancient Greek democracy. Ancient Greek democracy restricted election to the election of military officers, and there's no demand here for the election of military officers.

If we move to Russian social-democracy, we see already a watering-down of the radical ideas in the Erfurt program, although Lenin presented himself as a very orthodox follower of the Erfurt program. The program that the Russian social-democrats adopted is essentially a demand for the type of constitutional structure that became general in Europe after the second world war, of republics with an elected parliament being sovereign. Having a single legislative chamber is a slightly more radical demand, not all places have a single legislative chamber, but it is basically a model of electoral democracy. Now, that is not the original model of the Erfurt program. In terms Marx understood democracy and in which Aristotle understood democracy it is very questionable whether you could say what the Russian social-democrats under Lenin were demanding in 1905 was a democratic system.

The ideas that Lenin had were sharply influenced by the Russian revolution and the first world war, and the ideas that most of the left that descends from the communist left have of democracy are very heavily influenced by Lenin's modification of the Russian social-democratic program in 1917. This is the key section that was changed. Much of it is similar: the abolition of the standing army, universally armed people's militias. What is introduced that's new are three things. First, that parliamentary representation will be gradually replaced by soviet institutions. Secondly, the representatives must be subject to recall, and thirdly, that representatives will be paid no more than an average worker's wage. Those three objectives which were written into the Russian social-democrat program in 1917 are the orthodoxy that the communist movement and the extreme left have followed ever since. Now, I'm going to argue that they're actually very inadequate principles and dialectically contain their own negation.

Let's look at the principle of recall. This was derived by Lenin by looking at the experience of the Paris commune, and it was incorporated in the Soviet constitution and remained a part of the Soviet constitution till the overthrow of the Soviet Union in 1991, but also exist in surprising places like the state of Arizona in the United States that has this built into its constitution. And in the election that has just taken place in the United Kingdom all the major political parties, right and left said they were in favour of the right of recall of parliamentary representatives, and that is almost certainly going to be written into British law.

Now, it is of some use, but it is mainly of use in dealing with manifest incompetence or corruption. Individuals who are manifestly incompetent or corrupt can be replaced. The reason why it is of limited use is that in order to effect the right of recall you actually need to get an awful lot of signatures. You need to mobilise maybe 10 % of the electorate to sign a petition asking for a re-election. That may be worthwhile, it may be of some advantage, but my contention is that wherever this exists it doesn't radically change the class character of the political system. It's mainly a control on corruption.

If we look at soviets or people's councils, these are bodies which certainly at the base level, at the local level contain mass participation in a way that you don't get in electoral democracy of the sort that exists in

136

a country like Sweden or Britain. It is certainly arguable that the level of political participation by the general public in a country like the Soviet Union in terms of the number of people who participated in political bodies was higher that in the West, even up until the final collapse of the Soviet Union. But we have to ask: when do soviets arise? Historically they've been thrown up under very specific circumstances when military autocracies are overthrown, are defeated in war. The key examples are the overthrow of Napoleon III in 1871 by the Prussian army, and that military defeat discredited the imperial state and led the people's militias in Paris to take up arms to defend the city. Petrograd in 1917, or one could say St. Petersburg 1905, both brought about by Russian military defeats. The instability in Germany in 1919 and in Austria-Hungary, against brought about by military defeats. The last occasion that soviets, or something like soviets, where thrown up in Europe was in Lisbon in 1975 when the fascist regime in Portugal had lost a series of colonial wars and the army mutinied, and that created the circumstances to the soviets. And this is an absolutely crucial factor: they only become revolutionary institutions if there's an army mutiny. Army or navy has to mutiny. If the army or navy doesn't mutiny you don't get a revolution the soviets, or workers' councils, remain temporary institutions with little power. And the other thing is: even if they come into existence they only lead to a change in state power if they are actually led by determined insurrectionists. The Commune was successful due to the efforts of the Blanquists in the leadership of the Commune, due to the efforts of a group that had dedicated themselves for years to the idea of armed insurrection. And similarly the success in Russia 1917 – whereas in Germany in 1919 there was a failure, in Hungary 1919 there was a failure – it was because the Russian revolutionaries had dedicated themselves to the idea of insurrection and overthrow of the state. They were able to make use of the situation which came into being.

Now, I'm going to take an example here from physics. I don't know if you've ever tried this, but you can go home and try it. Get yourself a polystyrene cup and put cold water in it and put it in a microwave for about 60 seconds, maybe a bit longer. After this tip a spoonful of NÃ©scafe into it. What will happen is that the water will suddenly boil over when the coffee granules hit it because you super-heated the water above its boiling point and you put the coffee granules in, and it nucleates and starts to boil. Revolutionary situations are like this. External events, for example the privations of war and the suffering that comes from war, raises the emotional energy of the people. Then something apparently minor, a march for bread that's fired on by the cossacks, which is the nucleating event and suddenly the stored emotional energy bursts out in a turbulent event. So the whole thing contains at once a deterministic element, there has to be the build-up of emotional energy due to privation and hardship. But what happens after that is chaotic and indeterminate and turbulent. What happens after that is unpredictable.

The Leninist idea of a communist party being the workers' general staff can only be understood in terms of the mindset which was brought on by the first world war. There you're in the midst of a titanic conflict, nearly every country in the world is involved – all of Europe, South America, China, Japan, the United States, they're all war. And in that the economies are devoted to the task of destruction and overcoming one another, and they're led by general staffs. Now what that war taught was what has now become a military truism, that no battle plans survives first contact with the enemy. The Schlieffen plan to envelop Paris was all very well on paper, but in the chaos and turbulence of the real war soon proved to be failed. And a political party that goes into a revolutionary situation with a fixed program like the Schlieffen plan is bound to fail. It was only because the Bolsheviks were able to come up with concrete answers, economic answers to the problems people faced and understood what the imperial general staffs of Europe took four years to learn: to win in a war you have to encourage initiative and flexibility in a changing situation. They adapted to the changing situation, adapted very rapidly, and adapted more rapidly than any of the other political parties active in Russia and ended up the dominant party

I don't know whether people can see this, I've tried to draw a picture of the soviet structure, the structure of the Soviet constitution in the first years of Soviet power. These circles here represent about a thousand ordinary people, these people, each thousand people, were entitled to elect someone to the local soviet, local neighbourhood soviet. These local soviets then sent deputies to the all-Russian congress of soviets. Local people elected someone to the local soviet, the local soviet elected a delegate to the all-Russian congress of soviets. The all-Russian congress of soviets – thousands of members – then elects two hundred people to the central executive committee of the Soviet Union. The central executive committee then elects seventeen people to the council of people's commissars who effectively form the government. There's one, two, three, four levels of elections here before you get to the government. And what this system of indirection, of indirect election does is give an enormous advantage to a

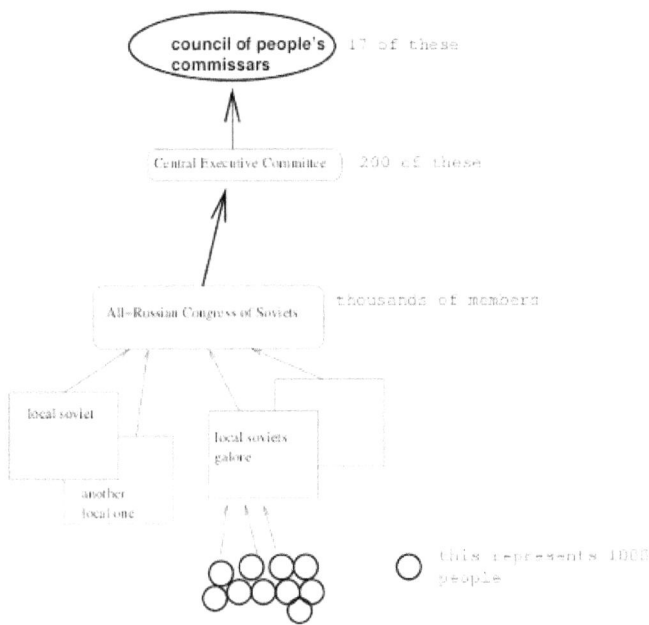

Figure 14.1.: Early Soviet form of government.

well-organised political party like the Bolshevik party. Suppose the Bolsheviks made up one in a fifty or one in a hundred of the Russian population. They're much more likely to put themselves forward as volunteers at this local level. They're much more likely to get elected at this level. Once they're in this level, the other Bolsheviks are much more likely to nominate them as the person to go forward. You get what in maths is considered an exponential process, a multiplicative process of probability. So the probability of an ordinary person who is not a member of any political party ever ending up in the council of political commissars runs down to practically zero, whereas the probability of that being dominated by one political party approaches one. Just the maths of it means that it is almost inevitable that one political party was to be completely dominant in the council of people's commissars. It's a matter of chance whether that was going to be the Bolshevik party or the Socialist Revolutionaries, it could have gone either way; as it happened, it was the Bolshevik party. If it had become the Socialist revolutionaries, we would have never heard of Lenin, he would have disappeared from history. As it is, it was the Bolsheviks that won. Now I've covered that.

Now if we look at the stages that Russia has gone through. Starts off as a Czarist monarchy. In the very early stages of the Russian revolution you have a soviet democracy of the type they are talking about in the RSDLP program. Extremely rapidly, certainly by 1918, it becomes a Bolshevik aristocracy in the sense of the original Greek use of the word aristocracy. The original Greek root *aristos* or best, for the word aristocracy meant rule by the best, rule by the wisest and the most conscious. That is essentially what the Bolshevik party took themselves to be, the wisest and the most conscious representatives of the working class. It became a Bolshevik aristocracy. It then degenerated into a revolutionary monarchy, where essentially power was held by one person, Stalin or Khrushchev. Eventually it became a bureaucratic oligarchy, and has now become a plutocratic oligarchy, an oligarchy of money. The question is not the surprise that soviet democracy collapsed, it was bound to collapse, it was bound to lead to aristocracy. We then have to ask: why did that aristocracy lead to a monarchy? Why is it so often the case that revolutions have ended up with monarchies? When I say monarchy, I'm meaning in the Greek sense again, with 'mono' meaning single ruler. It doesn't mean they have to call themselves king, they can call themselves First secretary of the communist party, they can call themselves President of the United States, it's still a monarchy.

There's several reasons for this. One of them is that from the point of view of the plebeian classes only a strong man with dictatorial power can hope to suppress the power of the rich and the existing propertied classes. That was the appeal of Caesar, that was the appeal of Napoleon, and that's partly the appeal of Stalin. Secondly, external enemies, the danger of war tends to militarise the state and raise the position of commander-in-chief of the armed forces to a critical position. We see this particularly in Cuba or Korea, where constant threat from the United States leads to a monarchical system of government – in fact, in both those cases to hereditary monarchy.

In addition, if you have a highly concentrated system like the council of people's commissars you have very powerful individuals who are very self-confident, very well educated, who argue with one another and there's a danger of instability. And all such political states with a cabinet system of government end up generating a prime minister or first secretary who dominates and breaks the deadlock. All of these things happened Russia. You needed to break the deadlock, there was a threat of war, and if you consider the popularity that Stalin had even after the fall of the Soviet Union, it's because people thought Stalin would sort out these oligarchs for us. The strongman would deal with it.

If that road fails, where do we go now? I think we have to a very long view of history. If you were looking at the world in 1820, after the fall of Napoleon, after the defeat of the French revolution, after the restoration of monarchy and autocracy across Europe you would think that the enterprise to set up bourgeois democracies or bourgeois states had failed, but it was a matter that the bourgeoisie had not yet found the form of constitution that would allow them to rule stably. In the future we will look back at China and Russia and say, OK, these were false starts. They were like Napoleon, they were like Cromwell, they were revolutionary movements which changed the society but they didn't find the stable form appropriate for the rule of that class. It's worth looking to the past when you do this. Our view of history shouldn't be limited to the 20th century, it shouldn't be limited to the bourgeois epoch. We should look at the whole of recorded history. When the American revolutionaries were trying to establish their state – and that is the stable form of bourgeois state that has survived – they looked at historical models. And there were two models available for them, there was Rome and Athens. They had to choose between these, and it is actually no accident that they chose Rome, that the United States constitution is largely based on the Roman ideas of constitution – it's a republic, it's not a democracy. It was constructed as a state by slave holders who saw what had been the most stable slave holder state in the past: Rome. And they modelled their state on that.

But there's another model, and that's the Athenian model of direct democracy, and the Greeks, over a period of hundreds of years, developed mechanisms to prevent aristocratic domination of the state. The first point was that there was no representative democracy. All political decisions had to be taken by the people as a whole by plebiscite. The plebiscite of course if a Roman term, but the power of the Roman plebs to exercise the plebiscite was very limited. In Greece all laws were passed by the assembly. This is exactly what the Erfurt program had been demanding in the 1880s. Secondly, the executive functions of the state were implemented by a randomly selected council, not by an elected body. The Greeks believed that only if you chose people at random – they actually used random number generators – could you guarantee that the council was unbiased and representative of the population as a whole – or representative of the citizens as a whole, because they're not the same thing. If you think how a polling organisation tries to determine public opinion, if a polling organisation wants to know what the public opinion is, do they go to the Swedish parliament and ask the opinion of the Swedish parliament? No they don't, they take a random sample of the population and ask that. If you had that kind of constitution now, the role of political parties would be radically different. They would no longer exist primarily as a body to mobilise support for a group of politicians. Their main job would be to mobilise public opinion towards specific ideological or social objectives, and the people who join the political parties would be joining just because they believe in it. They'd not be joining because there's covert calculation of their political careers; "if I join this party and work my way up, I can become prime minister". They'd be joining because they believed in it.

No movement which aims to change the world can do that unless it has a strategy, and strategies have to be tied to the political and economic structures that exist at the moment, and how to change these in ways that are favourable to the social class that the movement represents. And this means that you have to have a constitutional program and you have to have an economic program. This was understood by early social democracy. It has been forgotten essentially since the second world war by both the communist parties and the social-democratic parties.

First point here is that classical social democracy and to a large extent the communist parties as well were based around the nation state. The communist philosopher [Louis] Althusser goes so far as to say that political parties are part of the state's ideological apparatus. All political parties then existing were part of the legitimation mechanism of the state. But the nation state is no longer actually the focus of political power that it once was. In Europe the coexistence of the EU and the nation state means that nation states are no longer economically self-governing, and secondly, the prospect that was once held that if a social-democratic party of a communist party took power in one country it could install a socialist economy in that country. It's unrealistic, given the scale of modern production.

Back in the 1960s, Russia and Britain thought they could compete with the United States on almost any area of industry. In aircraft industry, what have you? Later it was realised that it was impossible, and in Europe for instance now only an all-European aircraft industry that can mobilise the technology to build modern airliners. In the EU at the moment the whole system is in crisis and it is very much up in the air as to whether it will survive. The problem is that the monetary union has deprived the nation states of economic control. Sweden and Britain are different because we raise our public debt in our own currencies, but any country that has joined the monetary union raises its public debt in Euros. If the public debt is raised in krona or in pounds, what it is being raised in is pieces of paper that the state itself prints and in the end the state can always print more of those to solve the problem. The British state has done exactly that. The Irish state is not allowed to print Euros. The United States raises its debt in dollars, and if it runs into problems financing its debt, it just prints more dollars. Greece, Portugal, Ireland – they can't do that. And when you have systematic inequalities between net exporters like Germany and importers and Greece and Portugal, certain states are bound to run a public sector deficit. If the run a public sector deficit, in the past they dealt with that by raising it in their own currency. Now they can't do that. In consequence the social and welfare provisions of the whole of Europe are now at ransom to the interests of the rentier classes in the creditor states.

I'm going to quote here from Abraham Lincoln:

> Any people anywhere being inclined and having the power have the right to rise up and shake off the existing government and form a new one that suits them better. This is a most valuable, a most sacred right, a right which we hope and believe it is to liberate the world.

What that basic democratic principle says is that people have a right to rebel, they have a right to overthrow the existing system of government, and the only way out of this, other than a degeneration back into national competition and to the kind of bloodshed that stained the 20th century, is to radically democratise the whole of the European Union and allow a democratic people's assembly to raise taxes which can redistribute income from one part of the Union to another. Unless that happens, the kind of crisis that's affecting Portugal, Spain, Greece at the moment will become general. If one was to apply the principles of the Erfurt program which, remember, was written in the time of Bismarck, in the time of autocracy in Germany, if one was to apply it to Europe now, you'd be saying that we need a sovereign people's assembly chosen at random from the citizens of Europe. We need taxes that can be raised by that assembly, that can be voted on by all the people of Europe, that the people of Europe can propose new laws and new legislation of any type which can then be voted on by the people as a whole. The only way you can do this would probably be to have a constituent assembly. This kind of thing could never be settled by negotiations between nation states.

What kind of economic measures would you need? You'd need democratic control over the European central bank. Instead of it being run essentially by bankers, it would have to be run by ordinary citizens, have a supervisory board run by ordinary citizens and perhaps with economists appointed by the parliament. If we are to abolish the tyranny of debt, abolish the power of the rentier class and finance capital over Europe you'd have to announce a general debt jubilee, you have to outlaw the payment of interest. At the moment, essentially, the European and American monetary authorities are being forced to do things like this: they're being forced to devalue the debt, they're devaluing it by quantitative easing. They're reducing the rate of interest close to zero in order to keep the economy going. But within that you see the keys to the real solution which is to get rid of debt altogether, to get rid of interest altogether. The European central bank should be placed under a legal obligation to stabilise the Euro in terms of labour, you should print on Euro notes how many minutes this actually represents. Currently a Euro represents about two minutes of labour, average European labour. Two minutes' labour creates a value of one Euro. We should be moving towards the sort of economic system that Marx advocated in his Critique of the Gotha program, where instead of money we use non-transferable labour credits.

In general the communist and social-democratic movements in the 20th century thought property was the essence of socialism, gaining control of the means of production was seen as the essence of socialism. I'm saying that's a misreading. The essence of socialism is abolishing the relation of wage labour. It is the abolition of wage slavery that is the key goal. And again I'm going to say that the historical precedent here was the most successful revolutionary if the 19th century, Abraham Lincoln, in the abolition of slavery. A constitutional amendment in the Unites States abolished slavery. The entire system of social relations on which the slave society had been based became unsustainable when the legal relation of chattel slavery was abolished. If the legal relation of wage slavery is abolished, the entire structure of capitalist civilization and exploitation falls.

Again, a quote from Lincoln:

> Labour is prior to and independent of capital. Capital is only the fruit of labour and could never have existed if labour had not first existed. Labour is superior to capital and deserves much higher consideration.

What would that actually mean? It would mean that the law must recognise that labour is the sole source of value added. That is scientifically the case: capital doesn't add any value, labour is the sole source of value added. Therefore the employees have both a moral and should have a legal right to all the value they add, and these rights should be enforceable by the courts. One of the key lessons of ancient Greek democracy is that when the people take hold of the courts of law, then they rule. So long as the courts of law are run by representatives of the upper classes, then the upper and propertied classes rule. So you'd need labour courts to be run by juries drawn from workers and judges elected by workers. Employees should therefore have the right to elect the majority of the board of any firm.

Now, these things don't actually take anyone's property away. They don't violate the protection of private property that's written into the European constitution. They just assert a higher right. They assert the right of labour not to be exploited, they assert one human right is higher than another. They don't take anyone's property away, shareholders would still have their shares, they'd just receive no income from them.

About the cancellation of debts. The basic cause of the current crisis was the extension of debt excessively as a relation to national income. And this inevitably occurs if you have a class who derived a majority of their income from capital. That class cannot consume all the income it receives. If it doesn't consume it, it saves it in the banks. If it deposits the money with the banks, somebody has to borrow it. The cause of the debt is the saving, the cause of the debt is the accumulation of credit. These are two sides of the balance sheet, one is inextricably associated with the other. The European banks had become insolvent by 2008 and it's quite cleat that many of them still are insolvent. Should the banks have been bailed out, or should they be allowed to fail? From the standpoint of the working class it is undoubtedly the case that the banks should be allowed to fail. The overwhelming majority of ordinary depositors with the banks were already protected by bank deposit insurance schemes which ran up generally to the order of 30 000 Euros per person. Very, very few people keep credit balances in the bank worth more than 30 000 Euros. On the other hand, there are huge credit balances in the banks held by the millionaire class, and the bailout of the banks was actually a bailout of the deposits held by the millionaire class which would not have been protected by the state deposit insurance schemes, had the banks failed. It was of no benefit to the majority of people, the majority of people's savings were safe. It was the millionaires and billionaires who would've lost, if the banks failed.

We should be calling for the cancellation of all debts, both public and private, other than three classes of debt that should be preserved. Firms should not be able to renege on back wages to workers; people should have up to one year's average income guaranteed in the deposit guarantee schemes; and companies and rich individuals should not be able to get out of the back taxes they owe. All of the debt should be cancelled, that includes credit card debt, mortgage debt, the state debt.

What would the effect of that be? The heavily over-levered firms, heavily debt-burdened firms would be able to resume economic activity. State finances would become solvent again. Consumers would be able to resume spending since they wouldn't be so heavily indebted. The banking system paradoxically would become much more liquid, since its ratio of liabilities to reserves in the form of deposits with the central bank would become much better, and the power of the rentier class would be broken.

So, in summary. I'm saying that the struggle for direct democracy is the lost memory of social-democracy. People forget what it stood for originally. The old forms that people have been obsessed with, the parliamentary republic or the soviet republic, are not appropriate to the 21st century. You could have direct democracy now easily with the mobile phone, everyone can vote easily on things, you don't have to gather everyone in the town square of Athens – you can have a virtual town square. We must win the battle for democracy in the original sense, if we are to make progress.

Questions and answers

Is Athens the only possible reference in terms of democracy, hasn't the human species lived hundreds of thousands of years in conditions of primitive democracy, in hunter-gatherer societies? Or what about the North American Iroquois? Is Athens such a good example, women couldn't vote, they had slaves etc.? And secondly, is it really possible to democratise the European Union? Shouldn't we rather smash it and build some kind of socialist EU?

OK, I'll try and answer that. You're correct to say that tribal society is in a sense democratic. What was unique about Greek democracy was that it was a democracy within a class society, within a society where there were contrasting class interests between the peasantry and the slave-owning class, and Unlike Rome, it was the peasantry that dominated through democracy. It was the peasantry and the artisans that dominated. Now you're quite right that there were four categories of people who didn't have the legal rights: children, women, foreigners and slaves. Now, no-one is proposing that we restrict political rights now. The point is that you take what was positive about that, which was the idea that – as CLR James put it – any cook can govern. Anybody is suitable to be chosen to be on the governing body, you don't need special qualifications to rule. Choose people at random and let them decide. So that is the positive lesson. Obviously I'm not proposing that we introduce slavery and other Athenian laws like that.

On the issue of the European Union. Think back to how the social-democrats in Russia and Germany were operating. At the time of the Erfurt program the German federation had just been established, but it had been established under very undemocratic terms. They could have had the option of saying, oh, we'll smash the German federation and go back to Bayern and establish socialism in Bayern and Wurttemberg. They didn't say that. They recognised that the ruling class had established a union and they would contend power in that union. If you look at Russia, they didn't say, let's smash it up into lots of small states, they said, OK, we'll give them the right to self-determination, because when they actually tried to have self-determination against socialist government it turned out to be not a good idea. So effectively they stood for the territorial union. I'm not saying that you keep the institutional structure of the European Union, but I am saying that it would be a disaster for the working classes of Europe if Europe is not united, if it's not a Union. And you change the constitutional structure, but to break it back up into nation states would be a disaster, and one must oppose any tendency to demonise the European Union that at the same time lets the nation state off the hook, because the nation state is worse.

A question about direct democracy. What about Switzerland, don't they have direct democracy, and yet isn't it a pretty normal conservative bourgeois state?

Democracy doesn't guarantee that the working class will rule. What it does is that it provides the most favourable conditions for the working class movement, it provides the least obstacle to the working class exercising power. You cannot offset the actual class structure of the society. If the class structure of a society is not favourable to the workers' movement, then it will not succeed even if it's got democracy. You could take examples from the United States where there are states which have very democratic constitutions as well, and because the overall class structure is not favourable and the ideological structure is not favourable. It doesn't mean that the working class rules, but it is preferable to have a system which, were the working class to be conscious, it can exercise its power that way.

Question: I don't have this is fresh memory, and it's along time [since] I read it, so I might mix up things. But you claim that this is in Marxist tradition, right, this whole presentation..?

I'm certainly claiming that the economic presentation is Marxist, and I'm claiming that the political presentation is the same as the proletarian left of the German social-democratic party pushed.

OK. Well, this whole idea with labour time receipts, didn't Marx in 'The Misery of Philosophy' criticise Proudhon for these ideas and again Engels in 'Anti-Duhring' against Eugen Duhring, this thing that it's just an equivalent, there's still an exchange, but the thing that we want to do is to socialize production and we want to establish use values that can't be bought and sold? Of course it's a transition . . .

You have to distinguish what Marx criticised and what he saw as positive. He criticised Proudhon, but he supported Owen. Owen also advocated labour tokens. The difference was that Owen advocated it under a system of the associated producers running society, rather than independent small producers. Now, the idea of establishing labour token economy here only becomes non-capitalist if wage labour is also abolished and in the long term if the tokens are made non-transferable. Talking about Owen's system, Marx said that Owen's labour tokens were no more money than a theatre ticket is money. The point is they don't circulate. Ultimately labour tokens would be issued by society to each individual in proportion to the number of hours they work. You receive back, Marx says, from the common stores goods which require the same amount of labour, and he says yes, this does still rest on the principle of equality that bourgeois society is based on. But there would be a long historical period during which that will exist before you move to a state where some other principle can occur. Now, we can see that in the case of information goods - like music from the web or free software - you can move to the free distribution now. But it is an illusion to think you could move to unlimited free distribution of goods which require environmentally limited resources. You can't do that, you have to have some proportionality between the effort someone puts in and what they get back.

What happens if someone works faster or better than someone else, are they going to get the same payment?

Marx says that if someone works faster or better, they get a higher income, they're actually doing more labour and therefore they would have more income, and therefore any principle of equality like that still rests on the inequality between human individuals; that some individuals, as Marx says, are stronger and swifter than others, and therefore they would have more income than others. But he says he'd move to a principle of "to each according to his need". Now, people often misinterpreted that "need" to mean free distribution. It doesn't mean that. It essentially means that if someone has a larger family, if someone is ill or disabled, [if] there's some objectively determinable need, they get compensation for that. But that is something which the labour movement has already won, in principle at least, in Europe – not in the United States, but in Europe most welfare states recognise the principle of need and distribution of need in a number of fields, in medicine and education etc. So the principle of need is not the critical thing, social-democracy has won that in many places, but what is hasn't won is the abolition of exploitation.

Isn't there a danger about electronic money going around?

That's why I say that Marx's idea of labour credits is that they're non-transferable. There's an account that you get through your labour [with] which you can withdraw goods from the common stores, or proportional to it. But you cannot use it to exploit other people, you cannot use it as capital. It's marked with your name on it, in that sense. It's just a matter of software, whether the software allows transfers.

[Question about David Schweickart, market socialism and its criticism.]

He's [the guy in the audience] asking whether I'm familiar with Schwe-

149

ickart's work on market socialism. I am. The first stages of what I'm proposing would not cause any objection by Schweickart, I don't think. I see in the longer term market socialism as being an unstable social form. You may initially establish worker-owned firms, but unless the European trade union movement push that to a rapid process of merger and the formation of European industrial syndicates, like a single European syndicate making yoghurt in which Farmelat, Danone and all the other yoghurt enterprises go into, a single European syndicate of railway workers dealing with all the railways, a single syndicate of airline workers running all the airlines, and abolish competition between sections, then there is a danger that independent cooperatives can regenerate much of the dynamics of a capitalist economy. So, unless the stage of cooperatives is a transitional phase to what Marx called the free association of the producers, the voluntary merger into great syndicates, then I don't think that it would sustain itself for more than about 50 or 60 years. It would generate the kind of tendencies which eventually occurred in Yugoslavia.

[Questions about general strike and strike committees, a lot of it inaudible; scepticism about "mobile phone democracy" replacing soviets etc.; in the end there's a question about exploitation rates that Cockshott and Cottrell calculated for Britain 20 years ago, are there more recent calculations?]

There was a lot of questions there ... David Zachariah, who's here [in the audience], I think has done calculations for Sweden for the exploitation rate, so you could speak to him, he has done calculation of labour values here. So, I'm passing the buck here. But there's obviously occasions when worker's councils have formed during general strikes, in big strikes. These a distinct from the soviets, though, because they're not organs of state power. They only become organs of state power when they're armed and command military forces, and that those military forces can enforce the will of the soviets and shoot anyone who doesn't go along with it. OK? The soviets in Russia could line the whites up against the wall. None of these other ones could do that, they weren't organs of state power. I think it is dangerous to extrapolate from a temporary organisation which doesn't have state power to a constitution of state power as the power to shoot people. And you can see the difference between a strike committee and the soviets when you look at Kronstadt.

When you talk about direct democracy and the planned economy and so on, this is very much up here [i.e. on an abstract level], what kind of mass movement, what kind of party, what kind of dynamic do you want to bring this forth, you have to have some sort of...

It is very difficult to say how you can produce change at a... society of a whole continent, the scale of a whole continent. But my feeling is that unless you have a vision of where you want to go, you'll never get there at all. As to stages, I would think that it is essential to form a single European socialist or left party that stands in the European elections as a single party, rather than as national parties affiliated to one another, and that you have to win the ideological battle for the principle of democracy. You have to make people think that yes, we could change things, we could rule ourselves, we don't need politicians to do it. I think that is a very big obstacle, because the Unites States has redefined democracy to be democracy in the American way, and it means a particular kind of government form, and that's not what it originally means. That a big ideological obstacle to overcome. So I think you actually need a European socialist party that has a program of radical democracy as its prime goal, and an attempt to win people other than just the working classes to that, because radical democracy has a broader constituency of potential support than just the working class. But beyond a very general statement like that I wouldn't like to say.

I think there was another question you didn't answer, from the former guy, what about this mobile phone democracy, that it is somewhat atomistic, you don't get much interaction and talking between people, collective interaction.

Some of these are real problems of scale. There are decisions which have to be made which are not local decisions. It's easy to say, OK, we will get the people within a village or a small town together to debate something. When you say you're going to get the people of even a country the size of Sweden together to debate a major national issue, you can't get them to do it locally. If you attempt to build it on a local basis and then though a series of indirect levels what you're actually doing is building a hierarchical structure of concentration of power when you want to devolve power to the mass of the people. I see no reason why you can't have debates, public debate between random audiences, randomly selected audiences, where the issues are debated on TV channels and people can vote afterwards. If you look at actual elections, the only interesting part of an election, is the comments of the studio audiences in the debates. If you have these debates without politicians at the front, but just people sitting in a circle with no politicians at the front, and debating the issue, I think that's the only way that you can overcome the problem of scale of modern society. We're not living in tribes, we're not living in individual city states, we need to do things differently, but we must learn the lessons of what has failed.

Question about the importance of psychological transformation of people, wouldn't old structures reconstitute themselves, if there's no psychological transformation as well, even if you've changed the external conditions?

I think the social values which would come to dominate in a different type of society would be different, but it's difficult to speculate exactly in what way before you have experience of it. But I think there's a risk that has been taken in the past by people like [Che] Guevara who in emphasizing new socialist morality want to make psychological change overcome the barriers of institutions and go beyond what the institutions can do. The risk if you do that [is] that you become like the Christian church, teaching people to be virtuous in a world that forces them to be otherwise. Unless you create a society that favour virtue.

I don't mean any global priesthood, but it seems to me that we need to reorganise our psyche as well, and I don't know if this reorganisation of the external conditions is enough. Obviously there's a need for, let's called it a spiritual or psychological transformation. Would you agree?

Whenever there is a serious revolutionary movement – and we can take three [examples]. If we take the English revolution, associated with that was a very strong ideological movement which took a religious form at that time. If we look at the revolution in Iran, again there was a spiritual, ideological movement which takes religious form again in that time. If you look at the Cultural Revolution in China, there was a very serious attempt then again to change psychology. So any major social revolution certainly generates attempts to change psychology. Now, how successful they are in the long run, I don't know, but it's an inseparable part of the process, I agree.

When you have a huge planned economy, one of the major problems can be the gathering of information to make wise decisions. Do you have any advice how to achieve that?

At one level, it's a technical question. The technical means of solving it is obviously there with modern communications and internet technology. The actual details of all inputs to every production process that goes on in the industrial world are recorded in the local computers of the companies that are ordering the parts. But commercial secrecy means that what's gathered locally is not publicly available, so a way to deal with it is you'd have to break down the commercial secrecy which exists and make this information openly available. And this is one of the great aims of [Victor] Glushkov, who was the Soviet computer pioneer who in the 1960s tried to persuade the Soviet Union to build what we now understand to be the internet. And he advocated things which now seem obvious, that in libraries and in public places there should be computer terminals where people could go to and look at any information. He was saying that all the information of the economy should be recorded on what is essentially an openly available internet. And I think basically that Glushkov was right, that is the way to go.

If I understand correctly you said we should not abolish private property but rather we should put our energies in abolishing wage labour. What are we to do with private property?

Well you have to ask yourself what does the private property amount to in the absence of the right to exploit labour. Let's suppose you're a rich resident of Savannah [in George, USA] in 1860 and you own shares in slaves on the slave plantations, OK? You can trade in those shares. And this did happen. As soon as slavery is abolished, your shares become worthless because they're the paper representation of a social relation which no longer exists.

But what about entire islands that are owned by families ...

There are actually three exploitation mechanisms that current society rests on. One of them is the direct exploitation of wage labour. The second is the exploitation of people through debt, and the third is rent, being able to charge rent for land. Ideally, one might want to nationalise all land. There are certain political risks for doing that if you are wanting to win support on a large scale in an area where a significant number of people are peasant farmers. You don't want to drive the peasant farming population into the hands of reaction by threatening to take their land away from them. So a more effective policy is to introduce what the land reform movement in the United States used to call full site value taxation, whereby you introduce a tax on land which is proportional to the rent that would be obtained on that land, proportional to a hundred percent, so effectively you confiscate rent incomes.

You mean to say that the more land you own, the more tax ...

Scotland still has a feudal pattern of land ownership, there's a small number of aristocratic families, dukes and earls, who own most of the country. They obtain their income by charging rent from tenant farmers. And if the tenant farmer gets an EU grant to improve their land, the duke will up his rent saying, oh, you're getting money from the EU now, well

153

you're getting 2 000 pounds this year from the EU, your rent's going to go up by 2 000 pounds. Now, that right to levy rent on land should be effectively neutralised by saying, we'll tax it to the hundred percent. So that you don't actually take the land off them, he can nominally retain it but he doesn't retain any income from it or power over it. That is just a political concession, you don't want to give the right the propaganda gain of saying, they're going to take your house away from you, these socialists, they're going to take your land away from you, they're going to take your car away from you. If you say you're going to abolish private property, that's what the right will say. You want to abolish exploitation. Put it that way, and who can say that it's a good thing to keep exploitation? If you say, I'm going to abolish private property, lots of people raise that as a bogey-man and it's a political risk to do it that way. You have to concentrate on what you want to achieve, not the form you want to achieve it on. You do it in a way which makes it the most difficult for the right to make propaganda against you. You want to achieve that effect, but you don't put it those terms.

You say the the European union is the alternative for Europe. I think the Union is highly undemocratic and expensive, and it's going further and further away from socialist thought, and it also has nationalist parties... so I wonder how can you say that the Union is the alternative for Europe?

The current constitution of the EU is radically undemocratic in that the parliament has very limited powers, it cannot initiate general legislation, it doesn't elect the commission from among its members, it cannot raise general taxes etc. And it's even aside from the limited nature of parliamentary democracy. But what I'm saying is that you have to focus on the geographical area that constitutes a unified economy and unite the working classes within that area for common rights and common goals which can only be achieved now at that scale. No individual nation state now can hope to stand up to global capital, you can only do that at a continental level. And to promote a strategy of saying, we will go it alone in Greece as the KKE says, I can understand their incentives to do that, but it would never work in the long run, that any independent country that claims to have a socialist government and tried to do that would be under such pressure from international capital that it would be unable to really have a socialist economy internally, that only by having a really large scale can you do it. China has a chance to do it, it's so vast. If there's a political movement in the left in China, then it could do it, no one could really stop China. But Sweden, Britain, Ireland, no, it's not viable on that scale.

Talk given in November 2010

Part IV.

Economics of Socialism

15. Venezuela and Socialist Economic Policy

In 1989 Paul Cockshott and Allin Cottrell wrote a book on socialism which was published three years later in English as *Towards a New Socialism*. This book was addressed at an audience in the USSR and East European countries because it dealt with the problems that socialism was then facing in these countries. It had been the intention to have it translated and published in Russian. The book presented a model of how to run a socialist economy based on clear economic and moral principles and re-asserted the basic values of socialism against the pro-capitalist measures being introduced under Gorbachov. Events moved too fast to allow it to come out in Russian before the USSR fell, but since then what it says has been recognised to be sufficiently important that publishers in Sweden, Germany, Czechoslovakia and Venezuela have published translations under a variety of national titles.

In June 2007 at a workshop in Venezuela to launch the Spanish translation entitled *Hacia el socialismo del siglo XXI*, Paul was asked how the principles in the book could be applied to the process of establishing socialism in that country. This report tries to answer that question.

Clearly an economic model designed to answer the problems of a mature socialist industrial economy like the USSR can not be applied immediately to Venezuela. What it can do, is give people some idea where the process of socialist transformation may end up. It can warn them about avoiding some economic mistakes that were made in the USSR and Eastern Europe: for those who do not learn from history are doomed to repeat it.

When a society undergoes a transition to socialism there are decisions that have to be made, forks in the road that have to be chosen. If the wrong set of turnings are chosen, you can end up going in a circle. Starting off going towards socialism, you can end up on a path that eventually leads back to capitalism. We all know that this happened in several 20th century attempts to go towards socialism. The worst thing is that the implications of decisions are not immediately obvious at the time they are made. This means that, almost up until the last moment, people can think that they are still on the right course.

This is not the place to repeat what was said in the book *Towards a New Socialism*, but let us summarise the three key features of the mature socialism that it describes:

1. The economy is based on the deliberate and conscious application of the labour theory of value as developed by Adam Smith and Karl Marx. It is a model in which consumer goods are priced in terms of the hours and minutes of labour it took to make them, and in which each worker is paid labour credits for each hour worked. The consistent application of this principle eliminates economic exploitation.

2. Industry is publicly owned, run according to a plan and not for profit. Stage retail enterprises for example, work on a break even rather than profit making basis.

3. Decisions are taken democratically, both at a local and a national basis. This applies in particular to decisions about the level of taxation and state expenditure. Such democratic decision making is vital to prevent the replacement of private exploitation with exploitation by the state.

When we compare this with Venezuela today, we see that all three key features still need to be built. On some features the progress towards socialism has not yet started, on others it has started but the country has only taken a few steps along the path.

Let us look at these points one at a time.

Still a money economy

The Venezuelan economy is still based on money. In his great book *Capital*, Karl Marx showed how money was at the root of the evils of capitalism. The essence of capitalism is to start out with a sum of money at the beginning of the year and end up with a larger sum at the end. Marx denoted this by $M \to M'$, where M might be $1,000,000 for example and M' might be $2,000,000.

Because capitalists have more money than working people, they can use this money to hire workers to work for wages. These wages are much much less than the value which workers create during the working week. Since the capitalist can sell the product for more value than they paid out

158

in wages, the capitalists become richer and richer whilst workers stay as poor as ever.

This process is still going on in Venezuela. It is the root cause of the difference between rich and poor, between the oligarchy and the masses.

On top of this there is a secondary form of exploitation that allows capitalists to increase their money: lending money at interest. This process allows the money-lender to get richer year by year by doing absolutely nothing. This again, still occurs in Venezuela.

Still an unplanned economy

In Venezuela, unlike for example the USSR, the supply of most goods and services is regulated by the market. Whilst this is not entirely a bad thing, since it does, to a limited extent allow supply to be adjusted to peoples wants, the drawback is that the provision of goods and services is systematically biased towards the wishes and desires of the rich. Venezuela currently lacks the mechanisms by which the structure of the economy as a whole can regulated by a conscious social plan both to achieve development and to equitably meet the needs of all citizens.

Towards a New Socialism, assumed public ownership of the economy. Most of the economy in Venezuela, is still privately owned, although this may be changing now.

Democratic revolution not yet complete

Whilst Venezuela has made great strides towards local participative democracy, it has yet to introduce participative democracy on key questions of national economic control. Issues relating to the raising of state revenue and the allocation of this revenue between major budget headings: defence, social care, infrastructure investment etc., are taken centrally rather than allowing the people as a whole to vote on them. If this is not addressed, it will in the long run, as the state comes to dominate more and more of the economy, be a serious danger. You could end up with a situation as occurred in the USSR where the state, and the bureaucracy of the state could be seen as being rather like a new exploiting class.

When we think of what happened in the USSR just before it collapsed, the desire of state bureaucrats to go from being like an exploiting class, to become outright capitalists like today's Russian oligarchs, must be counted as a key factor in the collapse.

How to effect the transformation

The great economist Keynes remarked that practical political men, whether they be cautious or bold, fond themselves unconsciously repeating the ideas of long dead economists. Politicians who advance neo-liberalism, whether they know it or not, are repeating the ideas of the reactionary Austrian economists Ludwig von Mises and von Hayek. The policies that we suggest below counter those ideas by drawing on the insights of others particularly the Scottish philosopher Adam Smith, the German economist Karl Marx, the Polish socialist economist Oscar Lange and the Englishman Maynard Keynes.

As economists and social scientists we can only sketch out possible courses of action and some of their likely consequences of these actions. Decisions on what course to take are essentially political and political community, the leaders and the citizens of the country concerned are responsible for their own destiny. What intellectuals can to is to suggest possibilities which influence the terms of debate.

In the last section we looked at key objectives in the socialist transformation of an economy and the extent to which they have been met in Venezuelan experience. We will now shift the focus to specific policy measures, which we will present one by one and whilst explaining how each of these helps to achieve the broader objectives we have described.

Currency stabilisation

There is, by world standards, a considerable degree of inflation in the Venezuelan economy. This is masked by administrative measures to stabilise prices of certain essentials of life but it is nonetheless real. Of itself, inflation is not necessarily against the interests of the poor and working classes, provided that wages keep up with prices. The people who are hit hardest by inflation are the rentier class whose holdings of money and interest bearing assets depreciate. Since these people are opponents of socialism anyway, a socialist government need not worry about any financial loss they suffer were it not for the other social effects of inflation.

Uncertainty about future prices can lead to a social psychology of instability leading to a loss of confidence in the government. We explain in an annexe how this sort of inflation played a role in the collapse of the USSR. For this reason alone, it will eventually be necessary for the Venezuelan government to take measures to regulate inflation.

However, if ones objectives are to establish a socialist economy based on the equivalent payment of labour, then currency reform can be a step towards this goal. What we suggest is that, following the introduction of the new strong Bolivar, the state place a legal obligation on the central bank to maintain a stable value of the currency in terms of labour.[1] A prototype for this could be the successful monetary policy of the British Labour Government after 1996. At that time the government placed monetary policy under a committee of expert economists ('The Monetary Policy Committee') rather than politicians and gave them a clear legal obligation to achieve a particular target rate of inflation. One might have expected this policy to be severely deflationary, but it has actually been very successful, because committee are legally obliged to avoid both deflation and inflation in their policy.

Where our proposal differs from British policy is in the goal it sets – we advocate fixing the value of the Bolivar in terms of labour not in terms of the cost of living index. The reasons for this goal are twofold:

1. As labour productivity rises, a Bolivar fixed in terms of hours of labour, will be able to buy more each year, cheapening the cost of living.

2. Once the value of the Bolivar has been stabilised in terms of labour, then the labour value of Bolivar notes should be printed on them in hours and minutes. This step would be an act of revolutionary pedagogy. It would reveal clearly to the oppressed just how the existing system cheats them. Suppose a worker puts in a working week of 45 hours and gets back Bolivars and sees that the hours printed on them amount to only 15 hours, then she will become aware that she is being cheated out of 30 hours each week. This will act to raise the socialist consciousness of the people, and create favourable public opinion for other socialist measures.

Instead of just having a committee of economists charged with regulating the value of the Bolivar, the principle of participative democracy implies that the 'Value Policy Committee' should be made up both of economists and delegates from the trades unions and consumers associations. The Value Policy Committee would have to commission surveys of how much work was being done in different industries, and how much monetary value added there was in these industries, in order to guide its stabilisation policy.

---

[1]This should be contrasted to the current policy of attempting to fix the value of the Bolivar in terms of dollars.

Reform of accounting and pressure for fair prices

All firms have currently to prepare money accounts, The government should make it a condition of their accounts being approved for auditing, that they also produce labour time accounts. and that they mark on all products that they sell their labour content.

Initially firms need not be legally obligated to sell their commodities at their true values. They could attempt to sell them for a price that is higher or lower than the true value. But since the consumer can now see when they are being overcharged, consumers will tend to avoid companies that sell goods at above their true value. This will put psychological and consumer pressure on companies that are overcharging. This too will be an act of socialist mass pedagogy to raise consciousness.

In the first few months, before all goods have their labour values printed on their price tags, firms will have to impute labour values to the goods they purchase using the printed exchange rate between Bolivars and labour hours. The will add to the labour value of their inputs, the number of hours of work that are performed by their employees to get a labour value for the final product.

We mentioned earlier the need to establish labour accounting in industry for pedagogic purposes. The government should also move towards having a dual system of national accounts, labour accounts alongside money accounts because, at the level of national economic policy, there are many issues on which labour accounts would be more informative than money accounts. Money accounts hide the fact that what government economic policy really does is re-allocate society's labour. Money is the veil behind which real labour allocation occurs.

Enshrine the rights of labour in law

Scientific evidence shows that in the capitalist world the money value of goods is overwhelmingly determined by their labour contents. Studies find that for most economies the correlation between labour values and prices are 95% or above. So Adam Smiths scientific hypothesis that labour was the source of value has now been statistically verified.

This scientific fact should be incorporated in law.

The law should recognise that labour is the sole source of value and that in consequence, workers, or their Unions will have a claim in law against their employers if they are paid less than the full value of their labour.

If we consider the previous measures and the revolutionary pedagogy that would follow from them, it should be relatively easy to pass a referendum on such a law.

Following such a law being passed, there would be a huge wave of worker activism as workers and their unions sought to end the cheating and deceit to which they and their ancestors had been subjected. It would also bring about a very large increase in real wages, cementing support for the socialist government.

The employing class, on the other hand would see sharp fall in their unearned incomes. Employers who were active factory managers would of course still be legally entitled to be paid for the hours that they put in managing the firm, just like any other employee.

The cumulative effect of the three measures outlined so far would be to substantially abolish capitalist exploitation in the workplace – at least in the short term. There will be long term difficulties if other measures are not taken, and we shall examine these later.

Eliminating other forms of exploitation

In addition to the exploitation of employees by employers, there are other forms of unearned incomes, the most economically important of which are interest and rent.

Usury

Interest, the getting of money from money itself, was regarded for thousands of years as being sinful. Philosophers like Aristotle condemned it. Papal encyclicals banned it. Islamic law still forbids it in Muslim countries. But in capitalist countries, such was the social power of the banks and other money lenders that this moral objections came to be forgotten.

In capitalist countries which were undergoing very rapid industrialisation, for instance, Japan in the 1950s or 1960s, lending money at interest did serve a necessary economic purpose, since it allowed peoples savings to be channelled, via the banks, to fund industrialisation. But once a country has industrialised, firms finance most of their investment from internal profits. Indeed they normally have more profit than they know how to invest. Instead of borrowing from the banks, industrial firms run a financial surplus, and they themselves lend to the banks. The banks now channel the financial surplus of firms into loans to the third world, or to Northern governments and consumers. Lending at interest looses the temporary progressive function that it had during industrialisation and reverts to being what morality and religion originally condemned: usury.

Socialism abolishes interest as a form of income. It has no class of rentiers – people who do no work but just live off the interest on their money. So it is clear that at some point, that a government seriously intent upon socialism has to pass a legislation banning the lending of money at interest. It could specify, for instance, that interest on debt could not be enforced in the civil courts. It could impose severe criminal penalties on those who used threats of harm to extort interest.

Before moving to a step such as this, a socialist government needs to put in place replacements for the economic functions still served by lending, and charging interest.

Investment

It will still be necessary to fund new investments. This could be done by interest free loans from the state bank. But if this is not done with care, the resulting expansion of the money stock will lead to the type of suppressed inflation which occurred in the USSR.

Investment on credit is based on the illusion that you can push the cost of investment into the future. Whilst this can be true for an individual borrower, for society as a whole, today's investment has to be made using today's labour. We can not get future generations to travel back in time in order to do work for us. Socialist economies should thus rely mainly on tax revenue to fund investment.

Regulating price levels

Capitalist central banks try to control inflation by adjusting the interest rate. If inflation is too high, they raise interest rates. The effect is to choke off investment, reduce demand, and so reduce inflationary pressures. If interest is banned, how is the price level to be regulated ? – or, in the light of what we said earlier – how would the Venezuelan Value Policy Committee ensure that the value of the Bolivar in terms of labour was held steady?

An alternative control mechanism would be to adjust the term on which loans are made. The state bank could set maximum durations for loans. For example, if the Value Policy Committee thought the value of the currency was in danger of falling it could shorten the period for which loans could be had. If loan periods were reduced from 10 year to 5 years, then monthly repayments rise, just as happens with interest rate rises today.

Another means of regulating prices is tax policy. Paper money, like the Bolivar, is inherently worthless – just printed paper. It has value imputed to it, from the fact that the government will accept its own currency for tax debts. The fact that people need money to pay their taxes, forces them to value it. If governments tax less than they spend, the money stock will rise leading to inflation. The second way to regulate prices is thus to fine tune tax levels.

Rent

Rent is another type of exploitation. Socialists regard it as immoral since the owner of land enriches himself, not by his own labour, but by the labour of others combined with the bounty of nature. Rent is however an inevitable phenomenon in a commodity producing society. If there is some product, be it crude oil, or corn, the efficiency whose production depends on the land being used, then rent incomes will arise.

Suppose the price of a ton of corn is $200, then any land on which the corn's cost of production is less than $200 will be worth cultivating. By the cost of production we mean the ultimate labour cost translated into money – including the cost of fertilizers. If land will yield corn at a cost of production of only $50 – say because of its great fertility – then its owner can rent it out to farmers for $150 and they can still break even selling corn at $200. The same applies to oil production. If on the marginal oil field – say the tar sands of Athabasca in Canada, oil can be produced for $50 a barrel, then a productive oilfield like the Venezuelan where costs are much lower, say $15, will yield its owner (the state in this case) a rent of $35 a barrel.

In a socialist economy all rent income should accrue to the state and be used for the good of the community in general. Socialist states have usually nationalised land, but have not always charged a rent for using the land. In the case of mineral extraction this made no difference, since this was done by state enterprises and rent would just have been a fictitious transfer between sections of the state. Failure to charge agricultural rents to collective farms will, however, accentuate differences in income between fertile and less fertile agricultural regions.

In the immediate situation in Venezuela, the nationalisation of land may not initially be politically opportune since it could drive the small farmers into alliance with large landowners. An alternative, which over the long term would produce a similar effect, would be to introduce a land tax on the rentable value of land. The threshold for the tax could be set high enough to ensure that small farmers paid nothing or only a token amount, but for larger more fertile estates it could be set at a level that would confiscate the greater part of rent revenue. The effect on the landowners would be similar to that which would be achieved by nationalisation – depriving them of their unearned income and making it available for communal uses – but it is ideologically harder for them to mount a campaign to justify tax evasion than it is to mount one to justify resistance to expropriation.

State finance and foreign currency

This brings us onto the general topic of state finance.

Socialist economies typically have a higher level of state expenditure than capitalist ones at a comparable level of economic development. It is essential that the state has an efficient revenue raising mechanism, with taxes that are easy to collect and difficult to avoid. Venezuela is unusual in having large oil exports, which helps somewhat, but the principle still remains.

Social democratic states like Sweden relied mainly on income taxes along with an efficient civil service. East European socialist states like the USSR relied upon turnover taxes on industry and on profits earned by state firms. Because of the importance of oil revenue to the Venezuelan state, it currently leans more towards the Soviet model.

Which of these models of tax revenue should be used is one of the major strategic issues that has to be faced by Venezuela as it moves towards a socialist economy.

In *Towards a New Socialism*, Cottrell and Cockshott argue that the Soviet model of taxation had several drawbacks, which, in the long run, contributed the final collapse of the Soviet socialist economy.

1. The use of indirect taxation, such as turnover or value added taxes [2] , and a-fortiori a reliance on profit income, puts the state in the position of being a collective capitalist vis a vis the workers.

---

[2]The German term for such taxes Mehrwertsteur translates incidentally as 'surplus value tax', encapsulating very well what its economic function is from the standpoint of Marxian political economy.

2. The use of indirect taxation, has also traditionally been opposed by socialists as these are regressive rather than progressive forms of taxation.[3]

3. It resulted in a distorted price structure that systematically undervalued labour to the detriment of economic efficiency.

4. Reliance on the profit of state industry is a hidden form of revenue, which is not easily amenable to democratic control.

In the case of Venezuela there is the additional complicating factor that profits from oil revenue are dependent on the very volatile world market price of oil. This can cause unexpected fluctuations in state revenue. The recent sharp rise in oil prices has been very beneficial to the government, but it must be remembered that prices can go down as well as up.

It is said Venezuelan government has plenty of money thanks to oil, but it is important to understand in what sense it has plenty of money. What it has is plenty of dollars. These are fine if the government wants to directly purchases manufactured commodities made in other countries. Dollars are also fine for giving aid to other countries. But dollars are no use for paying the wages of government employees or when the government wants to buy domestically produced goods, for these the government needs Bolivars not dollars.

The government can get Bolivars in several ways:

a. It can raise them from taxes.

b. It can issue bonds denoted in Bolivars and sell these on the money markets.

c. It could purchase Bolivars on the open market using it's dollar reserves.

d. It can get the state bank to extend it credit.

The fact that the black market rate for the dollar is well above the official rate, and that there is significant inflation indicates that the state has been relying excessively on the last of these methods of finance.

It must be realised that dollars can not be used to meet a shortfall of tax revenue in Bolivars so long as foreign exchange controls are retained. Dollar revenue can only be freely converted to revenue in Bolivars by the state

---

[3]A progressive tax is one which bears most heavily on people with higher incomes.

buying Bolivars on the open market. This in turn implies that Venezuelan citizens would have to be free to sell dollars in the open market.

It is understandable that the government maintains exchange controls to prevent the upper classes expatriating their Bolivar assets, and in the process using up the government's foreign exchange reserves, so there is obviously a dilemma here. This dilemma indicates that the government has not yet felt itself to be strong enough to face down the economic power of the oligarchy. We could suggest two possible policies under these circumstances:

1. Increases in higher rate income taxes and abolition of tax exemptions sufficient to fund government domestic expenditure from domestic tax revenues.

2. More radically, a sharp reduction in the amount of privately held Bolivars could be brought in along with the projected currency reform. If there was a limit to the amount that any one person could change from old Bolivars to new Bolivars – for instance this might be set at a certain number of months of average wages – then the money capital of the rich would no longer be sufficient for them to threaten the states foreign exchange reserves following the removal of exchange controls. It would also incidentally greatly reduce the social power of the capitalist class.

Each of these policies has obvious political risks involved, which have to weighed against the future benefits of a more stable system of public finance.

Foreseeable consequences

The policies described above would go a long way to transforming the economy into a new socialist one. However, since they undermine what are important functional components of capitalism there would be consequences if alternative mechanisms were not put into place.

★ Ending the production of surplus value by paying workers the full value they create would make employment unprofitable. There is a danger under these circumstances that capitalists would find it more profitable to leave their money in the bank and earn interest on it than use it to employ workers.

* It would thus be important that the payment of interest was abolished prior to introducing the right to the full value of labour.

* It would might well also be necessary to introduce the right for employees to be able to vote for their firm to be co-managed with a co-management committee having a clear majority of employees on it, in order to prevent owners asset stripping and closing the now unprofitable firm.

Written in June 2007

16. Economic Factors in the failure of Soviet Socialism

Paul Cockshott was asked by Gen. Jose Angel to elaborate on remarks made about the economic causes of Soviet Collapse. This is a very brief personal perspective on what is obviously a huge and very controversial subject.

The collapse of the Soviet and later the Russian economy under Gorbachov and then Yeltsin was an economic disaster that was otherwise unprecedented in time of peace. The world's second super-power was reduced to the status of a minor bankrupt economy with a huge decline in industrial production and in living standards. Nothing brings out the scale of the catastrophe than the demographic data which show a huge rise in the mortality rate brought about by poverty, hunger, homelessness and the alcoholism that these brought in their wake.

In determining what caused this one has to look at long term, medium term and short term factors which led to relative stagnation, crisis and then collapse. The long term factors were structural problems in the Soviet economy and required reforms to address them. The actual policies introduced by the Gorbachov and Yeltsin governments, far from dealing with these problems actually made the situation catastrophically worse.

Long Term

During the period from 1930 to 1970, and excluding the war years, the USSR experienced very rapid economic growth. There is considerable dispute about just how fast the economy grew, but it is generally agreed to have grown significantly faster than the USA between 1928 and 1975, with the growth rate slowing down to the US level after that.[1] This growth took it from a peasant country whose level of development had been comparable

---

[1]For more details see the attached appendix B which is reproduced from the website 21stCentury Socialism.

170

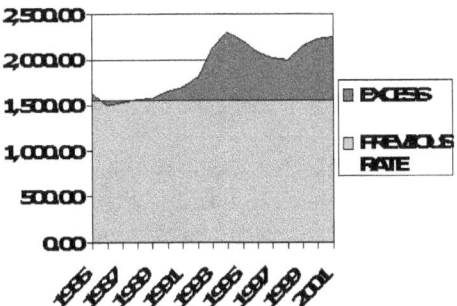

Figure 16.1.: Soviet Economic collapse let to huge increase in mortality
with 5.7 million excess Russian deaths 1991-2001. Vertical
axis 1,000 deaths per annum.

to India in 1922, to become the worlds second industrial and technological
and military power by the mid 1960s.

Observers have given a number of reasons for this relative slowdown in
growth in the latter period.

It is easier for an economy to grow rapidly during the initial phase of industrialisation when labour is being switched from agriculture to industry.
Afterwards growth has to rely upon improvements in labour productivity
in an already industrialised economy, which are typically less than the difference in productivity between agriculture and industry.

A relatively large portion of Soviet industrial output was devoted to defence, particularly in the latter stages of the Cold War, when they were in
competition with Regan's 'Star Wars' programmes. The skilled manpower
used up for defence restricted the number of scientists and engineers who
could be allocated to inventing new and more productive industrial equipment.

The USA and other capitalist countries imposed embargoes on the supply of advanced technological equipment to the USSR. This meant that
the USSR had to rely to an unusually high degree on domestic designs of
equipment. In the west there were no comparable barriers to the export
of technology so that the industrial development of the western capitalist
countries was synergistic.

Labour was probably not used as efficiently in Soviet industry as it was
in the USA or West Germany. In one sense, or course the USSR used

labour very effectively, it had no unemployment and the proportion of women in full time employment was higher than in any other country. But a developed industrial economy has to be able transfer labour to where it can be most efficiently used. Under capitalism this is achieved by the existence of a reserve of unemployment, which, whilst it is inefficient at a macro-economic level, does allow rapid expansion of new industries.

The Soviet enterprise tended to hoard workers, keeping people on its books just in case they were needed to meet future demands from the planning authorities. This was made possible both by the relatively low level of money wages, and because the state bank readily extended credit to cover such costs. The low level of money wages was in turn a consequence of the way the state raised its revenue from the profits of state enterprises rather than from income taxes.

Although Soviet industrial growth in the 1980s slowed down to US levels, this by itself was not a disaster, after all the USA had experienced this sort of growth rate (2.5% a year) for decades without crisis. Indeed whilst, working class incomes in the USA actually stagnated over the 1980s, in the USSR they continued to rise. The difference was in the position of the intelligentsia and the managerial strata in the two countries. In the USA income differentials became progressively greater, so that the rise in national income nearly all went to the top 10% of the population. In the USSR income differentials were relatively narrow, and whilst all groups continued to experience a rise in incomes, this was much smaller than had been the case in the 1950s and 1960s. This 2.5% growth was experienced by some of the Soviet intelligentsia as intolerable stagnation – perhaps because they compared themselves with managers and professionals in the USA or Germany. A perception thus took root among this class that the socialist system was failing when compared to the USA.

Again this would not have been critical to the future survival of the system were it not for the fact that these strata were disproportionately influential within the USSR. Although the ruling Communist Party was notionally a workers party, a disproportionately high proportion of its members were drawn from the most skilled technical and professional employees, manual workers were proportionately under represented.

The slowdown in Soviet growth was in large measure the inevitable result of economic maturity, a movement towards the rate of growth typical of mature industrial countries. A modest programme of measures to improve the efficiency of economic management would probably have produced some recovery in the growth rate, but it would have been unrealistic to expect the rapid growth of the 50s and 60s to return. What the USSR got however, was not a modest programme of reform, but a radical demolition job on its basic economic structures. This demolition job was motivated by neo-liberal ideology. Neo-liberal economists, both with the USSR and visiting from the USA promised that once the planning system was removed and once enterprises were left free to compete in the market, then economic efficiency would be radically improved.

Medium Term

The medium term causes of Soviet economic collapse lay in the policies that the Gorbachov government embarked on in its attempts to improve the economy. The combined effect of these policies was to bankrupt the state and debauch the currency.

One has to realise that the financial basis of the Soviet state lay mainly in the taxes that it levied on turnover by enterprises and on sales taxes.

In an effort to stamp out the heavy drinking which led to absenteeism from work, and to poor health, the Gorbachov government banned alcohol. This and the general tightening up of work discipline, led, in the first couple of years of his government to some improvement in economic growth. It had however, unforeseen side effects. Since sales of vodka could no longer take place in government shops, a black market of illegally distilled vodka sprang up, controlled by the criminal underworld. The criminal class who gained money and strength from this later turned out to be most dangerous enemy.

Whilst money from the illegal drinks trade went into the hands of criminals, the state lost a significant source of tax revenue, which, because it was not made up by other taxes, touched off an inflationary process.

Were the loss of the taxes on drinks the only problem for state finance, it could have been solved by raising the prices of some other commodities to compensate. But the situation was made worse when, influenced by the arguments of neo-liberal economists, Gorbachov allowed enterprises to keep a large part of the turnover tax revenue that they owed the state. The neo-liberals argued that if managers were allowed to keep this revenue, they would make more efficient use of it than the government.

What actually ensued was a catastrophic revenue crisis for the state, who were forced to rely on the issue of credit by the central bank to finance their current expenditure. The expansion of the money stock led to rapid inflation and the erosion of public confidence in the economy. Meanwhile, the additional unaudited funds in the hands of enterprise managers opened up huge opportunities for corruption. The Gorbachov government had recently legalised worker co-operatives, allowing them to trade independently. This legal form was then used by a new stratum of corrupt officials, gangsters and petty business men to launder corruptly obtained funds.

Immediate

The Soviet economy had gone through the stages of slowdown, mismanaged crisis and now went into a phase of catastrophic collapse, quite unprecedented in peacetime.

Following a failed coup by sections of the armed forces and security services, Yeltsin, instead of helping restore the constitutional government of President Gorbachov, seized power for himself. Acting on the instructions of US advisers he introduced a shock programme to convert the economy from socialism to capitalism in 100 days.

In the old USSR there was no capitalist class. In the west governments could privatise individual firms by selling them off on the stock market where the shares would be quickly snapped up by the upper classes, or in the case of Thatcher's privatisation, by sections of the middle class. But in the USSR things were very different. There was no class of individuals wealthy enough to buy up state companies by legal means. Also the scale of the privatisation was so vast, that even in a market economy, the savings of the population would have been insufficient to buy up the entire industry of the nation. Logic alone would predict that the only way that industry could pass into private hands was through corruption and gangsterism. This is exactly what happened, a handful of Mafia connected oligarchs ended up owning most of the economy.

Neo-liberal theory held that once enterprises were free from the state, the 'magic of the market' would ensure that they would interact productively and efficiently for the public good. But this vision of the economy greatly overstated the role of markets. Even in so called market economies, markets of the sort described in economics textbooks are the exception – restricted to specialist areas like the world oil and currency markets. The main industrial structure of an economy depends on a complex interlinked system of regular producer/consumer relationships in which the same suppliers make regular deliveries to the same customers week in week out.

In the USSR this interlinked system stretched across two continents, and

Table 16.1.: Output of Selected Branches of Industry in Russia in 2003 Compared to 1990 (1990 = 100). Source: Goskomstat, 2004, Table 14.3.

Total Industry	66
Electric power	77
Gas	97
Oil extraction	94
Oil refining	70
Ferrous metallurgy	79
Non-ferrous metallurgy	80
Chemicals and petrochemicals	67
Machine building	54
Wood and paper	48
Building materials	42
Light industry	15
Food	67

drew into its network other economies: East Europe, Cuba, North Vietnam. Enterprises depended on regular state orders, the contents of which might be dispatched to other enterprises thousands of miles away. Whole towns and communities across the wilds of Siberia relied on these regular orders for their economic survival. Once the state was too bankrupt to continue making these orders, once it could no longer afford to pay wages, and once the planning network which had coordinated these orders was removed, what occurred was not the spontaneous self organisation of the economy promised by neo-liberal theory, but a domino process of collapse.

Without any orders, factories engaged in primary industries closed down. Without deliveries of components and supplies secondary industries could no longer continue production, so they too closed. In a rapid and destructive cascade, industry after industry closed down. The process was made far worse by the way the unitary USSR split into a dozen different countries all with their own separate economies. The industrial system had been designed to work as an integrated whole, split up by national barriers it lay in ruins.

The following figures show how far the economy had regressed. These figures show how little recovery there had been, even after 13 years of operation of the free market.

If the economy had continued to grow even at the modest rate of the later Brezhnev years (say 2.5%) then industrial production would, on this scale have stood at 140% of 1990 levels. The net effect of 13 years of capitalism was to leave Russia with half the industrial capacity that could have been expected even from the poorest performing years of the socialist economy.

Key Economic Lessons

Ignoring for now, the political lessons, which we elaborated on at length in our book *Hacia el Socialismo del siglo XXI*, the key economic lessons are:

1. It is vital that the state maintain a strong, honest and efficient system of tax revenues.

2. It important that when attempting to rapidly change social relations that one does not dismantle the old economic mechanisms faster than new ones can be put in their place.

3. One should never overestimate the ability of markets to organise an economy.

4. One should beware the risk that a corrupt managerial strata attempts to divert state property into their own private domain.

5. Allowing the existence of criminal black markets is dangerous in the long run.

6. Until such time as money can be phased out and replaced by direct labour accounting, it is dangerous to allow prolonged inflation to take hold.

Written in 2007

17. Review: *Red Plenty* by Francis Spufford

This is a marvelous and unusual book. It sits in a remarkable way in between science popularisation, social history and fiction. The author describes it variously as a novel whose hero is an idea and a fairytale. The hero idea is that of optimal planning. The idea of running a planned economy in just such a way as to ensure that resources are optimally used in order to deliver the 'red plenty' of the title.

Combining real and imagined characters, politicians like Khrushchev, mathematicians and economists like Kantorovich and Nemchinov with fictionalised minor characters, it gives a gripping and apparently realistic picture of life in the USSR during the 1950s and 60s. It is not a single narrative as one expects from historical fiction. Instead it gives us a series of snapshots from the lives of individuals, separated by years. The common link is the project of the Cybernetic economic reformers, and the ambitions of Khrushchev to attain communist plenty.

The author shows real skill as a science populariser, explaining such diverse topics as how the Pentode valve logic of the early BESM computers worked, to the molecular mechanics of the carcinogenesis mechanism that eventually killed its designer. He vividly portrays the enthusiasm and self confidence of the USSR in the late 50s when Khrushchev's boasts that they would overtake the USA by 1980 and achieve communism seemed plausible. He gives a good didactic account both of the basic mechanisms of the Soviet Economy, and, through the lives of incidental characters paints a picture of its real operation that is more detailed and convincing than any academic history.

He traces the idea of cybernetic economic management from the hope of the 1950s and early 60s to its sidelining under Kosygin, and the eventual relegation of Kantorovich to the less ambitious task of optimisating steel tube output for the oil and natural gas industry. Ironically, says Spufford, as growth rates slipped in the 1970s, it was only the exploitation of petroleum for export that allowed Soviet living standards to rise.

This is a book that should be read by anyone who is seriously interested in the possibility of a different sort of economy from the one we now have. It shows both the strengths, and the hidden weaknesses of the most serious attempt so far to construct an alternative to capitalism, an attempt that was born when the idea of a communist future was taken very seriously by a whole society. To read it is to be convinced that whatever the truth of standard leftist criticism of the USSR as being undemocratic and bureacratic, there was much more than that at issue in this tragedy.

It raises real political and philosophical issues that would have to be faced by any future socialist project, and draws attention to a forgotten history that today's socialists ignore at their peril.

The bulk of what we read and hear about the USSR focuses on the 1920s and 30s. The remaining 50 years of its history fade before the glamour, grandeur and horror of the early years. But the early 1960s, when Russia was already an industrial country, with many areas of internationally competitive technology in aviation, space, computing holds more relevant lessons for the European left than its early years.

It is clear what lesson orthodox economists will draw:

It's a timely exploration, now so many people have gone off the idea of markets, of why the alternative is worse.

But such conclusions betray an unjustified and callous smugness. It is a smugness not justified by the elegaic last paragraph of the book. The restoration of the market mechanism in Russia was a vast controlled experiment. Nation, national character and culture, natural resources and productive potential remained the same, only the economic mechanism changed. If Western economists were right, then we should have expected economic growth and living standards to have leapt forward after the Yeltsin shock therapy. Instead the country became an economic basket-case. Industrial production collapsed, technically advanced industries atrophied, and living standards fell so much that the death rate shot up by over a third leading to some 5.7 million extra deaths.

If you were old, if you were farmer, if you were a manual worker, the market was a great deal worse than even the relatively stagnant Soviet economy of Brezhnev. The recovery under Putin, such as it was, came almost entirely as a side effect of rising world oil prices, the very process that had operated under Brezhnev.

But this does not excuse us from seriously considering the problems so vividly raised in the book. Spufford recounts how the attempt to follow the reformers' recommendations and raise the price of food to provide more income for farmers provoked strikes by industrial workers, which were suppressed with great brutality. The same scenario played itself out in Poland in the 70s and 80s, when any attempt to raise the ridiculously low subsidised meat prices led to strikes. Spufford brings out the disconnection between the recommendations of the reform economists and the real lives of the people that the reforms would impact on. Food subsidies were the bad conscience of inequality. They were necessary because without them, those on the lower wage rates could scarcely have survived. Marx had advocated that in the first stage of communism everybody would be paid in labour vouchers not money – 1 hour's work getting 1 hour's vouchers. Goods would be directly priced in terms of the labour required to make them and social expenditure would be met out of a tax or time-levy on incomes. Soviet prices deviated considerably from labour values for two reasons:

⋆ The well known subsidies on essential foods and housing.

⋆ The turnover tax was, I think, calculated on the basis of total turnover not just wages, as such it was similar to the fixed percent markup Marx posited for prices of production. Given that due to subsidies, wages underestimated the real value of labour power, this sort of markup would mean that the deviation of prices from labor value would actually have been bigger than under capitalism.

To have furthered Khrushchev's avowed aim of communism, Kantrovich would have had to propose egalitarian pay rates and a shift in state finance from turnover taxes to income taxes, before prices could be rationalised. Spufford gives greatest emphasis to the policies of those around Kantorovich and Nemchinov, who were advocating price reforms as part of a programme to allow optimal operation of the economy. Kantorovich argued that these prices – objectively determined valuations – arose out of the objective technical structure of the economy. If actual prices corresponded to objectively determined values, then the signals that these prices provided would guide individual factories to produce in accordance to what the plan needed. There is of course a strong similarity between this argument and that put forward by Western economists about the role of prices in guiding resource allocation in a market economy. It is probably no accident then that Kantorovich was the only Soviet economist to get a Nobel Prize for economics. But there was a fatal paradox in this whole notion, one that Spufford brought out in a meeting between Kosygin and a leading reformer: how were these optimal prices to be calculated? The maths was well understood, but the technical problems of handling that much data with 1960s computers were vast. And if Gosplan could concentrate the information and could have done the computations, then the indicative prices would have been unneccessary – the whole process of calculation could have been done in-natura with the Objective Valuations only having a fleeting existence as coefficients within the matrices of the planning computers.

So the programme of Kantorovich ended up requiring the same level of computing resources as that of his rival cyberneticist Victor Gluschov who apparently advocated the complete abolition of money – something superficially closer to Krushchev's vision of communism. In this context it is worth reading *InterNyet: why the Soviet Union did not build a nationwide computer network* by Slava Gerovitch. It would have been interesting had Gluschov appeared as a character in the book, rather than just as someone who is refered to indirectly. In the afterword it becomes clear why Gluschov remains such a shadowy figure to Spufford. Spufford reveals that he relied entirely on English language sources. What he knew of Gluschov came from Gerovitch's brief account. All in all, let me say again, this is a book that should be read by anyone with a serious interest in economic alternatives.

Written in May 2010

18. Against Mises

The first proponent of the claim that socialist economic calculation was impossible was the economist of the Austrian school von Mises. In his book *Human Action*[1] he devoted a chapter to arguing against socialism. He had two main arguments: on the one hand he said that the socialists themselves could not agree on what socialism meant, on the other he tried show that economic calculation would be impossible without a market.

The argument from discord

Mises notes that socialists have no uniform idea of what socialism is. Each socialist, or at least each group of socialists proclaims that only its view of socialism is right and that all others are misleaders, enemies of the people etc. Each socialist, he claims, implicitly assumes that the future socialist state will be headed by himself. True socialism is what he will decree. All other views are dangerous heresies best dealt with by the firing squad.

This seems to us to be a fairly accurate caricature of a substantial fraction of the socialist movement. Whilst the communist parties tended to have a fairly clear idea of what they wanted to achieve, based for the most part on an emulation of the USSR, other socialist parties have been loath to give a concrete view of how socialism should be organised. On all sides there has been a reluctance to examine the practical problems of organising a socialist economy.

Before the Russian revolution

Socialism arose first as philosophical movement by thinkers like Owen, and Fourier in the early 19th century. At that stage socialist thinkers were willing to advance quite detailed utopian plans for the reorganisation of society. Later it became a political movement of the working classes seeking a just society. Marx and Engels the socialist thinkers with the most lasting influence in the workers movement applauded the work of the early

---

[1] *Human Action*, L von Mises, 1949, Hodge and Company, London

utopians in establishing the socialist movement. They were in particular full of praise for Owen. But they were severely critical of the utopias of later philosophers like Proudhon and Duhring. They claimed that the later utopians were pale reflections of the earlier pioneers and that their utopias were for the most part internally inconsistent.

Marx took the view that as a scientist he could not put forward detailed theories about socialism, a form of society that did not yet exist. Economic and social research had to base itself upon the data provided by real society. He was ready to identify features of contemporary capitalism that revealed the potential for a future socialised production system but not to construct a detailed theory of socialism in the absence of data. He was willing to say that capitalism had generated a class struggle that would lead ineluctably to the dictatorship of the proletariat and thence to a classless society. As to what this society would be like, he was only willing to give sketchy predictions: that it would be based on planned production rather than the market, that it would not use money, etc.

After the Russian revolution

After the Russian revolution, and in particular after the mid-1930s the Communists held that Marx's views had been amply born out in practice. The dictatorship of the proletariat held sway, the economy was operated under a single plan and classes were being abolished. They had had to invent things as they went along. They had had to improvise and much of what they had done could not have been predicted in detail from Marx's writings. But this was to be expected, socialism was something born out of real life and history not the crystallisation of philosophers dreams. For the Communists, from the '30s to the '60s, if you wanted to know what socialism was you had just to look at Russia.

For other, non-communist, socialists the issue was more problematic. Although the great majority of socialists during the period from the '30s to the '50s took things at face value and accepted that Russia was socialist, there was always a minority who did not, and, in Western Europe during the last 30 years such views have probably come to represent a majority of socialist opinion.

The argument of the Social Democrats

From the early days of the communist revolution in Russia the Social Democratic parties in Europe argued that socialism could not be established by the methods of dictatorship that the Bolsheviks were using. They argued that the workers movement had during the previous decades struggled hard to win the franchise and for freedom of association and the press. To establish a one party dictatorship, impose censorship, imprison and execute political opponents went against everything that the movement had stood for.

Socialism they argued could only be established on the basis of a free press, free political parties and open parliamentary elections. A socialism that denied this was either not socialism or was not worth having. This is a clear and principled argument and the Social Democrats have stuck to it for seven decades. Its weakness was that the communists could simply retort: "Who says you can't build socialism using a dictatorship. That's just parliamentary cretinism. We have tried dictatorship and it works. You tried parliament and where is your socialism?"

On economic grounds, the Social Democrats had less to say against communism. Social Democracy has a 'liberal' definition of socialism both in the sense of looseness and in the Manchester sense. A mixed economy with social welfare legislation and some elements of industrial planning would certainly qualify, so their economic criticism of Soviet Communism is that it was not necessary to go so far. The economic direction was not in question, rather it was the council of moderation. Public ownership of the means of production, planning, welfare rights and an egalitarian income distribution were accepted as socialist objectives by both Communists and Social Democrats. The latter presented themselves as the democratic socialists without challenging the socialism of the latter, only their totalitarianism.

The argument of the Trotyskyists

Although there has been considerable overlap between Trotskyism and Social Democracy, with all Social Democratic parties worth their salt having Trotskyist fractions, their founder was a Communist and in consequence their arguments as to why the Soviet Union was not socialist start from different premises. The key points were:

1. Socialism in one country: a) It is in principle impossible to build socialism in a single country. b) The USSR is one country. c) It follows that the USSR could not be socialist.

2. The argument from plenty: a) Socialism is only possible in condi-

tions of abundance when mankind passes from the real of necessity to freedom. b) The USSR was plagued by shortages, which in turn stem from it being an isolated country. c) Hence the USSR could not be socialist.

Socialism in one country   What is the 'question' of socialism in one country? There seem to be not one but several possible questions. Here are some:

1) Is socialism possible in one country?

2) Is socialism possible in more than one country?

3) In the long term is socialism more stable in: a) A single country b) Many countries.

In short our answers to this would be 1) Yes, 2) Yes, 3) a. This may seem a bit paradoxical but our meaning will become clearer as the argument progresses.

From our perspective questions 1) and 2) are partly empirical. Only partly, because the meaning of the question still relies upon the interpretation on makes of the word country. This is commonly used to refer to a nation-state, but nations and states are not coterminous. The USSR was an international organisation of proletarian state power not a nation state in the old sense. If by country we mean explicitly a nation then it must be said that we lack empirical evidence to decide if socialism is possible in a single country. If by a country then we mean a single state power, then we have historical experience of the existence of a single socialist state from the early 1930s to the late 1940s. The time period given is determined by the point at which the distinguishing characteristics of a socialist economy came into being. On either definition of a country: nation, or unitary state power, then since the late 1950s it has been clear that a plurality of socialist countries can co-exist. We give the late 1950s as the crucial period here, since until then the People's Democracies of Eastern Europe were only nominally independent state powers, Communist Parties there were the effective agents of state power and the CPs remained so tightly co-ordinated that it was doubtful that the states could really be considered as independent. China, where the CP was independent of Moscow, had not established a socialist economy in the early 1950's. On the question of whether socialism is more stable in one country or several, it appears that it is more stable in one provided that by 'country' one means a unitary

184

state power. A unitary state power is better placed to present a united front to the hostile capitalist world, and best placed to coordinate the economic development of nations at different levels of development. One only has to consider what the chances of socialism's survival would have been had the USSR not been formed, and had there existed instead a multiplicity of sovereign nation-states on its current territory. The imperialist powers would undoubtedly have picked them off one by one. In the post war period, splits between socialist states: USSR/Yugoslavia or USSR/China or China/Vietnam have been exploited to disastrous effect by the USA and hamstrung socialisms economic development. In a paradoxical sense, it can be said that the abandonment of the policy of socialism in one country in the sense of a monolithic state by the communist movement in the late 1940s early '50s contributed to their collapse in 1990.

The argument from plenty The argument from plenty is convincingly dealt with by Nove[2] ,we can give a brief summary of its problems here. Consider the standards of life of the working classes of Europe when Marx or even Lenin were writing. Now consider what the conception of abundance would have been then: adequate and nutritious food, warm clothing and good dry shoes, houses with good heating and sanitation, access to education, culture, literature and leisure, an 8 hour day, free medical treatment. Given the conditions of life of the 19th century British proletariat, or the workers in Czarist Russia this would have seemed abundance.[3] Cars, televisions, home video cameras would not have featured. By the standards that the workers movement originally had in mind, the workers of East Germany, Czechoslovakia and to large extent the USSR were already entering into an age of abundance by the 1980s.[4] Despite this these economies were still clearly in the thrall of scarcity. This was true whether the measure of scarcity was the presence of queues, the budgetary constraints faced by the government or the aspirations of the population for oriental luxuries. The advance of technology had given rise to new aspirations which had yet to be met. In any technically advancing world this is bound to be the case. Newly developed technologies open

---

[2]*Economics of Feasible Socialism*, pp 15-20
[3]It would still be abundance to most of the worlds population. It is easy to forget, living in Western Europe, that the norm for the world capitalist economy is Mexico city rather than Berlin, Lagos rather than Stockholm.
[4]Whilst for significant sections of the population even a rich free market economy like the USA fails to provide abundance of such necessities.

up possibilities that can not immediately be met in unlimited quantities. It may well be the case that in market economies advertising artificially stimulates these needs, (which is the case against advertising), but even in the absence of adverts there was no lack of demand on the black market for Sony products in the USSR. Beyond this, it is an open question as to whether the current living standard of say France could be extended to the whole world population given the ultimately limited resources of the globe. It is even questionable whether the establishment of a socialist world economy would, in the short run at least, be helpful in alleviating scarcity in the USSR. Although its national income per head is below that of the leading capitalist countries, it is still well above average by world standards. As such, it might be expected that it would have to make substantial aid contributions to socialist countries in the third world. The contributions that it made to Vietnam, Cuba, Angola etc., were already a subject of some popular resentment.

The argument of the Left Communists

Another school of socialist thought was the Communist Left criticised by Lenin in his pamphlet 'Left Wing Communism'. Given his influence at the time, their views came to be largely discredited. Their most articulate theorist was Amadeo Bordiga, the founder of the Italian Communist party. Surprisingly enough, he remained politically active down to the 1960's. In 1952 Stalin published his booklet Economic Problems of Socialism in the USSR which set the terms of communist orthodox debate about the Soviet Economy. Shortly thereafter a publication by Bordiga appeared under the imprimatur of the International Communist Party, called Dialogue with Stalin. In this Bordiga argued against the idea that the USSR was socialist, holding instead that its economy was a form of state capitalism. Some of his arguments parallel those of the Trotskyists, that socialism was not possible in one country and that it demanded abundance. To this he added the argument that the USSR continued to be a commodity producing society. The Marxist vision of socialism had always been one in which commodity production was abolished, he argued. But in the USSR workers still worked for money wages and paid Roubles for goods in the shops.

At a formal level he was certainly correct in this. But the difficulties involved in establishing a genuine market economy in Eastern Europe after the counter revolution of 1990 indicate that the social reality behind money and prices in these countries was somewhat different from that in the West.

In the consumer goods markets, the prices bore little relation either to the amount of social labour required to produce them or to demand. In producer goods there was not really a market at all, since money alone did not suffice to ensure supply of a good if it had not been allocated in the plan. Bordiga was right in raising the existence of money and the commodity form as a potential problem, but like other left communists he was none to specific as to what alternative form of economic calculation should be used.

The argument of the Maoists

During the 1960s the Maoist section of the Communist Party of China started to argue that the USSR had reverted to capitalism. It was claimed that Khrushchev and then Kosygin, had taken the road to capitalism and that the USSR had passed from being a socialist state to being a social-imperialist one.

Given that the economic changes introduced by Khrushchev were fairly minimal this argument was hard to sustain. If, however, one views them as allegorical comments on an internal Chinese political debate about the appropriate way forward, then they make a lot more sense. Within China there was a fierce struggle between the Maoists and the followers of Liu Shaoqi and Deng. Liu was stigmatised as China's Khrushchev. Alternatively this can be seen as labelling Khrushchev as Russia's Liu.

If the economic policies followed by Deng after he came to power are indicative of what was being proposed in secret party debates during the 1960s then the charges of 'capitalist roadism' seem to have been accurate in the Chinese context. But until Gorbachov, those advocating similar measures in Russia were far from the centres of political power.

Summary

It is now a century and more since Marx was writing and there is much more historical evidence to go on. We have had extensive opportunities to observe societies that were by common understanding called socialist. we say by common understanding, being well aware that some people dissent from this, but whether one takes account of the constitutions of these societies, which proclaimed them to be socialist, the common view of their citizens who believed them to be socialist or the common view of the international press which declared them to be socialist that appears to have been the consensus view.

Many currents of thought in the socialist movement have dissented from this consensus, on the grounds that the conditions in countries of 'actually existing' socialism violated numerous socialist ideals.

This may well be true, but as materialists we can not judge the material world by the standards of the ideal. It is not the job of reality to materialise our ideals. Reality just *is,* in all its glories, horrors and contradictions. In judging the reality of socialism by comparing it with ideals advanced by its early advocates one is adopting an unusual criterion. We do not judge feudalism or capitalism by the standards of an ideal, were we to do that we would soon find that no real capitalist society corresponded in whole to this ideal. One may note here that it was a common argument by opponents of Marxism to say that since welfare state Britain differed in many respects from the ideal type of 19th century capitalism, it was no longer really capitalist.

If one advances a theory about a class of society before it ever comes into existence the scientific status of that theory is not strong. If the predictions of the theory come to conflict with later observation one can either decide that the theory needs modification or that reality has been misbehaving. If one adopts the later policy and says that socialism has never existed anywhere in the world, one may hope (we think vainly) to escape the current political unpopularity of existing socialism, but one has hardly advanced ones ability to practically intervene in the contradictions that led to this unpopularity. An ideal can be kept pristine but its very distance from reality vitiates its practical political force and one is left in precisely the predicament that Marx criticised in Utopianism.

We therefore take an empirical approach to determining what have been the distinguishing characteristics of socialist society.

1. The absence of a class of wealthy private proprietors in agriculture or industry.

2. The allocation of instruments of production by means of a system of state directives.

3. A consequent absence of capital goods or raw materials markets. Indeed one may question the meaning of the term capital goods in these societies.

4. The formal existence of a consumer goods market subject to the constraints that: i) A significant portion of consumer goods were

188

distributed by means other than purchase or sale. ii) The price mechanism in the consumer goods market was generally non-operative.

5. The absence of a market in land, and the absence of rent as an economic category.

6. A lower variance of incomes from the mean than was the case in capitalist countries at an equivalent stage of industrial development.

7. A distinct mode of extraction of the surplus product: the politically determined division of the concrete forms of the social product between the categories of current consumption, accumulation and unproductive consumption.

8. The relegation of taxation from a means of extraction of a surplus to means of securing monetary stability.

9. The existence of money and wage labour.

10. The absence of a reserve army of unemployed, often associated with chronic labour shortages.

These seem to be the significant structural features that marked off the socialist world from the capitalist. These are also the features that the advocates of capitalism in these countries wish to abolish.

Those socialists to the left of Social Democracy who deny that socialism has ever existed do not generally specify which of them are incompatible with socialism. One has to assume that the socialist systems they advocate would share most of these features. Exceptions to this are perhaps the Bordigist International Communist Party, who argue that the continued existence of money was a decisive factor in preventing the USSR etc. from ever having been socialist.

Our view is that although it is fruitless to question whether the USSR was socialist, it does not follow that one has to accept the political and economic policies followed by its government. If one abandons the utopian viewpoint and sees socialism as concrete form of society with its own contradictory forms of development, then one can start to ask just what economic and social policies should be followed in a socialist state. Any real society is fraught with contradictions, and is either destroyed by them or develops by resolving them.

By the 1930s it was widely recognised that liberal capitalism had reached a dead end and offered the world no prospect other than an appalling alternation of world war and economic recession. Not surprisingly many people concluded that only Nazism or Communism offered any hope for the future. By the 1950s that had all changed. The subordination of all other capitalist powers to the USA, Keynesian economics, GATT and the IMF had transformed its prospects.

The economic contradictions of the socialist world have been evident and growing for a couple of decades. It is now as self evident that socialism is finished as it was that capitalism was finished in the 1930s. As self evident and as false. Our opinion is that the crisis of socialism stems primarily from bad economic policies and can be resolved by a radical transformation of these policies. We do not put our views forward as an unvarying blueprint and anathematise every deviation from them. We do claim that they are more soundly based, and more likely to be successful than the economic policies followed by socialist governments in the recent past.

The argument from calculation

The director[5] wants to build a house. Now, there are many methods that can be resorted to. Each of them offers, from the point of view of the director certain advantages and disadvantages with regard to the utilization of the future building, and results in a different duration of the building's serviceableness; each of them requires other expenditures of building materials and labour and absorbs other periods of production. Which method should the director chose? He cannot reduce to a common denominator the items of various materials and various kinds of labour to be expended. Therefore he cannot compare them. He cannot attach either to the waiting time (period of production) or to the duration of serviceableness a definite numerical expression. In short, he cannot in comparing costs to be expended or gains to be earned, resort to any

---

[5]The 'director' is von Mises term for the dictator of a socialist state: a peculiar adoption of capitalist corporate terminology that is perhaps understandable for a book published in 1940. His argument however is not dependent on the planning process being subordinated to the will of a single individual, but is more general so that for 'director' one could read: planning agency.

arithmetical operations.[6]

Mises is concerned above all with the issue of the choice of techniques to be used in the production process. The claim is that only a market, by reducing all costs and benefits to the common denominator money allows rational comparison of alternative possibilities.

He reviews various possible ways in which this could be done and rejects them all.

* Calculation in kind is rejected because one can not add together quantities of different inputs unless one first converts them to a common unit of measurement like money. This is at first sight a reasonable argument but it involves certain presuppositions about the nature of calculation to which we will return.

* Calculation in terms of the labour theory of value is rejected in a single sentence:

> This suggestion does not take into account the original material factors of production and ignores the different qualities of work accomplished in the various labour-hours worked by the same and by different people.[7]

This is a somewhat brief treatment of the issue so our reply can also be concise. We have shown in other chapters that the labour theory of value does allow one to assign definite measures to the different value-creating powers of labours of different degrees of skill. The essence of the method is to cost the training of workers in terms of labour also and impute this to the work they do once they have been trained. As for the failure to take into account the original material factors of production, the classical theory of rent shows how the level of differential ground rent is governed by the marginal labour costs of production. There is no reason why this calculation can not be applied directly in a socialist economy. If this basis were followed, then the resulting environmental destruction should be no worse than that routinely produced by the application of the same principle in market economies.

Given the widespread environmental damage produced to the world's natural ecosystems from the bourgeois principle of valuing natural resources on the basis of marginal costs of production, we hope that a socialist planning agency would adopt somewhat stricter rules.

---

[6]*Human Action*, p.694.
[7]*Human Action*, p.699.

★ He rejects the suggestion that the unit of measure be utility on the grounds that this is not directly measurable. We would agree with this.

★ He rejects what is essentially the market socialist approach on the ground that the market is essentially the pursuit of self interest and that its effective operation implies the existence of risk taking entrepreneurs. If one accepts that the pursuit of self interest through the market is necessary for economic calculation then it is inconsistent to try and exclude the function of the entrepreneur. In the view of what has happened in USSR since Gorbachov, this was a politically astute observation. Once the socialists have conceded the virtue of the market it is hard to denounce the vice of the exploiter clothed as it now is in the shining raiment of enterprise.

★ He argues against the use of "the differential equations of mathematical economics" as a technique of socialist economic calculation. It is not clear exactly which differential equations he means, but they appear to be those of comparative statics. Modern economics tends to assume that a differential equation will involve derivatives with respect to time, and thus that its function is to capture the dynamics of an economy. We assume that Mises means simply the differential calculus which is used in neoclassical economics to deduce static equilibrium conditions. The gist of his argument is that the equilibrium condition dealt with in comparative statics is an entirely abstract construction which never really occurs. The economy is constantly in a process of change and current resources available to it are always a hangover from the past unsuited to current wants.

This is all true enough, but it does not prove that it is impossible to plan how best to use current resources to achieve a given future output. Our algorithm for plan balancing taking into account current stocks is one of probably many mathematical procedures that could be followed to achieve this end.

★ He also rejects what he calls the method of trial and error. This is the most interesting in our current context because it bears some relation to what we advocate.

We may assume that in the socialist commonwealth there is a market for consumers goods and that money prices for consumers goods are determined on this market. We may assume that the director assigns periodically to every member a certain amount of money and sells the consumer goods to those bidding the highest prices. ... But the characteristic mark of the socialist system is that the producers' goods are controlled by one agency only in whose name the director acts, that they are neither bought nor sold, and that there are no prices for them. Thus there can not be any question of comparing input and output by the methods of arithmetic.[8]

This mechanism is similar to that which we advocate for the distribution of personal consumer goods. Mises again concentrates on the alleged impossibility of applying arithmetical methods to comparing inputs with outputs in the absence of markets for means of production. Our answer is simple, the planning agency knows:

⋆ the labour contents of the different means of production,

⋆ the number of labour tokens that each consumer good will fetch on sale to individuals

from this it is possible to compare the social cost of producing something with the valuation put on it by consumers. Dealing with producer goods is a little more complicated. In this case we have no market to give us a measure of demand for the good, but we do have the more direct information derived from input/output analysis. We know how much of each intermediate good will be required to meet a given mix of final consumer goods. We do not need a market in intermediate goods to determine how much should be produced.

Throughout, Mises identifies calculation with arithmetic. This is understandable since commercial calculation and arithmetic have been strongly associated. Calculation[9] and arithmetical operations are practically synonymous. But calculation can be seen as a particular instance of the more general phenomenon of computation or simulation. What a control system requires is the ability to compute. This is true whether the control system in question is a set of firms operating in a market, a planning agency, an autopilot on an aircraft or a butterfly's nervous system. But it is by no means necessary for this computation to proceed by arithmetical means.

---

[8]Human Action, p.701.
[9]From calculus a pebble or stone used in counting.

The important thing is that the control system is able to model significant aspects of the system being controlled. Firms do this by means of the procedures of stock control and accountancy in which marks on paper model the location and movement of commodities. In preparing these marks the rules of arithmetic are followed. The applicability of arithmetic to the problem relies upon number theory being a model for the properties of commodities. A butterfly in flight has to control its thoracic muscles to direct its movement towards objects, flowers or fruit, that are likely to provide it with energy sources. In doing this it has to compute which of many possible wing movements are likely to bring it nearer to nectar. As far as can be determined it performs these computations without the benefit of a training in arithmetic.

To use economic terminology the butterfly has many choices open to it. Different sequences of muscle movement have different costs in terms of energy consumption and bring different benefits in terms of nectar. Its nervous system has to try to minimise the costs and maximise the benefits using non-arithmetical methods of computation. The continued survival of butterflies is evidence of their computational proficiency. A planning agency is likely to make widespread use of arithmetic and indeed, if one wants to make localised decisions on the optimal use of resources by arithmetic means, then Mises arguments about the need to convert different products into some common denominator for purposes of calculation are correct. This is exactly the role played by labour values in our proposal: they allow engineers to have a good estimate of what is likely to be a cheap method of production.

If, however, one is wanting to perform global optimizations on the whole economy, other computational techniques having much in common with the way nervous systems are thought to work are appropriate. These can in principle be performed without resort to arithmetic. Indeed Oskar Lange pioneered such approaches in the 1950's when he constructed a hydraulic model of the Polish economy for planning purposes. Mises, like many bourgeois theorists confuses the particular historical form in which a function is carried out with its essence. He reasons that:

1. Economies must optimize.

2. Arithmetic allows us to construct ordering relations over numbers, which can be used for optimization.

3. If one is to order numbers they must be of the same sort.

4. This requires conversion into a common unit of measure.

5. Money is a method of converting into a common unit of measure.

6. Hence all economies need money.

The problems with this argument lie in the steps 2 and 5. While propositions 2 and 5 are true, they do not support conclusion 6. To reach that conclusion we should need stronger claims:

2. Arithmetical orderings are the only way of achieving optimization.

5. Money is the only practical metric.

As we have shown, these stronger claims are false: there are non arithmetical methods of optimisation and money is not the only meth od of converting into a common unit of measure.

Written in 1992

19. A critical look at market socialism

Advocates of the market compare it to a system of voting which makes the consumer 'sovereign'. This it does, but as the consumers and the people are two different groups. Consumers are those with money. Only those who already possess something can have their wants satisfied. The unemployed, with only their unwanted labor to offer, have no votes in this system. If, however, we first assume a highly egalitarian income distribution this objection to the market would not apply. So long as the market is restricted to consumer goods, there is no reason why it should be incompatible with socialism. The basic principle of a socialist market in consumer goods can be stated quite simply. All consumer goods are marked with their labor values, i.e. the total amount of social labor which is required to produce them. But aside from this, the actual prices (in labor tokens) of consumer goods will be set, so far as possible, at market-clearing levels. Market-clearing prices are prices which balance the supply of goods (previously decided upon when the plan is formulated) and the demand. By definition, these prices avoid manifest shortages and surpluses. The appearance of a shortage (excess demand) will result in a rise in price which will cause consumers to reduce their consumption of the good in question. The available supply will then go to those who are willing to pay the most. The appearance of a surplus will result in a fall in price, encouraging consumers to increase their demands for the item.

Suppose a radio requires 10 hours of labor. It will then be marked with a labor value of 10 hours, but if an excess demand emerges, the price will be raised so as to eliminate the excess demand. Suppose this price happens to be 12 labor tokens. The radio then has a price to labor-value ratio of 1.2. Planners (or their computers) record this ratio for each consumer good. The ratio will vary from product to product, sometimes around 1.0, sometimes above (if the product is in strong demand), and sometimes below (if the product is relatively unpopular). The planners then follow this rule: Increase the target output of goods with a ratio in excess of 1.0, and reduce it for those with a ratio less than 1.0. The point is that these ratios provide a measure of the effectiveness of social labor in meeting consumers' needs (production of 'use-value', in Marx's terminology) across the different industries. If a product has a ratio of market-clearing price to labor-value above 1.0, this indicates that people are willing to spend more labor tokens on the item (i.e. work more hours to acquire it) than the labor time required to produce it. But this in turn indicates that the labor devoted to producing this product is of above-average 'social effectiveness.' Conversely, if the market-clearing price falls below the labor-value, that tells us that consumers do not 'value' the product at its full value: labor devoted to this good is of below-average effectiveness. Parity, or a ratio of 1.0, is an equilibrium condition: in this case consumers 'value' the product, in terms of their own labor time, at just what it costs society to produce it. This means that the objective of socialist retail markets should be to run at break even level, making neither a profit nor a loss; the goods being sold off cheap compensate for those sold at a premium.

There are therefore two mechanisms whereby the citizens of a socialist commonwealth can determine the allocation of their combined labor time. At one level, they vote periodically on the allocation of their labor between broadly-defined uses such as consumer goods, investment in means of production, and the health service. At another level, they 'vote' on the allocation of labor within the consumer goods sector via the spending of their labor tokens.

Payment in labor tokens

It was a common assumption of nineteenth-century socialism that people should be paid in labor tokens. We encounter the idea in various forms in Owen, Marx, Lassalle, Rodbertus and Proudhon. Debate centred on whether or not this implied a fully planned economy. The *Critique of the Gotha Programme* [marx1970mnp] contains a particularly clear account of the idea:

> [T]he individual producer gets back from society-after the deductions-exactly what he has given to it. What he has given it is his individual quantum of labour. For instance, the social working day consists of the sum of the individual hours of work. The individual labour time of the individual producer thus constitutes his contribution to the social working day, his share of it. Society gives him a certificate stating that he has

done such and such an amount of work (after the labour done for the comunal fund has been deducted), and with this certificate he can withdraw from the social supply of means of consumption as much as costs an equivalent amount of labour. The same amount of labour he has given to society in one form, he receives back in another.

With the enthusiasm of a pioneer, Owen tried to introduce the principle into England via voluntary co-operatives. Later socialists concluded that Owen's goal would be attainable only with the complete replacement of the capitalist economy.

Whilst Marx was very complimentary about Owen, he was critical of the schemes of Proudhon and Rodbertus. It is worth considering the Marxian critique of 'labour money' schemes; for there may appear to be a tension between the latter critique and Marx's own proposals. Indeed, the 'critique of labour money' is open to a (mis)reading which takes it as critical of any attempt to depart from the market system, towards a direct calculus of labour time. This reading has been made by writers as far apart as Karl Kautsky and Terence Hutchison.

The basic object of Marx and Engels's critique might be described as a 'naive socialist' appropriation of the Ricardian theory of value. If only, the reformers argue, we could impose the condition that all commodities really exchange according to the labour embodied in them, then surely exploitation would be ruled out. Hence the schemes, from John Gray in England, through a long list of English 'Ricardian socialists', to Proudhon in France, to Rodbertus in Germany, for enforcing exchange in accordance with labour values. Marx criticizes Proudhon's scheme in his *Poverty of philosophy* [marx1975pp], and deals with John Gray in his *Contribution to the critique of political economy* [marx1859], while Engels tackles Rodbertus's variant in his 1884 Preface to the first German edition of *Poverty of philosophy*. Between Marx in 1847 and Engels in 1884 we find a consistent line of attack on such proposals. From the standpoint of Marx and Engels, such schemes, however, honourable the intentions of their propagators, represent a Utopian and indeed reactionary attempt to turn back the clock to a word of ,simple commodity production' and exchange between independent producers owning their own means of production. The labour-money utopians failed to recognize two vital points. First, capitalist exploitation occurs through the exchange of commodities in accordance with their labour values (with the value of the special commodity labour-power determined by the labour content of the workers' means of subsistence).

Secondly, although labour content governs the long-run equilibrium ex-change ratios of commodities under capitalism, the mechanism whereby production is continually adjusted in line with changing demand, and in the light of changing technologies, under the market system, relies on the divergence of market prices from their long-run equilibrium values. Such divergences generate differential rates of profit, which in turn guide capital into branches of production where supply is inadequate, and push capital out of branches where supply is excessive, in the classic Smith/Ricardo manner. If such divergence is ruled out by fiat, and the signalling mecha-nism of market prices is hence disabled, there will be chaos, with shortages and surpluses of specific commodities arising everywhere.

One point which emerges repeatedly in the Marxian critique is this: ac-cording to the labour theory of value, it is socially necessary labour time which governs equilibrium prices, and not just 'raw' labour content. But in commodity-producing society, what is socially necessary labour emerges only through market competition. Labour is first of all 'private' (carried out in independent workshops and enterprises), and it is validated or con-stituted as social only through commodity exchange. The social necessity of labour has two dimensions. First of all, we are referred to the technical conditions of production and the physical productivity of labour. Ineffi-cient or lazy producers, or those using outmoded technology, will fail to realize a market price in line with their actual labour input, but only with the lesser amount which is defined as 'necessary'. Secondly, there is a sense in which the social necessity of labour is relative to the prevailing structure of demand. If a certain commodity is overproduced relative to demand, it will fail to realize a price in line with its labour value – even if it is produced with average or better technical efficiency. The proponents of labour money want to shortcircuit this process, to act as if all labour were immediately social. The effects within commodity-producing soci-ety cannot but be disastrous.

Now the lesson which Marx and Engels read to the labour-money so-cialists, concerning the beauties of the supply/demand mechanism under capitalism and the foolishness of the arbitrary fixing of prices in line with actual labour content, are obviously rather pleasing to the critics of so-cialism. It appears that Kautsky also read the critique of labour money as casting doubt on the Marxian objective of direct calculation in terms of labour content, so that by the 1920s the figure widely regarded as the authoritative guardian of the Marxian legacy in the west had effectively abandoned this central tenet of classical Marxism. From the account of the critique of labour money we have given, the limits of that critique should be apparent. What Marx and Engels are rejecting is the notion of fixing prices according to actual labour content in the context of a commodity-producing economy where production is private. In an economy where the means of production are under communal control, on the other hand, labour does become 'directly social', in the sense that it is subordinated to a preestablished central plan. Here the calculation of the labour content of goods is an important element in the planning process. And here the reshuffling of resources in line with changing social needs and priorities does not proceed via the response of profit-seeking firms to divergences between market prices and long-run equilibrium values, so the critique of labour money is simply irrelevant. This is the context for Marx's suggestion for the distribution of consumer goods through labour tokens.

The significance of labor tokens is that they establish the obligation on all to work by abolishing unearned incomes; they make the economic relations between people transparently obvious; and they are egalitarian, ensuring that all labor is counted as equal. It is the last point that ensured that they were never adopted under the bureaucratic state socialisms of the twentieth century. What ruler or manager was willing to see his work as equal to that of a mere laborer?

Labor tokens are payment for work done

The difference between a labor-token system and the hire of labor-power can be shown via some contemporary illustrations.

Suppose you engage a self-employed plumber to fix the toilet. The plumber will judge how long it will take and quote on that basis. On completion of the job you pay the plumber for parts and labor. You do not purchase his ability to work for a day, you pay for the actual work done. If he does not finish the job he does not get paid-it was up to him to judge how long it would take. Self-employed, he has an incentive to get his estimates right.

Suppose, on the other hand, you call out a repairman employed by a service company to fix the heating. You are likely to be charged for time actually taken. The service company need have no control over how hard or efficiently the repairman works, as the system of charging means that it can never lose. The company purchases his labor-power at $10 per hour and sells it on to you at $40. In this case you are being re-sold labor-power, not the labor actually performed.

Finally, suppose that you took out a maintainance contract for $80 per annum. The service company is now selling you the promise of work actually done, labor, and has the responsibility and incentive to ensure that the work is done efficiently and to time.

Payment in labor tokens implies payment for work actually done as in the first and third case. When Owen proposed such payment for artisans, this was unproblematic. Proof of work done was provided by the product delivered to the 'labor exchange'. In a modern economy it implies either a system of piecework, or detailed work study to arrive at estimates of time required under conditions of average skill to perform a task.

General argument against market socialism

Above sumarises the arguments about the role of the market under socialism that we presented in [cockshott93a]. *Towards a New Socialism* was written in the late 1980s when ideas of market socialism were comming to the fore under Gorbachov in the USSR. The book was in a way a polemic against market socialism. Whilst it recognised a necessary role for a consumer goods market, it took strong issue with any generalisation of the market to labour and capital goods. The argument was that advances in information technology allowed an efficient planning system to be constructed which could replace the market in the allocation of means of production, whilst socialist concerns for equity should prohibit a market for labour. We took this stand because we believed that the idea of market socialism was fundamentally corrosive. It would undermine such socialist achievements as had been built up during the 20th century and would legitimate a transition to capitalism. Subsequent events validated this intuition.

In this section we present general arguments against market socialism before going on to look at specific Western market socialist writers.

It has long been noted by socialists that economies based on simple commodity production tend to give rise to capitalism. Lenin wrote: "small production engenders capitalism and the bourgeoisie continuously, daily, hourly, spontaneously, and on a mass scale" [lenin1999lwc], a view he probably formed from his extensive sociological research on the Russian agrarian economy [lenin1967dcr]. This view led orthodox communists to oppose the extension of market relations [stalin1939fl, chunchiao1975ear, sayers1980fpa], even if these did not initially involve explotative labour contracts. The suspicion was that some people would get rich and others poorer if market relations were extended, and that over time these differences would solidify into a new class hierarchy.

Market economies are fundamentally chaotic. The incomes of individual economic agents, be these people, firms or cooperatives are subject to constant random variation. A seller of commodities will have good and bad months, good years and bad years. This random process means that even if there is initially no buying and selling of labour power income inequalities must arise.

In a market economy, hundreds of thousands of firms and individuals interact, buying and selling goods and services. This is similar to a gas in which very large numbers of molecules interact, bouncing off one another. Physics speaks of such systems as having a 'high degree of freedom', by which it means that the movements of all individual molecules are 'free' or random. But despite the individual molecules being free to move, we can still say things about them in the aggregate. We can say what their average speed will be (their temperature) and what their likely distributions in space will be.

The branch of physics which studies this is statistical mechanics or thermodynamics. Instead of making deterministic statements, it deals with probabilities and averages, but it still comes up with fundamental laws, the laws of thermodynamics, which have been found to govern the behaviour of our universe.

When the methods of statistical mechanics are applied to the capitalist economy [wright2005sac, wright2imm, farjoun], the predictions it make coincide almost exactly with the labour theory of value as set out in volume 1 of Marx's Capital [marx1]. Statistical mechanics showed that the selling prices of goods would vary in proportion to their labour content just as Marx had assumed. Because the market is chaotic, individual prices would not be exactly equal to labour values, but they would cluster very closely around labour values. Whilst in Capital I the labour theory of value is just taken as an empirically valid rule of thumb. Marx knew it was right, but did not say why. Here at last was a sound scientific theory explaining it.

It is the job of science to uncover causal mechanisms. Once it has done this it can make predictions which can be tested. If two competing theories make different predictions about reality, we can by observation determine which theory is right. This is the normal scientific method.

Farjoun and Machover's theory made certain predictions which went directly against the predictions made by critics of Marx such as Samuelson. In particular their theory predicts that industries with a high labour to capital ratio will be more profitable. Conventional economics predicts

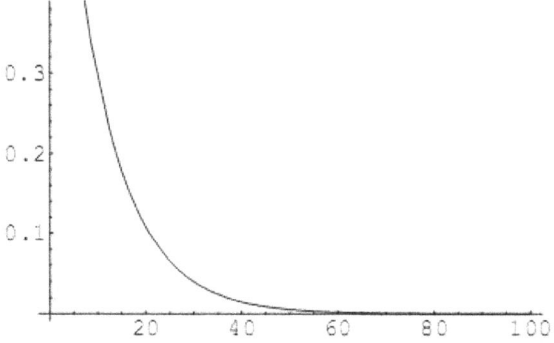

Figure 19.1.: The Gibbs-Boltzmann distribution, plotted on a linear scale. Contrast this with the Log scale image in Figure 5.2.

that there will be no such systematic difference between the profit rates in different industries. When put to the test it turned out that Farjoun and Machover were right. Industries with a high labour to capital ratio are more profitable [cockshott2003]. But this is exactly what we should expect if the source of profit was the exploitation of labour rather than capital. Their theory made predictions which not only turned out to be empirically spot on, but at the same time verified Marx's theory of the exploitation of the worker.

The next big advance was made by the phsyicist Yakovenko, who showed [dragulescu, cockshott:cee] that money in a market economy played the same role as energy in physics. Just as energy is conserved in collisions between molecules, so money is conserved in the acts of buying and selling. So far so obvious!

What was not obvious was what this implies. Yakovenko showed that the laws of thermodynamics then imply that the distribution of money between people will follow the same form as the distribution of energy between molecules in a gas : the so called Gibbs-Boltzmann distribution. This sounds very scientific, but what does it actually mean? What the Gibbs-Boltzmann distribution of money says is that a few people with end up with a lot of money and a lot of people with end up with very little money. It says that the distribution of money will be very uneven, just as we see in capitalist society. In fact Yakovenko showed that the distribution of wealth in the USA fits the Gibbs-Boltzman distribution pretty closely.

There is a tendancy to think that rich people owe their wealth to intelligence or effort, but physics tells us no. Given a market economy, then the laws of chance mean that a lot of money will end up in the hands of a few people.

In fact when we look at the USA we find that the distribution of wealth is even more uneven that we would expect from the Gibbs-Boltzmann law. If the Gibbs Boltzman law held, there would be millionaires but no billionaires. Why the disparity?

Yakovenkos original equations represented an economy that is rather like what Marx called simple commodity production. It assumed only buying and selling. More recent work by Yakovenko and Wright [dragulescu02a, wright2005sac], has shown that if you modify these equations to allow either the earning of interest on money, or the hiring of wage labour, then the equations predict a polarisation of the population into two groups. The great bulk of the population, the working class and petty bourgeois, follow a Gibbs-Boltzmann income distribution. But there is a second class, those whose income derives from capital, whose wealth with follow a different law, what is called a power-law. Again, look in detail at the distribution of wealth in and you provide exactly the distribution predicted by Yakovenko's theory. This, says Yakovenko, proves that Marx was right when he said that modern society was comprised of two distinct and opposed classes : capitalists and workers.

What conclusions can we draw from this with respect to market socialism?

The first point is that as soon as you have a set of private agents, be they individuals, firms or cooperatives engaging in monetary trade, the laws of thermodynamics mean that the maximal entropy (most probable) distribution of money between the agents will be very uneven. Since, as Adam Smith said, money is the power too command the labour of others, this uneven distribution of money translates into an uneven distribution of social power. Those agents with more money are in a position to hire other agents under contractual terms favourable to the hirers. As soon as this happens the process of differentiation of income accelerates, and you move from the Gibbs Boltzman to the even more unequal power-law distribution of income characteristic of capitalist society.

This is a prediction that arises from simulation models of economies, but if we look at a real examples of a socialist economy taking the market socialist path – China under Deng, we see in reality the sort of income inequalities the models predict.

It may be argued that in China the introduction of market relations went much further than is advocated by some market socialists. That may well be true, but this sort of process acquires its own dynamic:

> My own work, inspired by the reform experience, contributed additional arguments for refuting the Lange-theory. It seems to be highly improbable to generate the strong cost-minimizing or profit-maximizing incentive, taken as granted in the world of Lange's theory, in a public firm under a soft budget constraint regime.
>
> It is impossible to couple an arbitrarily chosen ownership structure and an also arbitrarily chosen set of coordination mechanisms. There is close affinity between certain ownership forms and certain coordination mechanisms. Decentralized market and private ownership belong together. A further important counter-argument comes from the political and ideological sphere. The smooth functioning of the market depends on the "climate". It requires a market-friendly environment. If the politicians ruling a country are sworn enemies of genuine decentralization, the market will be banned to the black and grey area of the economy and cannot become the fundamental coordinator and integrator.) [kornai,200]

The converse of this is that if we want to stop a highly undequal distribution of income, we either have to remove the mechanism that generates it, or do work to reduce the entropy of the system. Marx's proposal for abolishing money and instituting labour accounts which do not circulate, do not function as money, removes the underlying random process which generates inequality. The Swedish model works to reduce entropy through redistributive taxes. It has to constantly work against the tendancy of the market economy to generate a high degree of inequality, and can at most partially mitigate this inequality.

An evaluation of Yunker

In a series of articles, for instance [yunker1979mea, yunker1988npm], Yunker has made out the case for a form of market socialism. In these articles his main concern has been to defend market socialism against the criticisms of neo-classical economists who may be favourable to a capitalist economy. Since readers may not be familiar with his ideas we will give a brief summary of his proposals and his defence of them, before going on to make a critical assessment of them.

Yunker envisages what he calls a profit oriented model of socialism. The economy would be run, as now, by companies whose legal status would be largely unchanged. The companies will be able to engage in the full range of commercial transactions currently engaged in by US firms. These firms would employ people under the same sort of labour contracts as a present, and attempt to maximise their profits. Firms would be allowed to own shares in or make loans to each other as at present. The only limitation on capitalist activity would be that beneficial ownership of shares could not be vested in individuals. Instead, all shares not held or managed by other companies would be vested with a public body which he terms the Bureau of Public Ownership (BPO). The BPO would be obliged to maximise the return on the capital that it held. Capital income would then be distributed by the BPO to all employees in the economy as a percentage supplement to their wage incomes.

It is evident that the form of socialism advocated by Yunker is very similar to capitalism. Whether it should be termed socialism or state owned capitalism is a moot point, but Yunker's intention is evidently to deflect much of the criticism that capitalist inclined economists level at socialism by saying: look, socialism could be pretty much like the capitalism you know and love, so your criticisms of socialism are mostly ill founded.

Yunker devotes considerable attention to the problem of incentives for socialist managers as compared to private capitalists. An owner manager gains the full benefit from any increase in profit which would not be the case for a salaried manager under market socialist conditions. Yunker points out that in practice most lareg firms today are already run by salaried managers so that in some ways the situation would be no different. The issue then becomes whether the fund managers of the BPO would pursue the efficient use of capital as well as private shareholders do?

Again one of his responses is to say that already a large portion of shares are held by institutional investors who pay salaries and bonuses to fund managers, so the situation is again not dissimilar.

He has done empirical studies of the effort that private shareholders have to expend to influence the rate of return that they get on their capital [yunker1974iai], from which he concludes that they needed only to spend 9 hours a month in order to get close to the maximal rate of return on their capital. He therefore concludes that the BPO could be expected to earn close to the maximal rate of return with only a relatively small effort of fund management.

He goes on to construct a relatively elaborate theoretical economic model which purports to help us understand the relationship between return on capital and the effort put in by managers, and concludes from this that efficient management could be obtained at much lower levels of incentives than are typical for CEOs in American companies.

Assessment

Yunker's work has to be assessed from the standpoint of the ideological milieu in which it is embedded, for its theoretical and scientific cogency and finally in terms of its social and political implications.

Ideological The ideological context of his writing is very clearly that of mainstream academic economics in the USA. The economics profession in the USA is probably as hostile to socialism as that of any other country. This means that Yunker swims against a tide of hostility to any form of socialism, and exists within a universe of discourse that is quite quite different from that of Marxian socialists. He could have opted out of the milieu of neo-classical economics and formulated an external critique of capitalism, but he has chosen instead the path of internal critique. He uses the familiar conceptual apparatus of his opponents and the familiar institutions of American capitalism to make his case for socialism. In a sense this is to be expected. Spontaneously developed socialist critiques of the existing order can be expected to start out from the dominant economic ideas of the day. Owenite and Marxian socialism built themselves on a critical appraisal of classical British political economy, so it is not surprising that a modern socialism, arising in the USA builds itself on the conceptual framework of the dominant neo-classical economics. The advantage of this approach is that Yunker's socialism may be harder for neoclassicals to simply dismiss than Marxian socialism. The disadvantage is that his approach is unlikely to appeal so much to grass-roots activists, because it seems to offer a society that is only slightly different from today's. Even a cursory examination of current activist web discussion of socialism, as opposed to discussion in academic journals, shows that Yunker's vision has generated much less interest than the more radical vision of Michael Albert [albert1991pep] for example.

Theoretical But ideological reception is not everything. One also has to asses the scientific status of his arguments. From our standpoint as Marxian socialists, we would want to know why Yunker chooses to reject planning as part of socialism. Support for planning as opposed to market competition has been the prevalent position among socialists, so one would expect that Yunker would devote some energy to justifying his rejection of it. On the contrary in [yunker1988npm] he contents himself with a single sentence:

> Among Western economists, it is virtually axiomatic that the "market capitalist" economy of the United States is highly efficient relative to the "planned socialist" economy of the Soviet Union. ([yunker1988npm], page 71)

He then goes on to assume that this belief is justified and build all his further arguments on this assumption. His formulation is revealing in many ways. Firstly his use of the term "Western economists". By saying this he can not just have meant economists who lived to the west of the Iron Curtain, since there existed at the time he was writing, a small, but still real, fraction of Marxian economists in Western countries. These economists would not have taken it as axiomatic that market capitalism was more efficient than planned socialism. By Western economists he meant those economists, wherever they lived, who adhered to the neo-liberal Washington Consensus. It was a reference to, and affirmation of ideological allegiance rather than geography that he was making.

The next revealing thing is his use of the word axiomatic. One has to ask why he thinks axioms are relevant to an empirical study like economics?

The place for axioms is in formal theories such as set theory, number theory or predicate logic. Axioms and laws of inference provide a means by which it is possible for the validity of some, but not all, propositions within such a theory to be evaluated. Given a set of axioms and rules of inference it is possible to use a deterministic procedure to divide propositions into those that are provably true, those that are provably false, and those for which no deterministic answer can be obtained. People constructing formal theories are at liberty to select axioms, and by selecting different axioms different formal theories arise, the most famous historical example probably being the alternative axiomatisation of geometry by Riemann in 1854.

Yunker's reference to "virtually axiomatic" reveals the bias that neo-classical economists have towards treating economics as a formal system rather than an empirical science. Neoclassical economics proceeds by a discourse of proof from axioms rather than by the contrasting method of the empirical sciences: hypothesis, experimental or observational tests, modification of hypothesis. Biology does not proceed in an axiomatic fashion, why should economics?

Is it not possible that the axiomatic approach says something about the social role of neoclassical economic theory?

Couldn't it be the case that the function of the theory is to prove certain political propositions – that all is for the best in best of all possible worlds?

But then there is the adjective: virtually. It is "virtually axiomatic" that market capitalism is superior to planned socialism. Why the qualification?

Because neoclassical economists have not been able to prove the superiority of market economy to planned economy from their prior set of axioms. On the contrary, for the century since Barone [barone1908imd], it has been evident that the axioms of neo-classical economics could be used to show that planned socialism was just as efficient as market capitalism. So it becomes necessary for "Western economists" to add a final "virtual axiom"; to assume what they want to prove in the first place.

Yunker seems to have felt uneasy about disposing of hitherto existing socialism in one sentence, so he adds a footnote to the work of Bergson [bergson1978pas] who is claimed to have empirically validated this virtual axiom. But Bergson's work uses data from the 1960s and 1970s. It claimed to show that the Soviet economy was less efficient in its use of resources than the US one. Such comparisons are bedeviled by the difficulty of compensating for factors other than the social system that distinguish the two countries: stage of industrialisation, available level of technology, level of technical culture in the workforce, differences in national cultures etc. But such debates from the 70s are now history. We have the results of a controlled experiment in Russia to go on. From 1989 the Russian government took the advice of American economist who took it as virtually axiomatic that replacing the planned economy with a free market would result in an enormous improvement in economic efficiency. Had these economist been right, were it the case that the main thing holding back the Russian economy was the constraints imposed by central planning, then we should have expected a Russia to have experienced a leap in prosperity and economic growth post 1989. In fact the effect was completely the opposite. The institution of a market economy led to a catastrophic decline in overall economic output, (Table 1).

TABLE 1. Decline of Russian GDP following the switch
from a planned to a market economy.

year	GDP in 1990 US $Millions
1990	569709
1991	541224
1992	462746
1993	422487
1994	368831
1995	353709
1996	340948
1997	345657
1998	327182
1999	347962

We are not saying that the Soviet planning system, or its system of economic calculation and valuation were adequate. We argue in TNS that
considerable inefficiencies arose from the under-valuation of labour in the
USSR; that planning was based on aggregate rather than detailed targets;
that it failed to make effective use of modern computer and telecoms technology; that consumer goods prices often diverged excessively from labour
values. But our response, writing in 1989, was not to advocate market
oriented reforms, which we considered would have catastrophic consequences for the working classes of the USSR. Instead we advocated a
modernised, technologically sophisticated, and democratic model of planning. We think, in retrospect, that our scepticism about the market socialist reforms then being advocated in the USSR have turned out to be well
founded. In contrast the 1990s seem to have passed Yunker's by. He seems
to have nothing to say about the signal failure of Gorbachov's market socialist trajectory. He still holds to a rejection of planning based on little
more than US cold war prejudices.

One of the key points of Yunker's arguments concerns the role of management unders socialism and capitalism. He is concerned to show that
salaried employees of the BPO would be as effective in the efficient management of publicly held capital assets as current fund managers or individual capitalists are with privately held funds. His concern here is with
efficient use of capital as a key component of overall efficiency. He takes
return on capital employed to be the key indicator of economic efficiency,
and argues that if socialist industry were to be oriented towards this, it

would be as efficient as current capitalist industry, whilst allowing for greater equity.

There are several theoretical questions to be addressed here:

1. What is meant by the management of capital?

2. Could a single agency like the BPO operate in a manner analogous to multiple private fund managers?

3. Is profit really a good indication of capital efficiency?

4. Is the return on capital determined by the effort of capital managers or by quite other factors?

In Yunker's empirical study of capital management [yunker1974iai] he focused on individual 'investors'. But these were investors only in a very limited sense. They did not engage in the direct purchase of plant or equipment, instead they bought and sold financial assets. They were what used to be called rentiers, people whose wealth consisted in paper titles to future income streams. Management of capital, understood this way, is a much simpler task than efficient management of real capital assets and real capitalist production processes. But it is the latter which affects the productivity of a real economy. The former does affect the income of an individual rentier, but in a zero sum game. When a Mr A sells a low performing stock and buys a high performing one, he gains, but only at the expense of a Mr B who bought the low performing stock, and a Ms C who sold him the high performing stock. Contrast this with the task of organising the production of the A380 super jumbo jet. This requires the efficient coordination of a huge number of distinct labour processes, spread across multiple nations and using a vast variety of capital equipment. Efficient execution of this sort of management directly affects aggregate welfare. It determines the timeliness of delivery of the jets. I determines their reliability and safety. Such management decisions influence their fuel consumption, etc. So there are two quite different sorts of capital management involved here, one of which has purely selfish implications, the other has social implications.

In the sort of economy that Yunker advocates, with only one ultimate owner, the BPO, the private rentier type of capital management would be irrelevant. The state is the ultimate owner of all shares and can not affect its income by portfolio adjustments. So Yunker's empirical studies are irrelevant to the issue he is addressing.

He might object that whilst buying and selling existing stock may be a zero sum game, the same can not be said about new issues of stock. Here, a consequence of stock purchase is the funding of real capital investment, and judgements by the market as to whether or not to fund such stock issues, have a real effect on future production. It is in this context that we have to ask: could a single agency like the BPO operate in a manner analogous to multiple private fund managers?

No.

The BPO as the only ultimate shareholder will have a synoptic view of the investment plans of all firms in the economy. Since the investment plans of one firm will affect other firms, the BPO must take this into account. Knowing the planned investments of all airlines for example, and knowing the best projections available to these firms for the growth of the airtravel market, it will be in a position to judge if the overall investment plans are excessive. It will thus be subject to none of the 'animal spirits' that motivate private investors during a bull market. A system of capital investment funded by a BPO will be much less likely to engender the bubbles which have time and again caused disastrous waste of real capital in the US economy, from the railway bubble of the late 19th century to the real-estate bubble that collapsed so dramatically in 2008. Many would judge this a good thing. But note that in the process, the BPO will have to act more and more like GOSPLAN.

If it is to make sound investment judgements, it will have to construct increasingly sophisticated econometric input-output models of the whole US economy. Only then will it be in a position to assess whether or not a particular investment in new stock issues is likely to give a good overall return. In will, in other words, have to plan.

Social and political implications of Yunker's model

Given the position of the USA in the world economic and political system, and given the absence of any significant socialdemocratic workers movement there, discussion of American Socialism has a slightly artificial air. However, it is not inconcievable that during the course of the 21st century this will change. The USA has moved from being the world's greatest creditor to its greatest debtor. In China it is faced for the first time with an industrial rival with the population resources to potentially overtake it. At the time of writing (March 2009) it is entering what looks like being its worst recession in three generations. All of these factors could lead to a serious socialist or social democratic movement taking root in the USA over the next quarter century. But would the ideology put forward by Yunker's be a plausible basis for such a movement?

We believe not.

Yunker's proposals are too timid to inspire a new generation of working-class organisers. Although his ideas would, if somehow put into practice, mean some improvement in the income of workers, they would leave most of the structure of society unchanged. The very top stratum of capitalists would be removed, but the rest of the class structure would remain. The managerial and professional classes would retain their position vis-a-vis the working class. Workers would be employed by the same companies, managed in the same way but with the sole difference that the state would be the ultimate shareholder. Because his proposals do nothing to narrow income differentials arising from wages and salaries, because they provide no guarantee of full employment, they would be seen as having little to offer to the working class. They might perhaps win a certain middle class following, but in the ideological struggles that would take place within a growing working class socialist movement, they would be displaced by more radical doctrines.

One has to realise that for socialism to become 'on the agenda' in the USA will presuppose

1. A political movement at least comparable to classical German or Swedish social democracy, or the large communist movements of the post WWII period,

2. A major war resulting either (a) in a defeat, comparable to those suffered by France in 1870, Russia 1917 or Germany 1918/45, or (b) a pyrrhic victory that could only be won after years of national sacrifice, in which the social democratic movement avanced its position like Britain in 1945.

In these circumstances, different socialist doctrines, memes to borrow Dawkin's term, will contend for extended reproduction. The laws of evolution will favour those best suited to the new political and economic environment. Yunker's doctrines have been tailored to a particular evolutionary niche on the margins of American economic orthodoxy, in a climate of US world domination. It seems unlikely that they will sucessfully reproduce themselves in a working class movement in a defeated or declining USA.

Written in 2009

References

AH91 M. Albert and R. Hahnel. The Political Economy of Participatory Eco-nomics. Princeton University Press, 1991.

Bar08 E. Barone. II ministro della produzione nello stato collettivista', Englishtranslation ('The Ministry of Production in the Collectivist State') inFriedrich von Hayek. Collectivist Economic Planning: Critical Studieson the Possibilities of Socialism by NG Pierson, Ludwig von Mises,Georg Halm, and Enrico Barone, pages 245 90, 1908.

Ber78 A. Bergson. Productivity and the Social System: The USSR and theWest. Harvard Univ Pr, 1978.

Cc75 C. Chun-chiao. On exercising all-round dictatorship over the bourgeoisie. Foreign Languages Press, Peking, 1975.

CC92 Allin Cottrell and Paul Cockshott. Towards a New Socialism, volumeNottingham. Bertrand Russell Press, 1992.

CC03 W. P. Cockshott and A. F. Cottrell. A note on the organic compositionof capital and pro t rates. Cambridge Journal of Economics, 27:749 754, 2003.

CCM+09 P. Cockshott, A. Cottrell, G. Michaelson, I. Wright, and V. Yakovenko. Classical Econophysics: Essays on classical political economy, thermodynamics and information theory. Routledge, 2009.

DY00 A. Dragulescu and V. M. Yakovenko. Statistical mechanics of money.The European Physical Journal B, 17:723 729, 2000.

DY02 A. Dragulescu and V. M. Yakovenko. Statistical mechanics of money, income and wealth: a short survey, 2002.

FM83 Emmanuel Farjoun and Moshe Machover. Laws of Chaos, a ProbabilisticApproach to Political Economy. Verso, London, 1983.

Key36 J. M. Keynes. The General Theory of Employment Interest and Money.Macmillan, London, 1936.

Kor J. Kornai. Socialism and the market:conceptual clari cation.

Len67 V.I. Lenin. The development of capitalism in Russia. Progress publishersMoscow, 1967.

Len99 VI Lenin. " Left-wing" communism: an infantile disorder. ResistanceBooks, 1999.

Mar54 Karl Marx. Capital, volume 1. Progress Publishers, Moscow, 1954. Orig-inal English edition published in 1887.

Mar70 K. Marx. Marginal Notes to the Programme of the German Workers'Party (*Critique of the Gotha Programme*). Marx and Engels SelectedWorks, 3, 1970.

Mar71 Karl Marx. A Contribution to the Critique of Political Economy. Lawrence & Wishart, London, 1971.

Mar75 K. Marx. The poverty of philosophy (1847). Marx and Engels, collectedworks volume VI, pages 105 212, 1975.

Say80 S. Sayers. Forces of Production and Relations of Production in SocialistSociety. Radical Philosophy, 24:19 26, 1980.

Sta39 J. Stalin. Foundations of Leninism. International Publishers New York,1939.

Wri I. Wright. Implicit Microfoundations for Macroeconomics. Economics:The Open-Access, Open-Assessment E-Journal, 2.

Wri05 I. Wright. The social architecture of capitalism. Physica A: StatisticalMechanics and its Applications, 346(3-4):589 620, 2005.

YK74 J.A. Yunker and T.L. Krehbiel. Investment analysis by the individualinvestor. Quarterly Review of Economics and Business, 28:90 101, 1974.

Yun79 J.A. Yunker. The Microeconomic E ciency Argument for Socialism Re-visited. Journal of Economic Issues, pages 73 112, 1979.

Yun88 J.A. Yunker. A New Perspective on Market Socialism. Comparative Eco-nomic Studies, 30(2):69 116, 1988.

20. Towards a New Socialism

Transcription of a video by O. Ressler, recorded in Glasgow

My name is Paul Cockshott; I am the co-author of the book *Towards a New Socialism*, I wrote with my friend Allin Cottrell. We wrote it in response to a political situation in the 1980s, where the Soviet Union was obviously getting into difficulties, and within Britain pro-market ideas were spreading in the Labour Party. Particularly influential at that time was the professor [Alec Nove] for Soviet studies at the Glasgow University who wrote a book advocating market socialism. He was an expert in the Soviet economy, so his arguments seemed convincing, and they certainly convinced the leadership of the Labour Party in Britain. But we thought we could refute those using ideas from modern computer science and also from classical political economy – and that's what our book was about.

We are in the 21st century and people start to think again about the viability of socialism. It seems to me that there are now a number of people coming together and saying that there are three key ingredients to a viable socialism today.

One of them is the replacement of money and prices with value-based economics, with economics based on labor time. The other is the use of the much more advanced information technology we now have, to make rational and detailed planning of the economy envisionable in the way it wasn't before. And finally, the principle I think most modern socialists would advocate, is the replacement of representative democracy with some form of participatory democracy, to give the majority of people real control over the disposition of national income.

I

The question why socialism would be preferred to capitalism can't be answered in the abstract, in general, because not everyone is going to prefer it. Who is going to prefer it, is going to depend on, basically, if you are rich or poor. The studies we've done on the distribution of income in Britain indicate that if an egalitarian system of payment was introduced, the over-whelming majority of the population would benefit. We calculated, in the early nineties, how much a person would get, if an egalitarian system of payment was introduced. And the only section of the population, which would lose out was the top 25 percent of men in office jobs. All manual workers, male or female, would win out, all quartiles or female workers would win out, and three quarters of male office workers would win out. The people who would lose out are a small minority of the best-paid people and an even smaller minority of people driving their income from property.

One of the points that Alex Nove brought out in his book was the inability of the Soviet planners to plan in detail. You can take examples: They could set up a plan for the pairs of trousers they are going to make, but they did not necessarily get the right plan for the number of zips they are going to have for the pairs of trousers, so that you end up with trousers without zips or shoes without laces. That kind of thing came from the fact that the plan targets were set in aggregate terms. The plan targets were set for a couple of thousand categories for goods, and they were set in money terms. They were not set in terms of the actual physical products that were going to be made. You contrast that with the system of product codes, which was introduced in the capitalist world in the 70s, a bar code system that enables every single individual product to have a unique identification number. The modern supermarkets have a feedback system, whereby they know exactly how many of every product has been sold. You need a planning system that goes right down to the product code level, if it is going to be efficient.

I have done experiments with a modest computer costing maybe 5,000 Pounds, which our department has, and found I could solve the equations of an economy roughly the size of the Swedish economy in about two minutes. If one had used the types of computers, which the Physics department here or any weather forecasting center has, then it would be a very easy matter to solve the equations.

The remaining problem is the problem of obtaining the information, collecting the statistics. And that also is becoming a lot easier, because when you think of it, every production facility nowadays uses computers for ordering its components. It uses computerized spreadsheets for calculating its costs. The data is already being entered into computers and into databases. In many cases, users and suppliers share these databases already in the capitalist world. At the same time, companies like Google have developed the technology to send spiders across the web and concentrate enormous amounts of information in their servers. Were it the case that companies generated web pages containing the information about what they needed to produce each of their product, then that could easily be captured by systems analogous to Google. What stops it to be done at the moment is obviously commercial secrecy. Companies don't want others to know what they are doing. But if we envisage a system of publicly owned enterprises, there is no reason why they shouldn't publish their resource requirements as web pages or by some appropriate submission system to a database, and collect the data that are required for planning.

II

The idea of using labor vouchers, instead of money, goes back a long way in socialist thought. The first person to propose it was Robert Owen, who proposed it in probably the 1830s or so. His idea was that you get rid of banknotes and people would be paid in labor notes. If someone had worked, let's say five hours during the day producing something, they get labor notes denoted in five hours, and you could then go to a corporative store and buy goods that have taken five hours to make. If you did that, the middleman would have been cut out, no profit would have been made, either for the shop, or by the employer and therefore the main cause of exploitation would be got rid of in one stroke. The idea was adopted also in one form or another by Lassalle, Proudhon and Marx. All the nineteenth century socialist leaders advocated it.

Another difference between labor vouchers and money, however, is that money can circulate between people. And that is the basis on which capitalist exploitation is based: Employing people, and then giving them back only half the value they produce. In order to prevent this, Owen's scheme was, that these labor vouchers would not circulate, they would be canceled out, once people had handed them in to the corporative store, they could only be used once. And therefore, you couldn't get a circulation of capital arising. Nowadays, you wouldn't necessarily have to do that with paper, you would obviously use a kind of electronic accounting system, similar to credit cards, but the same principle applies.

One of the problems, which socialists always encounter, is people saying that if you reduce income differentials, there would be no incentives. If you take this in the case of labor vouchers, you have to realize what the labor vouchers are been given for. They are been given for people performing work of average intensity, and where it is possible to measure physical productivity. If one person is physically turning out more goods in an hour than another person, then it is possible to pay one person more than another, because you know they are physically producing more. When it comes to highly collective work, where a lot of people collaborate, then it is not so easy to say that one particular person has contributed more or less to that. Under those circumstances, you can't rely on that kind of incentive. But if you think that only monetary incentives are relevant, you have to explain two very important features of the modern world: One of them is the success of the Japanese economy, where people are not paid monetary incentives in the companies, but they tend to be paid a salary which depends on the number of years service. And, this does not stop Japan having the most productive workers in the world.

Then you take another example and look at two people: You look at Bill Gates and Linus Torvalds. Bill Gates owns a company whose developers produce Windows, and Linus Torvalds wrote the original Linux operating system. Linus Torvalds and the other developers of Linux do it for love of workmanship. They do it from love of producing something useful. And, in the end, they have produced something more useful than the people with monetary incentives like Bill Gates. If you look at the Internet now, it runs largely on Linux servers. It runs using Apache web servers. All of this is software that has been written by people just for the love of doing it. One should not underestimate the extend to which people have a pride in their work and want their work to be done well, and they are willing even to do this, as the free software movement shows, without being paid at all, if the satisfaction of the work is enough.

If you had a system of people being paid by labor vouchers, the average person would get roughly twice as much as he gets now; or twice, before taxes, the income they get now. Because it is a general feature of most capitalist economies that income tends to divide roughly 50/50 between wages and profits. It is a slightly lower level of profits than that in Britain; but historically, over time, it tended to be roughly 50/50, so that you can see roughly a doubling of real incomes. You always have to pay taxes on top of that, but the pre-tax income would roughly double.

The question is: Whether people who had more education should be paid more? In a capitalist economy, they get paid more if there is a short-age of that particular skill. Particularly, for example, if you look at doctors in the United States. They are paid extremely highly, because the American Medical Association acts to restrict the supply of doctors. If, on the other hand, you have in a capitalist economy, a profession, which requires education but there is a lot of people educated for it, like media studies, for example, – a lot of people have been educated to do media studies at the moment – and the salaries that they get from that are not what you get as an average manual worker. The reason is the supply and demand of that case. But, more generally, if you take professions, which are paid highly in the capitalist world, it tends to be the case that the education is expensive and only rich families can afford to send their children to get that education, and therefore the supply is restricted. If the education is paid for by the state and people are paid a salary once they are students, then there is no particular reason why the individual should benefit from that. The costs of education have not been met by the individual, but they have been met by the taxpayer. If the restriction on entry due to lack of wealth is removed, one would expect to see the shortage of supply to be removed as well. If one compares the situation of doctors in the United States with doctors in the Soviet Union, doctors in the United States were relatively scarce and highly paid, doctors in the Soviet Union and Cuba are plentiful and not particularly highly paid. But it doesn't stop people wanting to become doctors, because many people want to become doctors for humanitarian reasons.

One of the key differences between a socialist economy and a capitalist economy is that in a capitalist economy, there is always unemployment. This unemployment acts as a stick to beat the worker to work harder. In a socialist economy, where the allocation of resources is being planned, you tend to get full employment. You had full employment in all the socialist economies, when they existed. However, full employment could come in two forms: It could either come because, in the economy as a whole, there was sufficient demand for labor to take up all people who are willing to work, or it could come because people had a right to work at one particular workplace where they started work. And if you had the latter form, you run the danger that the economy will become set in concrete. It becomes very difficult to reallocate resources to new industries and to run down old industries, as taste or technologies change. So, it has to be the case that the state guarantees people a job, but it does not necessarily guarantee them a job at the same place indefinitely. If factories are being closed down, the state must guarantee to create an equal number of jobs elsewhere in the economy, before they close those factories down, so that people can transfer. But it does not mean that you keep on running the same factories as you run in the year 2000 till the year 2050.

III

Originally democracy meant rule by the mass of the people – especially Aristotle makes this clear – it means rule by the poorer mass of the people. The system we have now is called democracy, but is actually a system of electoral rule, which according to Ancient Greek political theory at least, should be better described as an aristocracy or meritocracy than a democracy. Because any system based on elections is based on a principle of selecting people who appear to be the best to rule.

Who appears to be the best in any society? The people who appear to be the best are always the rich and better educated. Aristotle says, the better educated, the more vocal are nearly always the richer sections of society. And you can see this most clearly in the United States, where to become a political candidate for the presidency, you either have to be a millionaire yourself or have the backing of millionaires. But even if one were to look at a European parliament, or take the European Parliament, and look at the cross-section of the population who is represented in the European Parliament, look at the percentage of men and women, look at the percentages of people from different social classes, look at the percentages of people from different races. Does this actually represent the population of Europe? It clearly doesn't. Anybody who had a job from a polling company and selected the Euro MPs as a group to poll to get a representative sample of opinion in Europe, would be fired from his job. It is clearly grossly unrepresentative.

There is a scientific way of getting a representative sample, and this is random selection. And that is actually how the Greeks did it. If you go to the museum in the Agora of Athens, you can actually see the old voting machines the Ancient Greeks used. They were made out of marble, and the brass parts have long since disappeared. But they were based on the principle, you put your ID card into the machine, turn the handle, or an assistant turns the handle, and if a white ball emerged, you were elected, and if a black ball emerged, you won't. They randomly selected, whether you were going to be a member of the council or not. And that is the only way you can get a representative sample to form a deliberative body.

The other system they had in Ancient Greece was a town meeting, where votes would be held on major issues by the show of hands. Obviously, nowadays, you can't get the whole of a country together into a square to vote on something. But you can get the whole of a country together to vote who is going to stay in the Big Brother house or other television reality shows by using their mobile phones. The same technology could be used on important issues that have to be decided by the population as a whole. The sorts of issues, which really demand that kind of democracy, I think, are issues like war or peace, whether or not taxes should go up, the major outlines of the national budget. Major issues like that should be put to the population, as a whole, in a referendum.

One of the possible drawbacks, I suppose, of a democracy is that you can't predict what people are going to decide. But all that one can say is that decisions made by a large number of people tend to be better decisions than decisions made by one or two people. In general, the more people were asked their opinion about something, the more people who decide on something; if you average these decisions, the decision you get tends to be better than the decision taken by one person. The best hope, I think, for getting ecologically sensible decisions is, firstly, to raise the decision from a private decision, which is made by the individual, to a social decision, which is made collectively, and, secondly, to involve as many people collectively as possible in making that decision. If a lot of people are engaged in making a decision it raises debate and discussion about the issue. If people have a say on something, they will take more interest in that and deliberate on their decisions.

A transition to a socialist economy has to go though an intermediate stage of a transition to a cooperative-based economy. The very first issue is an issue of democracy. The very first issue is an issue of the undemocratic nature of the current state and the need to replace it by a more democratic state, because we don't think that you can get the really radical changes in society that we advocate unless you have a much more democratic state structure. So, the first type of movement is a movement against the existing state and for direct democracy. Economically, however, we envisage the first stage of a transition being legislation, which allows a vote of the employees in an enterprise for that enterprise to be transformed into one that is a worker-managed enterprise, in which a majority of the managing board are elected or selected, by lot, from the workers, and a minority are appointed by the shareholders. Such a managing board is likely to want to pay considerably less dividends to the shareholders than the existing ones. The process of actually transforming the economy to a fully socialist economy cannot be done too rapidly, because you need to first put in place an alternative planning system. You have to set up a shadow planning system first. And you will then need to have a shift from a monetary economy to a labor-value economy. Now we have seen that in an analogous way occurring in Europe, where there was a shift from the national currencies to the Euro after some years planning. And what occurred was, that beyond a certain date the national currencies ceased to be recognized as a legal means of paying debts and taxes. The same process would have to occur: You would have to say that beyond a certain date all payments would have to be made in labor-vouchers.

An effect of that is that it would be a debate of whether such a law should be passed, which would be enormously polarizing. Because those people, who hold large amounts of money in the old system, would lose out, and those people, who have large debts – or even small debts – in the old system would benefit. In a modern economy, where the majority of people are debtors, I think that is potentially a very significant factor in a vote to abolish money and move to labor money, because the majority of people would benefit from that, whereas the millionaires who hold large amounts of money at the moment would obviously lose out. Their money would become worthless. So it poses the issue of wealth and poverty in a particularly sharp fashion, and it poses the issue of debt and credit in a particularly sharp fashion. I see that is an important final deciding issue.

Talk given in 2006

List of Figures

List of Tables